Adobe® Premiere® Pro For Dummies®

W9-DIB-329

Cheat Sheet

Playback Controls

Action	Windows
Play (press L again to increase speed)	Spacebar *or* L
Play backward (press J again to increase speed)	J
Pause	Spacebar *or* K
Frame forward	Right arrow
5 frames forward	Shift+right arrow
Frame back	Left arrow
5 frames back	Shift+left arrow
Beginning of Timeline	Up arrow *or* Home
End of Timeline	Down arrow *or* End
Previous edit point	Page Up
Next edit point	Page Down

View Controls

Action	Windows
Zoom in on Timeline	+ (plus sign)
Zoom out on Timeline	- (minus sign)
Zoom out to show entire Timeline	\
Move up one video track in Timeline	Ctrl++ (plus sign)
Move down one video track in Timeline	Ctrl+− (minus sign)
Move up one audio track in Timeline	Ctrl+Shift++ (plus sign)
Move down one audio track in Timeline	Ctrl+Shift+− (minus sign)
Toggle between Timeline, Monitor, and Project windows	Ctrl+Tab
Toggle between Source and Program in Monitor	Ctrl+`

For Dummies: Bestselling Book Series for Beginners

Adobe® Premiere® Pro For Dummies®

Cheat Sheet

Editing Controls

Action	Windows
Use Selection tool	V
Use Track Select tool	M
Use Ripple Edit tool	B
Use Rolling Edit tool	N
Use Rate Stretch tool	X
Use Razor tool	C
Use Slide tool	U
Use Slip tool	Y
Use Pen tool	P
Use Hand tool	H
Use Zoom tool	Z
Match Timeline edit line with original source-clip frame	T
Insert Edit	,
Overlay Edit	.
Export Movie	Ctrl+M
Undo	Ctrl+Z
Redo	Ctrl+Shift+Z
Slide Edit One Frame Right	Alt+right arrow
Slide Edit One Frame Left	Alt+left arrow
Begin Work Area at Edit Line	Alt+[
End Work Area at Edit Line	Alt+]

Marker Controls

Action	Windows
Clear In point	D
Clear Out point	F
Mark In point	I
Mark Out point	O

Copyright © 2004 Wiley Publishing, Inc.
All rights reserved.
Item 4344-X.
For more information about Wiley Publishing, call 1-800-762-2974.

For Dummies: Bestselling Book Series for Beginners

Adobe® Premiere® Pro

FOR

DUMMIES®

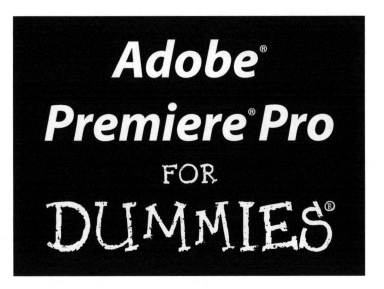

Adobe® Premiere® Pro FOR DUMMIES®

by Keith Underdahl

WILEY

Wiley Publishing, Inc.

Adobe® Premiere® Pro For Dummies®

Published by
Wiley Publishing, Inc.
111 River Street
Hoboken, NJ 07030

www.wiley.com

Copyright © 2004 by Wiley Publishing, Inc., Indianapolis, Indiana

Published by Wiley Publishing, Inc., Indianapolis, Indiana

Published simultaneously in Canada

For general information on our other products and services or to obtain technical support, please contact our Customer Care Department within the U.S. at 800-762-2974, outside the U.S. at 317-572-3993, or fax 317-572-4002.

Wiley also publishes its books in a variety of electronic formats. Some content that appears in print may not be available in electronic books.

Library of Congress Control Number: 2003113190

ISBN: 0-7645-4344-X

10 9 8 7 6 5 4 3 2 1

WILEY   is a trademark of Wiley Publishing, Inc.

About the Author

Keith Underdahl is a digital-media specialist residing in Albany, Oregon. Professionally, Keith is an electronic publishing specialist for Ages Software, where he serves as program manager, interface designer, multimedia producer, graphic artist, programmer, customer support manager, resident Portable Document Format (PDF) guru, and when the day is over, he even sweeps out the place. Mr. Underdahl has written numerous books, including *Teach Yourself Microsoft Word 2000*, *Microsoft Windows Movie Maker For Dummies*, *Macworld Final Cut Pro 2 Bible* (co-author), and *Digital Video For Dummies, 3rd Edition*.

Dedication

My beloved brethren, let every man be swift to hear, slow to speak, slow to anger.

— *James 1:19*

Author's Acknowledgments

So many people helped me complete this project that I hardly know where to begin. First and foremost I wish to thank my family for allowing me to work two full time jobs as I completed *Adobe Premiere Pro For Dummies*. My wife Christa has been my entire support staff, head cheerleader, creative advisor, and inspiration throughout my entire writing career. She was the one who urged me to start writing for a small motorcycle magazine in 1995, and that endeavor has led to so many great adventures and challenges in the years since. I owe everything to Christa.

My undying gratitude also goes out to my two very favorite movie subjects, Soren and Cole Underdahl. Not only do my boys take direction well, but they are also incredibly intelligent and look great on camera! I also received help both on-screen and behind the scenes from Ryan and Wendy Holbrook, and havoc23.

I wish I could take full credit for the quality and content of *Adobe Premiere Pro For Dummies,* but many other kind folks contributed to this work to make it what it is. I'd like to thank Steve Hayes for hiring me once again to write this book, my project editor Linda Morris, my technical editor Dennis Short, my copy editor Barry Childs-Helton, and the many other folks at Wiley Publishing who toiled to make this one of the best references on Adobe Premiere Pro to be found.

Finally, thanks to Liz McQueen, Jill Devlin, and all the folks at Adobe for inviting me to help develop this excellent video-editing tool; I've been on the user side of Adobe software for so long that it was great to finally get a chance to contribute and be useful!

Publisher's Acknowledgments

We're proud of this book; please send us your comments through our online registration form located at www.dummies.com/register/.

Some of the people who helped bring this book to market include the following:

Acquisitions, Editorial, and Media Development

Project Editor: Linda Morris

Senior Acquisitions Editor: Steven Hayes

Copy Editor: Barry Childs-Helton

Technical Editor: Dennis Short

Editorial Manager: Leah Cameron

Editorial Assistant: Amanda Foxworth

Cartoons: Rich Tennant
(www.the5thwave.com)

Production

Project Coordinator: Courtney MacIntyre

Layout and Graphics: Seth Conley, Lauren Goddard, Stephanie D. Jumper, Shelley Norris, Heather Ryan, Shae Wilson

Proofreaders: John Tyler Connoley, Dave Faust, Angel Perez, Carl William Pierce, Christine Sabooni, Charles Spencer

Indexer: Joan Griffitts

Publishing and Editorial for Technology Dummies

    Richard Swadley, Vice President and Executive Group Publisher

    Andy Cummings, Vice President and Publisher

    Mary C. Corder, Editorial Director

Publishing for Consumer Dummies

    Diane Graves Steele, Vice President and Publisher

    Joyce Pepple, Acquisitions Director

Composition Services

    Gerry Fahey, Vice President of Production Services

    Debbie Stailey, Director of Composition Services

Contents at a Glance

Table of Contents

Introduction

Some of you young folks may not remember all the way back to the twentieth century, but the waning years of that century were a heady time indeed. Hyped up on $4.00 coffee drinks and biscotti, overdosed on cathode rays, we'd spend hours sitting around and making wild predictions about the future. Through a fog of whipped soymilk we foresaw that humans (or possibly mutants) of the year 2004 would buy all their groceries online, check e-mail on their refrigerators, and edit high-quality movies on devices that fit inside most overhead storage bins. Of course, all these predictions were contingent upon whether or not the apocalypse came at the turn of the millennium.

Thankfully, many of our predictions proved untrue. We don't have to trust Joe DotCom to pick out firm tomatoes, we don't wonder if the light stays on when we close the door on our elceBoxes, and doomsday appears to be delayed at least until February 2012 (the end of the Mayan calendar) if not longer. We can, however, easily edit movies on devices that fit into most overhead storage bins. Those devices are called *laptop computers,* and they're even affordable. Hey, we got one prediction right. I think I'll take the rest of the day off.

Okay, I'm back.

As you've probably heard, movie editing is one of the hottest topics in the computer business today. High-quality digital camcorders are now widespread, and computers capable of editing the video shot by those camcorders are now affordable, if not downright cheap. Software vendors are rushing to provide programs that can take advantage of all this new hardware, and Adobe Premiere Pro is among the best.

If you recently purchased a computer that has a FireWire (IEEE-1394) interface, it probably also came with some free movie-editing software. Windows XP includes a modest little program called Windows Movie Maker. Countless other low-cost programs are available from companies like MGI, Pinnacle, and Ulead. You might have gotten one of these programs with a video capture card or FireWire card that you recently bought. Are those programs any good? Sure, but Adobe Premiere Pro is better. Premiere Pro is widely recognized as one of the best midpriced video-editing programs available for Windows platforms. If you want professional-grade video-editing capabilities but don't want to spend thousands of dollars, Premiere Pro is an excellent choice.

Why This Book?

Adobe Premiere Pro is an advanced program, so you need an advanced reference. But you do not need a gargantuan textbook that causes your bookshelf to sag. You need easy-to-follow, step-by-step instructions for the most important tasks, and you need tips and tricks to make your work more successful. You need *Adobe Premiere Pro For Dummies*.

Needless to say, you're no "dummy" or else you wouldn't be reading this book and trying to figure out how to use Adobe Premiere Pro correctly. Video editing is fun, and it is my hope that you'll find this book fun to use as well. I have included instructions on performing the most important video editing tasks, including lots of graphics so that you can better visualize what it is that I'm talking about. You'll also find tips and other ideas in this book that you wouldn't otherwise find in Adobe's own documentation.

Adobe Premiere Pro For Dummies doesn't just help you use the Premiere Pro program. If you're relatively new to moviemaking, you'll find that this book will help you choose a good camcorder, shoot better video, publish movies online, and speak the industry technobabble like a Hollywood pro.

Foolish Assumptions

I've made a few basic assumptions about you while writing this book. First, I assume that you have an intermediate knowledge of computer use. Movie editing is one of the more technically advanced things you can do with a computer, so I assume that if you're ready to edit video, you already know how to locate and move files around on hard drives, open and close programs, and perform other such tasks. I also assume that you have Windows XP, because (unlike previous versions of Premiere) Adobe Premiere Pro isn't available for the Apple Macintosh — and it won't run on Windows Me, Windows 2000, or any older versions of Windows.

Another basic assumption I made is that you might not (yet, anyway) be an experienced, professional video editor. I explain the fundamentals of video editing in ways that help you immediately get to work on your movie projects. Most of the coverage in this book assumes that you're producing movies as a hobby, you're working in a semiprofessional ("prosumer") environment, or you plan to use Premiere Pro for video production in a corporate environment. Typical projects might include wedding videos, company training videos, school projects, kiosk videos, professional presentations, or even programs destined for broadcast.

Conventions Used in This Book

Adobe Premiere Pro For Dummies helps you get started with Premiere Pro quickly and efficiently. The book serves as a reference to this program, and because Premiere Pro is a computer program, you'll find this book a bit different from other kinds of texts you have read. The following are some unusual conventions that you encounter in this book:

- ✐ File names or lines of computer code will look like THIS or this. This style of print usually indicates something you should type in exactly as you see it in the book.

- ✐ Internet addresses will look something like this: www.dummies.com. Notice that I've left the http:// part off the address because you almost never have to actually type that into your Web browser anymore.

- ✐ You will often be instructed to access commands from the menu bar in Premiere and other programs. The menu bar is that strip that lives along the top of the Premiere program window and usually includes menus called File, Edit, Project, Clip, Sequence, Marker, Title, Window, and Help. If (for example) I'm telling you to access the Save command in the File menu, it looks like this: Choose File⇨Save.

- ✐ You'll be using your mouse a lot. Sometimes you have to click something to select it. This means you should click *once* with the left mouse button after you've put the mouse pointer over whatever it is you're supposed to click. I'll specify when you have to double-click or right-click (that is, click once with the right mouse button).

How This Books Is Organized

Believe it or not, I did put some forethought into the organization of this book. I hope you find it logically arranged and easy to use. The chapters of *Adobe Premiere Pro For Dummies* are divided into five major parts, plus an appendix. The parts are described in the next section.

Part I: Introducing Adobe Premiere Pro

Adobe Premiere Pro is a highly advanced program, and if you're new to video editing, many of its parts may seen unfamiliar. Part I helps you get started with your movie-making adventure by introducing you to Adobe Premiere Pro. You'll begin by touring the Premiere Pro program and getting familiar with its tools and basic features. Because Premiere Pro is just one of many tools that you will use to produce movies, I will spend some time helping you prepare your production studio. I'll also show you how to prepare Premiere Pro for use with a variety of media formats.

Part II: Gathering Footage

After you're comfortable with Adobe Premiere Pro, you should familiarize yourself with the basics of video production. The first chapter in Part II introduces you to the fundamentals of moviemaking, a thorough understanding of which is crucial if you want to produce great movies. Next, you start new projects in Premiere Pro and manage the media and content that Premiere uses. I also show you how to import and manage material in Premiere Pro so you have something to work with when you start editing.

Part III: Editing in Premiere Pro

Adobe Premiere Pro is, first and foremost, a video-editing program, so this part could be considered the heart of *Adobe Premiere Pro For Dummies*. Here you edit clips, create movies using the Timeline, and give your project a high-quality soundtrack. You also utilize Premiere Pro's more advanced editing features. You perform advanced color corrections on video clips, create and manipulate transitions between scenes in the movie, create and use special effects, and get a crack at combining (or *compositing*) multiple video scenes into one, much the same way special-effects pros do in Hollywood. You also create title screens that tell viewers the name of the movie and who is responsible for it.

Part IV: Wrapping Up Your Project

All your editing work is for naught if you don't share your movies with others. This part helps you wrap up a movie project and then distribute it on the Internet, on videotape, or on DVD.

Part V: The Part of Tens

I wouldn't be able to call this a *For Dummies* book without a "Part of Tens" (really, it's in my contract). Actually, the Part of Tens always serves an important purpose. In *Adobe Premiere Pro For Dummies,* it gives me a chance to show you ten great moviemaking tips that you can use in Adobe Premiere Pro, ten Premiere Pro plug-ins and accessory programs that you may find useful, and ten toys, er, *tools* to help you make better movies.

Part VI: Appendix

Video editing is a technical subject with a language all its own, so I've provided a glossary to help you quickly decrypt the alphabet soup of video-editing terms and acronyms.

Icons Used in This Book

Occasionally you'll find some icons in the margins of this book. The text next to these icons includes information and tips that deserve special attention, and some warn you of potential hazards and pitfalls you may encounter. Icons you'll find in this book are easy to spot:

Although every word of *Adobe Premiere Pro For Dummies* is important, I sometimes feel the need to emphasize certain points. I use Remember to occasionally provide this emphasis.

Tips are usually brief instructions or ideas that aren't always documented but can greatly improve your movies and make your life easier. Tips are among the most valuable tidbits in this book.

Heed warnings carefully. Some warn of situations that can merely inconvenience you; others tell you when a wrong move could cause expensive and painful damage to your equipment and/or person.

Computer books are often stuffed with yards of technobabble, and if it's sprinkled everywhere, it can make the whole book a drag and just plain difficult to read. As much as possible, I've tried to pull some of the deeply technical stuff out into these icons. This way, the information is easy to find if you need it, and just as easy to skip if you already have a headache.

Where to Go from Here

You are about to enter the mad, mad world of video production. Exciting, isn't it? Video editing is *the* hot topic in computer technology today, and you're at the forefront of this multimedia revolution. If you still need to set up your movie studio or need some equipment, I suggest that you start off with Chapter 2, *"Setting Up Your Production Studio."* If you aren't quite ready to start editing yet, you may want to spend some time in Chapter 4, *"A Crash Course in Video Production."* Otherwise, you should go ahead and familiarize yourself with Adobe Premiere Pro, beginning with Chapter 1.

Part I
Introducing Adobe Premiere Pro

"I found these two in the multimedia lab morphing faculty members into farm animals."

In this part . . .

*I*t wasn't so long ago that moviemaking was "magic" that came from the shining temples of Hollywood. But thanks to the home-video revolution that got started in the mid-1990s, anyone with a reasonably modern personal computer, an affordable digital camcorder, and a video-editing program like Adobe Premiere Pro can now produce a high-tech motion picture.

This part of *Adobe Premiere Pro For Dummies* begins the moviemaking adventure by exploring Adobe Premiere Pro and finding out just what this program can do. It also looks at what's needed for your personal video-production studio, and walks you through configuring Premiere Pro to make movie magic.

Chapter 1

Getting to Know Premiere Pro

*T*he field of video-editing software is getting pretty crowded these days. Premiere Pro is now just one of many pro-caliber editing programs in the $500-to-$1000 price range, a field now populated with such offerings as Apple Final Cut Pro (for the Macintosh only), Avid Xpress DV, Pinnacle Edition, and Sonic Vegas. Adobe Premiere now has more than ten years of experience in the realm of PC-based video editing— but to be honest, it has been upstaged by some of its rivals in recent years. Thankfully, the newest version of Premiere Pro answers questions that almost everyone was asking, bringing it once again to the forefront of the video-editing scene.

This chapter introduces you to Adobe Premiere Pro by showing you what this program is designed to do and what it has to offer. You also get a tour of Premiere Pro to help you find your way around this feature-packed program.

What Is Adobe Premiere Pro?

Adobe Premiere Pro is, first and foremost, a video-editing program — although that term is almost too modest, given the versatility of Premiere Pro. Editing movies on affordable PCs has been a dream since multimedia-ready computers became common in the mid-1990s. For years, the *reality* of affordable video editing lagged well behind the dream. But today, video can be easily edited on computers that cost less than $1,000, and powerful programs like Premiere Pro give you editing tools that were previously available only to video and film professionals, working on systems that cost hundreds of thousands — if not millions — of dollars. With Adobe Premiere Pro, you can skip the glitz and get right to the gist:

- Capture audio and video from your camcorder or video deck (if your computer has the right hardware).

- Pick and choose scenes to include in a movie. You can move frame by frame through video to precisely place your edits.

✔ Make use of up to 99 separate video tracks that can be composited and combined to make a single image.

✔ Add and edit audio soundtracks to your program. Up to 99 separate audio tracks can be added to the program.

✔ Create titles and add still graphics to your movie projects. Titles and graphics can be animated in a variety of ways.

✔ Apply one of 73 different transitions to video. Transitions can be used in any video track.

✔ Modify your movie with 94 video and 22 audio effects.

✔ Improve and adjust color using an advanced new Color Corrector.

✔ Use powerful new audio tools to mix audio, whether it's mono, stereo, or 5.1 channel surround.

✔ Work more flexibly than ever with multiple, nestable timelines.

✔ Preview edits immediately in real time, without having to wait for rendering.

✔ Record movies to videotape at full broadcast quality.

✔ Export tightly compressed movies for the World Wide Web in RealMedia, QuickTime, Windows Media, or one of many other available formats.

✔ Output movies directly to DVD.

Even these hefty capabilities are only a smattering of what you can do with Adobe Premiere Pro. It's one of the most versatile programs you'll ever use.

Where's the Mac?

Previous versions of Adobe Premiere (version 6.5 and earlier) were available for both Macintosh and Windows computers. Adobe's announcement that Premiere Pro (technically version 7 of Premiere) would run only in Windows XP was met with some shock and surprise, especially considering that only a few years ago, Adobe was considered a very Mac-oriented software company. Exactly why Adobe chose not to develop a Mac OS X-compatible version of Premiere Pro is a subject that will probably forever remain a mystery to those of us who aren't part of the inner circles at Adobe.

If you have a Macintosh, you might be considering running Premiere Pro on your Mac using a program that emulates the Windows operating system. I do not recommend this workaround: As I describe in Chapter 2, Premiere Pro relies heavily on a technology called *SSE* — a set of multimedia instructions only found in the latest computer processor chips from AMD and Intel. If those exact instructions are not present, Premiere Pro will crash hard and crash often — and as of this writing, no Apple processors include the SSE instruction set.

Taking the Grand Tour

As you might expect from a program that can do so many things, the Adobe Premiere Pro program interface may seem complex and intimidating the first time you look at it. When you launch Premiere Pro, you see a welcome screen that looks like Figure 1-1. The area under Recent Projects gives you quick access to any projects you've been working on recently. (If this is the first time you've launched Premiere Pro, you probably won't have anything listed under Recent Projects.)

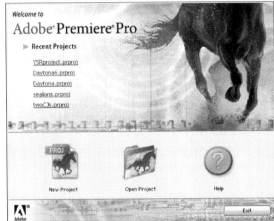

Figure 1-1:
Welcome to
Premiere
Pro!

If you don't have a previous project to open and continue work on, you have to start a new project if you want to see Premiere Pro in action. Click the New Project button in the welcome screen to open the New Project dialog box (as shown in Figure 1-2). This dialog box is a little complicated because you have to actually make a decision about what kind of project you want to create. This is where you choose a *preset* — a standard collection of settings that apply to a certain kind of video or medium.

Which preset you choose depends on the video you're working with; preset settings are specific to frame size, frame rate, audio quality, and the video broadcast standard for your area. For example, if you live in North America and will be editing video you recorded with your digital camcorder, you'll probably choose DV-NTSC⇨Standard 48kHz. If you aren't sure what to choose, click Standard 48kHz (under either DV-NTSC or DV-PAL), type a name for your project in the Name field, and then click OK. (For more on choosing presets, turn to Chapter 5.)

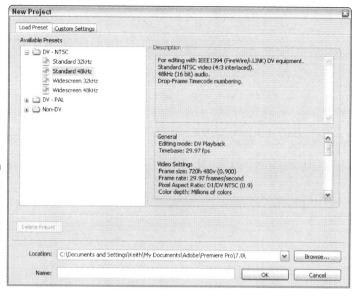

Figure 1-2:
This dialog box helps you start a new project in Premiere Pro.

When you have chosen a project preset, Premiere Pro opens (at last) to the editing workspace. The exact appearance of your workspace depends upon the current screen resolution setting on your computer, but the basic appearance should resemble Figure 1-3. Although the *exact* appearance varies, you still see at least the three fundamental windows that make up the Premiere Pro interface — the Project window, the Monitor, and the Timeline, as shown in Figure 1-3. These three windows are explained in greater detail in the following sections.

Project window

Think of the Project window as a sort of filing cabinet that helps you organize the various files and clips you use in your project. Whenever you capture video from your camcorder or video deck, import still graphics, or capture audio from an audio CD, the files show up in the Project window. If you're working on a big project, you'll end up with many different files in this window; a full project window looks similar to Figure 1-4. You can create new bins in the Project window to help organize your files. Bins work like folders in your operating system. To create a new bin, follow these steps:

1. **Click in the Project window to select it and make it active.**

2. **From the menu bar at the top of the Premiere Pro screen, choose File⟳New⟳Bin.**

   A new bin appears in the Project window with the name highlighted.

Project window   Monitor

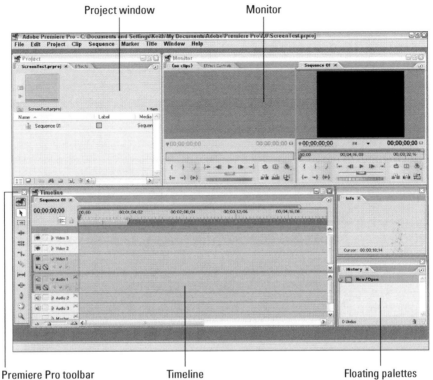

Figure 1-3:
Premiere
Pro's
interface
consists of
several
important
windows
and
palettes.

Premiere Pro toolbar   Timeline   Floating palettes

3. Type a name for your new bin and press Enter.

Your new bin now appears in the Project window. Click the bin to view its contents. To add items to a bin, simply click-and-drag them into the bin elsewhere in the Project window. Figure 1-4 shows a Project window for a project I'm working on; as you can see, I've imported and captured a lot of files into it.

Although the Project window is primarily a storage place, you can also use it to

✓ **Review data about a file.** What's the frame size of the image? Is the file an audio clip, video, or a still graphic? How long is the clip? Columns in the Project window provide many different kinds of information about your files.

✓ **Preview the file.** If you click a file in the Project window, a preview of it appears in the upper-left corner of the Project window (as shown in Figure 1-4). If you click the little Play button under the preview, you can play audio and video clips to get a better idea of what's in them.

Use bins to organize files

Preview

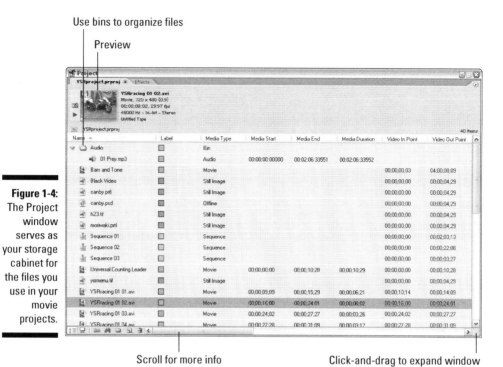

Figure 1-4:
The Project window serves as your storage cabinet for the files you use in your movie projects.

Scroll for more info

Click-and-drag to expand window

Monitor

Try to imagine editing video without being able to look at it. Your task would be daunting. Thankfully, Premiere Pro makes sure you can always see exactly what your movie looks like as you work on it. The Monitor window is where you view your work. The Monitor window has controls for playing video and audio clips and for performing other editing tasks. In the Monitor, you

✓ Play through clips you plan to add to a movie project. As you play each clip, you decide which portions to add to the movie by setting *In points* and *Out points*. When you set In and Out points, only the portions of the clip between those two points will be added to your movie program.

✓ Play through the edits you have already made in your project.

The Monitor shown in Figure 1-5 has two panes. The left pane is called the Source view, and this is where you review clips before you edit them into the movie. To load a video file into the Source view, simply drag the file from the Project window and drop it on the Source view side of the Monitor.

The right pane of the Monitor is the Program view, which shows what's in the actual movie project you're assembling in the Timeline (a feature described in the next section).

Monitor window menu

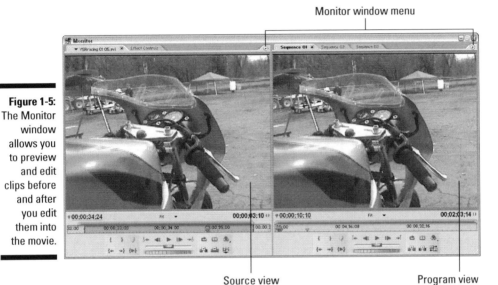

Figure 1-5:
The Monitor window allows you to preview and edit clips before and after you edit them into the movie.

Source view   Program view

If you're trying to conserve screen space, you can switch the Monitor to a single pane view if you wish. To do so, click one of the Monitor window menu buttons (as shown in Figure 1-5, it looks like a tiny little right-pointing arrow) and choose Single View from the menu that appears. If you choose Single View from the Source side of the Monitor, the Monitor will switch to a single pane showing only the source clip. If you choose Single View from the Program side, the single pane displayed is your video program as currently edited.

Timeline

The Timeline could be considered the heart and soul of Adobe Premiere Pro. As with virtually every other video-editing program, Premiere Pro's Timeline is the place where you craft your movie by putting its pieces in the desired order. You assemble clips, add effects, composite multiple clips on top of each other, and add sound. As you can see in Figure 1-6, the Timeline shows audio tracks on the bottom and video tracks on top. You can have up to 99 video tracks and 99 audio tracks in the Premiere Timeline. A new feature in

Premiere Pro is the possibility of multiple *sequences* in the Timeline. Sequences appear as tabs in the Timeline window. Each sequence functions like its own separate Timeline, which you can work on by itself. Sequences can be combined (or *nested* in the official terminology of Premiere Pro) or used separately.

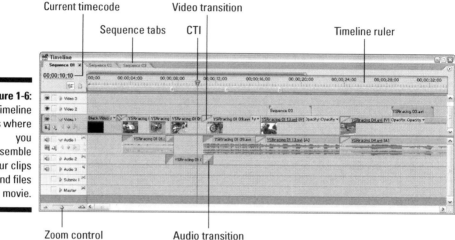

Current timecode   Video transition

Sequence tabs   CTI   Timeline ruler

Figure 1-6:
The Timeline
is where
you
assemble
your clips
and files
into a movie.

Zoom control   Audio transition

I can't completely explain the Timeline here. That would fill a chapter all by itself. (In fact, it does — Chapter 8.) However, I do want you to know that by using the Timeline, you can

- Expand the view of a track by clicking the right-facing arrow on the left side of the Timeline.

- Figure out where you are in the project by using the Timeline ruler.

- Use the CTI (Current Time Indicator) to set the current playback and editing location in the Timeline.

- Control aspects of a clip directly in the Timeline. You can set keyframes for effects or adjust audio levels using audio rubberbands. (See Chapter 12 for more on working with effects; Chapter 13 shows you how to work with audio.)

- Use the Zoom control to zoom your view of the Timeline in and out.

- Move items by simply dragging-and-dropping them to new locations in the Timeline. If your clip calls for some effects and transitions, you can add them by dragging them to the Timeline as well.

Palettes

Admittedly, the Project window, the Monitor, and the Timeline are the three primary components of Adobe Premiere Pro. An introduction to Adobe Premiere can't stop there though. You should also know about palettes. Premiere stores some of its advanced features and effects in small floating windows called *palettes*. If you're familiar with other Adobe programs such as Photoshop and Illustrator, you're probably already familiar with palettes. To view a couple of palettes, do this:

1. **Choose Window⇨History.**

2. **Choose Window⇨Info.**

You should now have two floating palettes on your screen that look something like the ones in Figure 1-7. You can move these palettes around by dragging the title bar, or close them by clicking the little Close (*x*) button in the upper-right corner. Use the Window menu to re-open the palettes again. To resize a palette, click-and-drag an edge or corner of the palette.

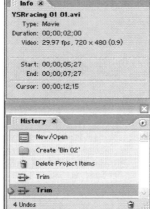

Figure 1-7: Premiere Pro stores some commands on floating palettes.

Commanding the interface

As I mention in the "Foolish Assumptions" section of the Introduction, one of the assumptions I make about you is that you already know how to open and close programs on your computer. You probably also know how to open menus, click buttons, and resize or minimize windows.

That said, Adobe Premiere is so advanced (and video editing is so demanding of a computer's resources) that I suspect you've recently bought a new computer — and there's a good chance you've recently "switched camps" from Macintosh to your first Windows PC. To help ease your transition, I want to provide a brief overview of the basic interface controls in the Windows versions of Adobe Premiere Pro.

Adobe Premiere Pro requires Windows XP. Either the Home or Professional edition will suffice. You can't run Premiere Pro in Windows 2000, Windows Me, or any previous version of Windows. If you're new to Windows XP, I suggest you purchase a book with more detailed information on using and managing the system. I recommend *Windows XP For Dummies,* by Andy Rathbone (published by Wiley Publishing, Inc.).

The fundamental look and feel of the Microsoft Windows interface has not changed significantly since Windows 95 was released in (ahem) 1995, although the cosmetics were modernized a bit with the release of Windows XP. Figure 1-8 shows a typical Premiere Pro screen. To launch Premiere Pro, click the Start button to open the Start menu and choose All Programs➪Adobe Premiere Pro. If you use Premiere Pro a lot, it will probably show up in the list of commonly used programs that appears when you first click Start. Basic controls include

- **Start menu:** Use this menu to access programs on your computer, as well as shut down and restart controls. The Start menu is similar in concept to the Apple menu on a Macintosh.

- **Taskbar:** All currently open programs will have a button on the Taskbar. Click a program's button on the Taskbar to open it. The Taskbar is similar in concept to the Mac OS X Dock.

- **Minimize:** Click this to minimize a window. When a program is minimized, it becomes a button on the Taskbar. Use this button like you would the Collapse or Minimize buttons on a Mac.

- **Restore/Maximize:** Use this button to change the window size. Restore/Maximize works like the Zoom button in the Mac OS.

- **Close:** Click this to close a program or window.

If you don't like digging through the Start menu every time you want to launch Premiere, right-click the Adobe Premiere Pro link in the Start menu and choose Send To➪Desktop (create shortcut) from the menu that appears. Doing so creates a desktop icon that you can double-click when you want to launch Premiere Pro.

Restore

Minimize | Close

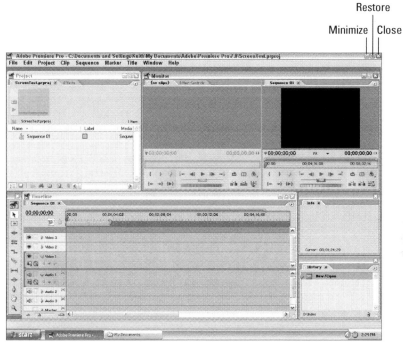

Figure 1-8:
The Windows interface is similar across all modern versions of Microsoft Windows.

Chapter 2

Setting Up Your Production Studio

- -

- -

*N*ot so long ago, the price of a good video-editing system could have bought you a pretty nice home in the suburbs. But thanks to programs like Adobe Premiere Pro, many of those suburban homes now *have* good video-editing systems — and the owners of said homes didn't have to take out second mortgages to purchase the equipment. Adobe Premiere revolutionized video by providing professional-grade editing capabilities in a software package that runs on affordable computers.

Another revolution has been the newfound affordability of digital video (DV) hardware. Amateur videographers can now shoot near-broadcast-quality video on cameras that cost less than $1,000. Then Apple created the FireWire interface a few years ago — and suddenly digital video can be edited on personal computers — both Macintoshes *and* Windows PCs — because the interface is fast enough to handle large video files at full playback speed. These three things — video-editing software, digital camcorders, and FireWire — have come together and created a synergy that is changing the way we think about and use moving pictures.

When you have the software (Adobe Premiere Pro), you need the hardware to go with it. This chapter guides you through the process of finding a computer to serve as a video-editing platform. You also get a look at digital cameras and other hardware that you may need or want as you get serious about video.

Selecting a Computer

Although video-editing systems have certainly become affordable, you should be aware that you can't expect to edit video on just any old computer. That PC your parents bought you for college ten years ago, for example, won't cut it. In fact, almost any computer that is not new or has not been significantly upgraded in the last year or so is probably barely adequate when using Adobe Premiere Pro. The following sections help you identify what kind of computer you need, including specific system requirements.

Macintosh computers have long been favored by video professionals, but as of this writing, Adobe Premiere Pro is a Windows-only program. This is a departure from previous versions of the software, which were both Mac and Windows compatible up through Adobe Premiere 6.5.

Identifying your needs

First, you need a computer that will run Adobe Premiere Pro without crashing. Beyond that, your computer should run Premiere efficiently without making you wait for hours on end while it performs a simple action. You need lots of storage space for your video files. And you need special hardware tailored to video editing. The next two sections describe the computer that you need.

Minimum system requirements

Like virtually all software programs, Adobe Premiere Pro has some minimum system requirements that your computer must meet. You'll find them emblazoned on the side of Premiere Pro's retail box, as well as in the "INSTALL READ ME" file located on the Premiere Pro CD-ROM. The minimum requirements are surprisingly low. The minimum requirements for the Windows version are

- ✔ Pentium III processor, 800 MHz or higher
- ✔ Windows XP
- ✔ 256MB of RAM
- ✔ 24-bit video display
- ✔ DirectX compatible sound card
- ✔ 300MB of free hard-drive space for program-installation files

You must be logged in to Windows XP — with administrator rights — to install the software. You must also be able to restart and re-log-in to Windows with administrator rights to complete installation.

The real system requirements

You've seen the *minimum* system requirements, but good luck actually trying to try to edit video on a system that exactly meets those minimum specs! It would be an exercise in futility. Video editing puts unusually high demands on a computer. Video files require massive amounts of disk space, as well as special hardware to capture video and lay it back to tape — and the computer's memory and processor are utilized to their maximum capabilities when you render video for playback. Premiere Pro works computer hardware especially hard as it displays effects and other complex edits in real-time.

Whether you are buying a new computer or upgrading, you really need some relatively souped-up capabilities:

- ✔ **A seriously powerful processor:** The *central processing unit* (CPU) can be thought of as the brain of the computer, and a faster processor affects how well everything else runs. The faster the processor, the less time you'll spend twiddling your thumbs as your video renders, and the better real-time previews will play. Adobe recommends an Intel Pentium 4 3GHz (or better) processor, but an equivalent AMD Athlon XP processor will work as well. Any processor you use with Premiere Pro should support the SSE instruction set, a set of CPU instructions that helps the processor better handle multimedia data. This means that you should stick with a Pentium III, Pentium 4, or Athlon XP processor. Older AMD Athlons (without the XP suffix) and Durons may cause system crashes or other stability problems during certain video-editing operations. The very best editing performance will be found with an Intel Pentium 4 because that processor includes an even more powerful instruction set called SSE2.

- ✔ **Lots of memory:** Your CPU uses *random-access memory* (RAM) as its working space. More RAM means you can run more programs, and processes like video rendering and real-time previews happen much more efficiently. Although Adobe says that 256MB is the bare minimum, they recommend at least 1GB of RAM for use with Premiere Pro, and I think that is a good recommendation.

- ✔ **A big, fast hard drive:** Video requires *lots* of storage space. You can get a good start with 80GB (gigabytes) of disk space, but more is always better. If your computer uses IDE hard drives (check the spec sheet), always choose 7200-rpm drives over 5400-rpm drives. I recommend installing a second hard drive in your system, and dedicating it solely to video storage.

- ✔ **A large monitor:** Premiere takes up a lot of screen real estate. Unless you want to spend half your life scrolling back and forth in the Timeline and moving windows and palettes this way and that, you need a monitor that can display a screen resolution of *at least* 1024 x 768 pixels, or preferably 1280 x 1024 pixels or higher. If you try to work at 800 x 600 pixels on a small 15-inch monitor, your workspace will be cramped and confusing like the one shown in Figure 2-1. Thankfully, big monitors are pretty cheap these days. You should seriously consider a dual monitor setup if your budget and desk space allows. Some advanced video display cards support dual monitors, meaning that you have two monitors connected to your computer. Placed side-by-side, these dual monitors behave like a giant desktop that basically doubles your digital workspace. Premiere Pro works quite nicely on a dual monitor setup. You can seamlessly move the mouse and various Premiere program elements back and forth between each monitor as you see fit.

✔ **FireWire interface:** FireWire ports are essential for working with digital video. Even if you don't currently have a DV camcorder, you will probably need a FireWire port before long. Many new PCs come with FireWire (IEEE-1394) adapters built-in, but double-check before you buy. FireWire adapters can be added to most PCs for less than $100.

✔ **A clean installation of Windows XP:** Adobe claims that Premiere Pro has been optimized for Windows XP. Windows XP Pro is "recommended" although you can run Premiere Pro in Windows XP Home as well. Premiere Pro is *not* recommended for systems running Windows 2000, Windows Me, or any other earlier Microsoft operating system. I further recommend that you only run Premiere Pro on a system where Windows XP was installed "clean." That is, Windows XP should have been installed on a blank, freshly formatted hard drive. If you bought your computer new with Windows XP preinstalled, this shouldn't be a problem. But if you have upgraded your computer to Windows XP from Windows Me or Windows 2000, you may encounter stability problems. Check out a book such as *Windows XP All-in-One Desk Reference For Dummies* by Woody Leonhard (Wiley Publishing, Inc.) for more on installing Windows XP.

Figure 2-1:
This is what Adobe Premiere Pro looks like with a screen resolution of 800 by 600. Good luck trying to get any work done in this cramped workspace.

What about flat-panel monitors?

I haven't mentioned flat-panel monitors yet, which may seem hard to believe because these advanced displays are all the rage today. Most flat-panel monitors use LCD (liquid crystal display) technology to generate the display, and they offer several advantages over CRT monitors, including these:

✔ LCD monitors use less electricity.

✔ LCD monitors generate less heat.

✔ LCD monitors usually cause less eyestrain.

✔ Flat-panel monitors take up less space on your desktop.

Sounds great, right? Unfortunately, just like with conventional CRT (cathode ray tube) monitors,

not all LCD monitors are created equal. Many LCD monitors still tend to be rather dark compared to CRT monitors, and the screen resolution is often not as fine. This does not mean that flat-panel monitors cannot be superior. Apple showed the way in the Mac world with its fabulous 21-inch Widescreen Studio Display monitor, and some PC-based LCD monitors now offer brilliant quality as well.

Clearly, flat-panel monitors are the wave of the future. But I recommend that you observe any monitor in action before you make a purchasing decision. You'll want bright, clear images when you fine-tune your video — and that means a high-quality monitor is crucial.

A lot of interesting hard-drive alternatives have appeared in recent years. These include external hard drives that plug into FireWire or USB ports. I recommend against using such drives for video storage when you're editing in Premiere Pro. External drives are seldom fast enough to keep up with video's demands, meaning you may experience *dropped frames* (that is, some frames of video are skipped and lost) and other problems when you try to output your video.

Choosing PC

Don't let anyone tell you that Macs are always better for video editing than Windows PCs. Yes, most new Macs are great video-editing machines right out of the box. But a properly equipped PC running Windows XP can be just as effective. You just need to take a bit more time (and spend a bit more money) to make sure you're getting the right kind of system, if only because when you are shopping for a Windows machine, you have so many more choices.

When shopping for a Windows-based video-editing system, follow the system recommendations I made earlier, and also look for the following:

✔ **A fast processor.** I can't think of a reason to buy any new PC these days with less than a 3 GHz CPU. Adobe recommends a Pentium 4 processor for use with Premiere Pro, although I have had success with an AMD Athlon XP processor as well.

✔ **A big hard drive.** Cheaper PCs usually have smaller hard disk. If you are ordering a more affordable PC, ask about upgrading to at least a 100GB hard disk, and if possible try to get two hard drives so that one can be dedicated solely to video editing. (And make sure you get a 7200-rpm drive!)

✔ **A good video card.** Many new PCs have the display adapter built into the motherboard. When you're reading the spec sheet, you may see something like "32MB on-board AGP video." I usually don't like on-board video because it almost always uses up some system RAM, and many on-board display adapters perform quite slowly. The better solution is to buy a system with a separate video card in an expansion slot, like PCs have had for over a decade. I recommend a video adapter card with at least 64MB of video RAM.

Speaking of video cards, many good cards (such as the ATI All-In-Wonder cards) include composite or component video inputs/outputs. This means that the video card can also be used to capture analog video. This feature is worth paying a little extra for.

✔ **A FireWire card.** Many PCs still don't come with built-in FireWire (IEEE-1394) adapters, so double-check to ensure that the PC you buy has FireWire.

If you get a computer without a FireWire adapter, you can usually add one for less than $100. FireWire adapters should be Microsoft-certified and OHCI-compliant. This information should be noted in the documentation that comes with the computer or adapter card.

✔ **A DVD recorder.** Many Windows PCs now include DVD recorder (also called a DVD *burner*) drives. For video editing, a DVD burner is virtually mandatory these days. As you shop around you'll notice that some DVD burners are called DVD-R drives, whereas others are called DVD+R drives. The use of a dash (–) or a plus (+) actually denotes unique, competing standards, each one supported by a list of manufacturers. Neither format has a clear technical advantage over the other, except perhaps that blank DVD-R discs seem to be a little cheaper than DVD+R blanks. Whatever format you choose, make sure you buy blank discs that match your recorder. DVD-R blanks won't work in a DVD+R drive, and vice versa. Some newer drives support both –R and +R formats, so if you buy one of these drives, blank disc format is less of a concern. DVD-RAM is a third recordable DVD technology that is of limited value for digital video work, so I don't recommend paying extra for it.

Some of the most powerful computers built today are designed as gaming systems. Modern computer games require massive amounts of disk space, memory, CPU power, and powerful graphics capabilities. So if you see a computer advertised to gamers ("The Ultimate Gaming System — this thing will blast your socks off!"), you can bet that system will probably make a great video-editing computer as well. Just make sure you get that FireWire option and DVD burner option!

Buy a PC or build your own?

If you are considering a Windows PC, you can either buy a complete system or build your own from parts. Building PCs from scratch (or upgrading an older PC) has been a vaunted geek tradition for years, and many people — myself included — still practice it. Components are available from mail-order companies, Web sites, and some retail electronics stores.

For most PC users, building a computer from scratch doesn't make a whole lot of sense anymore. You must purchase a case, power supply, motherboard, processor, RAM, sound card, video card, modem, network card, FireWire card, hard drive, DVD-R drive, floppy drive, keyboard, mouse, monitor, some cooling fans, speakers, Windows software, various cables, and plenty of coffee to sustain you through a long night of PC wrenching and tweaking. Expect to go back to the computer shop at least three times to get the things you forgot. Now you have a pile of parts that you must put together, and that pile probably cost hundreds of dollars *more* than a pre-assembled unit from a PC maker like Dell or Hewlett-Packard. And unlike your homebuilt computer, that affordable pre-made PC from Dell or H-P comes with a pretty good warranty and technical support.

But for some maniacs — like me — building your own PC can be a lot of fun. Besides, if you need a video-editing system, building your own can help you ensure that you're getting the best possible components. A pre-assembled unit is bound to include some cost-cutting measures to give it more mass-market appeal. Furthermore, because mass-produced computers usually use proprietary case and motherboard designs, gutting them for an extensive upgrade in the future may not be practical.

If you have never built a computer from scratch, this probably isn't a good time to start. I couldn't possibly tell you how to do it in this sidebar, because PC building and upgrading is a subject that fills many books. (May I recommend *Building a PC For Dummies* by Mark L. Chambers, from Wiley Publishing, Inc.?) But if you are comfortable with PC upgrades and construction — and want to build your own video-editing system — follow the system-requirements guidelines listed earlier in this chapter when you pick out your components. And remember, get as far above the minimums as you can afford.

One of these days you'll unplug your FireWire cable from your camcorder, only to have the loose cable fall down behind your desk. Then you'll have to get down on the floor and fish around behind your PC to retrieve the stray cable. Not fun. To address this, I like to have FireWire connectors right on the front of my computer case. If you are ordering a computer, contact the builder to find out if this feature can be added. If you are building your own, check your local PC parts retailer for a front plate kit for your FireWire connectors.

Choosing Video Gear

So you have a fantabulous new computer that is ready to edit video at blazing speeds. Don't worry: You're not done spending money just yet. You still have a lot of cool — and really important — gear left to buy. Well, okay some of the gear covered in the next few sections is pretty mandatory — a camera, for instance. Video can be kind of hard to record without a video camera. Other gear — video decks, audio recorders, and capture cards — may be less mandatory, depending on your needs and budget.

Cameras

No single piece of gear is more precious to a budding videographer than a good video camera. Most modern video cameras are actually *camcorders* because they serve as both a camera and a recorder. Older video cameras connected to separate VCR units on which to record video. Often these VCR units were hung by a strap from the videographer's shoulder. Bulky.

When buying a new camcorder, go digital. The quality of digital video is higher, and it is a lot easier to transfer video from a digital camcorder into a computer. And these days you don't have to take out a second mortgage to afford a digital camcorder — consumer-grade digital camcorder prices start as low as $400.

Of course, if you *want* to spend more money, plenty of high-end camcorders are available as well. The best digital camcorders have three *charged coupled devices* (CCDs) — the eyes in the camera that actually pick up light and turn it into a video image. These include camcorders like the Canon GL2, Panasonic PV-DV952, and the Sony DCR-TRV950. These cameras provide superior color and resolution, as well as features that the pros like such as usable manual controls and high-quality microphones. Be prepared to spend $2,000 to $5,000 for these high-end digital camcorders.

When you're shopping for a new digital camcorder, check the following:

- ✔ **Audio:** For the sake of sound quality, the camcorder should have some provisions for connecting an external microphone. Most camcorders have a standard mini-jack connector for an external mic, and some high-end camcorders have a 3-pin XLR connector. XLR connectors — also sometimes called *balanced* audio connectors — are used by many high-quality microphones and PA (public address) systems.

- ✔ **Batteries:** Make sure that spare batteries are readily available at a reasonable price. I recommend you buy a camcorder that uses Lithium Ion batteries—they last longer and are easier to maintain than NiMH (nickel-metal-hydride) batteries. Buy plenty of extra batteries when you buy your camcorder. If you'll be doing long "on–location" shoots, also consider a battery charger that plugs into a car's accessory power socket.

✔ **Digital Video connections:** Virtually all digital camcorders use a FireWire port for capturing video from the camcorder onto your computer. FireWire is also called IEEE-1394 or i.Link by some camera manufacturers. Some camcorders also have USB connectors, although I don't recommend using USB for video capture unless both your camcorder and your computer supports the USB 2.0 standard (check the documentation). Even *with* USB 2.0, I think you'll find that FireWire is just plain easier to work with.

✔ **Manual controls:** Auto focus and automatic exposure controls are great, but as you get more serious about shooting video you may want more control over these features. The easiest manual focus and exposure controls are ones that are manipulated by a ring around the lens body. Tiny little knobs or slider switches on the side of the camera are more difficult to use.

✔ **Storage media:** Make sure that tapes are affordable and widely available. MiniDV is now the most common recording format, and tapes are affordable and easy to find.

✔ **Zoom:** You'll see "400X ZOOM" splashed across the side of the camera. Such huge numbers usually express *digital* zoom, which is (in my opinion) virtually useless. Check the fine print next to the digital zoom figure and you should see a figure for *optical* zoom. Optical zoom is something you can actually use, and most mass-market digital camcorders offer around 10X to 25X optical zoom.

When you start spending over $1,500 for a camcorder, some people begin to look at you differently. They don't think you're crazy; they think you're a "professional." Actually, true "professional" videographers are shooting the 11:00 o'clock news with cameras that start at $20,000. So there you are with your $4,000 Canon XL1S — not quite a professional, but not exactly a typical consumer either. While I hesitate to slap a label on anyone (I hardly know you!), industry people obsessed with categorizing customers would refer to you as a *prosumer* (a buyer in-between pro and consumer). Don't slap them; you will often see "prosumer" used to describe higher-quality gear in the video world.

Video decks

The first time I heard the term *video deck,* I thought it referred to the deck on a cruise ship where everyone goes to watch movies. Not so. *Video deck* is actually just a fancy term for a *videocassette recorder,* which you may know as a VCR. If you want to talk like a true video geek, however, *video deck* must become part of your lexicon.

Why do you need a video deck? A high-quality deck becomes really useful if you plan to distribute your movies on tape. With the proper electronic connections, you can output a movie directly from your computer to videotape. Also, if you have a deck that uses the same tape format as your camcorder, you can save wear and tear on the camcorder's tape mechanism when you capture video into your computer. Good video decks aren't cheap, however, and a typical VHS VCR will not offer much in the way of quality or editing capabilities. When looking for a video deck, consider the following:

- **Format:** S-VHS decks are good for outputting movies to VHS tape, and provide decent quality. MiniDV decks and other formats are also available from a variety of sources. Some decks even offer both S-VHS and MiniDV in the same unit.

- **FireWire:** Some newer decks have FireWire connections. As with camcorders, this greatly simplifies the process of interfacing with your computer.

- **Device control:** You might be able to control the video deck (for example, fast-forwarding and rewinding) using controls in Adobe Premiere Pro. FireWire greatly simplifies this process, but some high-end editing decks can use a serial cable for device control as well.

If you're just starting to get involved with video editing, a video deck may seem like an extravagance. But the more time you spend capturing and outputting video, the more useful a good video deck can be. And like I said, using a video deck to capture and export video can save a lot of wear and tear on the tape drive in your expensive camcorder.

Audio recorders

All modern camcorders have built-in microphones, and most digital camcorders can record decent-quality audio. However, you may find that the built-in audio recording never exceeds "decent" on the quality scale. There are two simple solutions to recording better audio:

- Use a high-quality accessory microphone.
- Record audio separately.

If you want to connect a better microphone to your camcorder, the best place to start is with your camcorder's manufacturer (you'll need a *really* long cable — just kidding). Usually accessory microphones are available from the manufacturer. These accessory units make use of connections, accessory shoes, and other features on your camcorder.

Separate sound recorders give you more flexibility, especially if you just want to record audio in a certain location but not video. Many professionals use DAT (digital audiotape) recorders to record audio, but DAT recorders are usually quite expensive. Digital voice recorders are also available, but the amount of audio they can record is often limited by whatever storage is built into the unit. For a good balance of quality and affordability, I recommend one of the new MiniDisc recorders. For more on MiniDisc recorders, see Chapter 21.

Capture hardware

A digital camcorder and a powerful computer equipped with Adobe Premiere Pro won't do you much good if you can't get video from the camcorder into the computer. For this you need capture hardware, so called because it captures audio and video into your computer.

FireWire (IEEE-1394) devices

FireWire is a high-speed interface developed by Apple Computer and first released in 1996. *FireWire* is actually Apple's trademark name for the technology officially known as IEEE-1394, named for the international standard to which it conforms. Sony and a few other companies call the interface "i.Link." All DV-format camcorders have a FireWire interface. Although Apple originally developed FireWire with digital video in mind, the IEEE-1394 interface is also used by other devices including external hard drives, still cameras, and scanners.

A FireWire interface makes capturing digital video really easy. You just connect a cable between the FireWire port on your computer and the FireWire port on your camcorder, and then capture video using Premiere Pro. It's easy because all Premiere really has to do is copy digital video data from the camcorder onto your hard drive.

Why is the process of getting video from a camcorder tape onto your hard disk called *capturing* instead of just *copying*? Digital video is recorded onto a camcorder tape in an endless stream of data. The tape does not contain data files like those found on a computer hard drive. When you capture some of that video, you are basically taking a chunk of the video data and "capturing" it into a file that can be stored on your hard drive and used by your software programs (including Premiere Pro).

Many new Windows-based PCs come with FireWire ports, but some don't, so double-check your own PC. You should see a 6-pin FireWire port that resembles Figure 2-2. If you don't see one, you can purchase a FireWire expansion card from many electronics retailers. Installing a FireWire card in your PC has three indispensable prerequisites:

✔ Windows 98 Second Edition (SE) or higher (This shouldn't be a problem because you have to use Windows XP with Premiere Pro anyway.)

✔ A vacant expansion slot in your computer

✔ PC hardware expertise

Figure 2-2:
The FireWire port on your computer should look something like this.

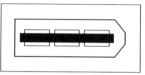

If you aren't familiar with expansion slots and don't have experience with hardware upgrades, consult a professional PC technician. If your computer is still under warranty, don't even *look* at a screwdriver until you've reviewed the warranty terms to determine whether — and how — upgrades should be performed.

Analog video capture devices

Analog video is a bit trickier than digital video to get into your computer because it must first be digitized. Capture cards are available to help you do this bit of magic, but they tend to be expensive. If you don't already have Adobe Premiere, you may find that one cost-effective way to buy a high-quality analog capture card is to get one that already comes bundled with Premiere Pro. Pinnacle used to sell some high-quality capture cards that came packaged with Adobe Premiere, but now that Pinnacle has its own high-end video editing program (Pinnacle Edition), that company is understandably averse to distributing a competitor's software. The Matrox RT.X100 is an excellent capture card that retails for about $1000. Although that may sound like a lot, it *does* include a full version of Adobe Premiere.

Whatever capture card you decide to use, review the specs carefully before you make a buying decision. Many FireWire cards are marketed as "video capture cards" even though they can only capture video from digital camcorders.

For light-duty usage, a good solution to the analog/digital conundrum may be an external video converter. A video converter is a box that sits on your desktop. The box has connectors for analog inputs. The types of inputs vary, but most have at least S-Video and composite inputs. The converter box then connects to your computer via a FireWire port. Electronics inside the box digitize analog video, which is then sent to your computer's FireWire port where it can be captured as regular DV-format video. Some popular video converters include the Canopus ADVC-100, Data Video DAC-100, or Dazzle Hollywood DV-Bridge. If you don't feel like tearing open your computer and dealing with expansion cards, this is a great way to capture analog video. (Video converters are described in more detail in Chapter 21.)

What is Bluetooth and do I need it?

As you shop for camcorders, you'll notice that some newer models advertise that they incorporate a technology called *Bluetooth*. This is a new wireless networking technology that allows various types of electronic components — including camcorders and computers — to connect to each other using radio waves instead of cables. Unfortunately the maximum data rate of current Bluetooth technology is still comparatively low (less than 1 megabit per second). In practical terms, that means Bluetooth won't be suitable for capturing digital video from your camcorder for the foreseeable future. A few camcorders incorporate Bluetooth technology anyway, and that may (or may not) come in handy if you still own the same camcorder a few years from now. But for now, Bluetooth isn't terribly useful in a camcorder, and I don't recommend spending a lot of extra money to get it.

Chapter 3

Getting Premiere Pro Ready to Work

In This Chapter

▶ Getting comfortable in your workspace

▶ Tweaking program settings

▶ Customizing windows in Premiere

▶ Installing plug-ins for Adobe Premiere

*I*f you've been using computers for a while, you have probably gotten used to just opening a program and getting right to work. If you have to type a memo, you launch your word processor, type a few paragraphs, and click Print. If you want to peruse the Internet, you launch your Web browser and start clicking away at links. But Adobe Premiere Pro might be a bit of a switch for you; you can't always just open the program and start making a movie. Some preparation is in order when you start working in this program.

Why does Adobe Premiere have to be set up before you can use it? The main reason is that Premiere Pro is an advanced program that can work with many different kinds of video. Premiere Pro accommodates a variety of editing styles, and you can configure Premiere to use your preferred style. Premiere also offers some options that you should review to ensure that your movie comes out right. This chapter helps you configure Premiere Pro for editing, take charge of important program settings, and get familiar with some useful options.

Setting Up Your Workspace

Look around at the workspace in your office, or wherever it is you plan to use Adobe Premiere Pro. You probably have the computer set up a certain way, the mouse is in your favorite spot, and a ring on the desktop reminds you where you normally place your coffee cup. You have everything just where you like it, and it works.

When you work in Adobe Premiere Pro, it presents a virtual workspace on the screen. Just like the physical workspace around your desk, you can customize Premiere and set up its workspace just the way you like it. You can move windows around, close some items, and open others. Premiere also offers a couple of preset workspaces. To begin exploring them, start by launching Adobe Premiere Pro. To do so, click Start➪All Programs➪Adobe Premiere Pro. After you've launched the program a few times, it should appear in the list of frequently used programs in the Windows XP Start menu.

When you see the Premiere Pro Welcome screen, click the New Project icon. In the New Project window that appears, choose Standard 48 kHz under either DV-NTSC or DV-PAL (it doesn't really matter which one for now). Give the new project a name in the Name field (any old name will do) and then click OK. Premiere Pro opens.

Using workspace presets

If you have used other Adobe programs such as Photoshop or Illustrator, you know that Adobe likes to organize program features into floating windows, toolbars, and palettes. These items can be moved around all over the screen, just like you might rearrange your desk several times through the course of a workday. Completed tasks get moved off to the side to make way for your next task.

With all these windows and toolbars and things floating around, the Premiere Pro workspace can start to look cluttered after a while. Fortunately you can quickly and easily reorganize screen elements using one of several pre-designed workspaces. To open a workspace, choose Window➪Workspace and then choose a workspace from the submenu that appears. The four standard workspaces are

- ✔ Editing
- ✔ Effects
- ✔ Audio
- ✔ Color Correction

Each workspace is designed to accommodate a certain kind of work. The next few sections describe each workspace in greater detail.

If you have used previous versions of Adobe Premiere, you may be wondering what happened to the A/B Workspace. Simply put, Adobe gave it the axe. Premiere Pro's Editing workspace is almost identical to the Single-Track Editing workspace found in previous versions of Premiere. The A/B Workspace was an alternative editing workspace, and after surveying a variety of users,

Adobe decided that the A/B Workspace had fallen out of favor. Other changes to Premiere Pro — in particular, the availability of transitions you can use in any video track — make the A/B Workspace kind of moot anyway.

The Editing workspace

The Editing workspace (formerly known as the "Single-Track" workspace in previous versions of Adobe Premiere) is where you'll probably spend most of your time as you work in Premiere Pro. It's the default workspace that appears when you start a new project, and if you've switched to another workspace, you can bring back the Editing workspace whenever you want by choosing Window⇨Workspace⇨Editing. You should see a workspace similar to Figure 3-1.

Project window   Dual view monitor

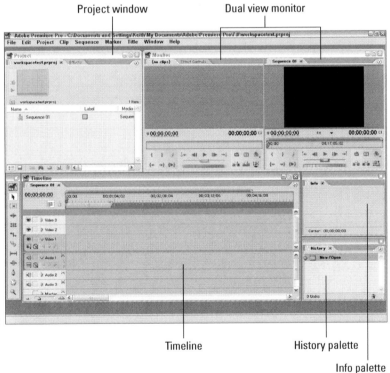

Figure 3-1:
The Editing workspace is a good place to perform most edits.

Timeline   History palette

Info palette

Key features of the Editing workspace include

- ✔ **Dual-View Monitor:** The left pane of the Monitor window is the source-clip area. This is where you decide which portions of a clip you actually want to edit into the Timeline. The other Monitor pane shows the video program that you're actually assembling in the Timeline. You may find that being able to see both clips simultaneously makes them a lot easier to edit into the Timeline.

✔ **History/Info palettes:** Just to the right of the Timeline you'll notice a couple of floating palettes. These palettes are marked History and Info. The History palette is useful because it shows a running record of the last 100 editing actions that you have performed. Figure 3-2 shows a History palette from a project I have been working on recently. I really like the History palette because it provides a log of all your actions — so if your cat steps on the Delete key while you aren't looking, there will be a visible record of Fluffy's dastardly deed right there on the screen.

Figure 3-2: The History palette provides a running log of all your editing actions.

The Effects workspace

Another preset workspace provided by Premiere Pro is the Effects workspace (Window⇨Workspace⇨Effects). This workspace has a single view Monitor, with the left pane of the Monitor replaced by effect controls as shown in Figure 3-3. Quick access to the effects controls is handy because fine-tuning is an essential part of working with effects. The Project window also switches in the Effects workspace to show the folders containing effects and transitions. (See Chapter 9 for more on working with transitions.) Chapter 12 shows you how to use video effects, and lucky Chapter 13 described audio effects.

Effect controls   Single view Monitor

Figure 3-3:
The Effects
workspace
provides
quick
access to
effects and
effect
controls.

The Audio workspace

Video is so exciting that it's easy to forget how important a good soundtrack is in a movie project. If you want your project to make a positive impression, you'd better put some time into editing your audio. Premiere Pro provides the Audio workspace (Window⟶Workspace⟶Audio) to help you get it done. Although you can edit audio in any workspace, the Audio workspace is custom-tailored specifically for audio work.

The Audio workspace (shown in Figure 3-4) includes

- Single-view Monitor
- Audio Mixer

With the Audio Mixer, you can tailor the overall level of your audio to fit your video, as well as mix the levels of individual audio tracks. So (for example), if you have a dialog track that goes with some video, and a musical soundtrack that should play in the background, you can control how loud or quiet the music is relative to the dialog. (See Chapter 13 for more about working with audio.)

Audio Mixer

Figure 3-4:
The Audio
workspace
includes the
Audio Mixer
controls.

The Color Correction workspace

One of the most important new features of Adobe Premiere Pro is an
advanced Color Corrector video filter. This filter provides advanced control
and monitoring over color adjustments for video. A special Color Correction
workspace is available (Window➪Workspace➪Color Correction). As you can
see in Figure 3-5, the Color Correction workspace isn't radically different from
the Editing workspace. The left (source) pane of the Monitor is replaced by a
Reference Monitor, which in the figure I have set to display some reference
monitors that provide technical information about the light and colors in
your video image. (See Chapter 10 for more on using the Color Corrector
filter and understanding the monitors.)

Creating your own custom workspace

Don't like any of the predesigned workspaces provided by Adobe? No problem! You can make your own. If you find that you're constantly re-arranging

windows and palettes a certain way in Premiere Pro, you may want to consider saving the layout as a custom workspace. After it's saved, you can call up your saved workspace from the Window↝Workspace menu, just as you would any other workspace. To save a workspace, follow these steps:

1. **Arrange the windows, palettes, and other program elements exactly the way you like them.**

2. **Choose Window↝Workspace↝Save Workspace.**

3. **Provide a name for your workspace in the Save Workspace dialog box that appears.**

4. **Click Save.**

That's all there is to it. You can create and save as many custom workspaces as you like, and they will all appear in the Window↝Workspace menu. If you ever decide to get rid of a saved workspace, you can simply choose Window↝Workspace↝Delete Workspace and then choose which workspace you want to delete from the Delete Workspace dialog box.

Reference Monitor

Figure 3-5:
The Color
Correction
workspace
helps you
monitor and
adjust video
color.

Adjusting Program Settings

Adobe Premiere Pro offers a plethora of settings, and you could easily spend a day or two trying to sort through them all. Some settings are immediately relevant to your work; some won't be used until you perform more advanced work. The next few sections show you some key settings that help you make more-effective use of Premiere Pro on a daily basis.

Setting up your scratch disks

I hear some of you scratching your heads. "What in the Wide, Wide World of Sports is a scratch disk?" The *scratch disk* is the disk on which you store all your video stuff. When you capture video onto your computer, you capture it to the scratch disk. Likewise, many transitions, timelines, effects, and edits must be *rendered* — that is, they are actually applied to the clips — before those clips can be exported as part of a movie. The rendered clips are stored as *preview files* on the scratch disk. The scratch disk is your Premiere storage place — your video data bucket, so to speak.

If your computer has just one big hard drive, you won't necessarily have a separate scratch disk. Your scratch disk will actually be a folder on your main hard drive. But if you can get a separate hard disk to use exclusively as a Premiere scratch disk, I strongly recommend it. Because big and fast hard drives are so cheap these days, there is almost no reason to *not* have a separate scratch disk.

A scratch disk must be not only big but fast. I recommend a 7200rpm IDE drive at the very least, or if you can afford it, a SCSI drive. If your disk isn't fast enough, you'll drop frames during rendering and when you try to output video to tape. (See Chapter 2 for more on selecting hard drives.)

You can choose different scratch disks and folders for different types of files. Premiere Pro will always use whatever location you specify. To set up your scratch disks, follow these steps:

1. **On the Premiere Pro menu bar, choose Edit⇨Preferences⇨Scratch Disks.**

   The Scratch Disks section of the Preferences dialog box appears, as shown in Figure 3-6.

2. **Use the Captured Video and Captured Audio menus to adjust the scratch disk's setting for media that you capture using Premiere Pro.**

   When you capture movies from a camera, video deck, or other source, this is where the video files are stored. The default location for all scratch disks is a setting called Same as Project — which means the same location where you save your project file when you create a new project. If you have a separate hard drive that you want to use just as a video scratch disk, choose Custom from the drop-down menu next to each item, and then click Browse to choose a specific drive and folder.

3. **Choose a scratch disk for previews from the Video Previews and Audio Previews drop-down menus.**

   When you want to preview or export part of your project or the whole thing, Premiere Pro usually must render several preview files. Just like with Captured Video and Captured Audio, the default location for these preview files is Same as Project, which as the name suggests is the folder where your Premiere Project (.PRPROJ) file is saved. You can select a different folder if you want.

4. **Choose a scratch disk for conformed audio files from the Conformed Audio drop-down menu.**

   Conformed audio files store track information and other audio changes made by Premiere Pro. (I recommend using the same setting here that you used for your audio and video previews.) Conformed audio is described in Chapter 13.

5. **Click OK when you're done adjusting your Scratch Disk settings.**

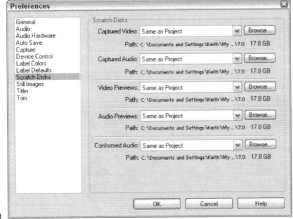

Figure 3-6:
Configure
your storage
space using
the Scratch
Disks
settings.

If your computer is on a network, you can choose network drives on other computers when you set up your scratch disks. However, I strongly recommend against using network drives as scratch disks. Most networks are not fast enough or reliable enough to adequately handle large video files without dropping frames and causing other problems.

Customizing other options

Premiere Pro has many options and preferences that you can fiddle with to make the program work the way *you* want it to. The new Preferences dialog box (shown in Figure 3-6) is a lot easier to use than in previous editions of Premiere because you can quickly jump to different groups of settings by simply clicking a category in the list on the left side of the dialog box. To open the Preferences dialog box, choose Edit⇨Preferences and then choose any item from the submenu that appears. Preferences are organized into the following groups:

✔ **General:** The most important General settings are the Default Duration settings for video and audio transitions — these determine how long a transition takes when you first apply it to an audio or video clip. Of course, you can always adjust the duration for any transition; you may find it useful to change the default settings. The duration for video transitions is expressed in *frames*, and the default duration for audio transitions is expressed in *seconds*. A slider control in General preferences also allows you to make the Premiere Pro program window brighter or darker.

✔ **Audio:** Here you can specify the audio automatch time as well as the default mixdown format for 5.1 (surround-sound) audio tracks. See Chapter 13 for more on working with audio.

✔ **Audio Hardware:** If you have multiple audio input/output sources on your computer, you can tell Premiere Pro which ones to use by setting the Audio Hardware preferences.

✔ **Auto Save:** Choose whether Premiere Pro automatically saves your projects, and control how often those auto-saves occur.

✔ **Capture:** Here you can tell Premiere Pro to simply abort video capture if any frames are dropped. (I strongly recommend that you leave the Report Dropped Frames option checked; if frames get dropped, you'll want to know.)

✔ **Device Control:** Set control options for your video-capture and output hardware here. (See Chapter 6 for more on working with device-control settings.)

- ✔ **Label Colors:** Do you like to color-code your work? Then you're in luck because Premiere Pro lets you apply color-coded labels to all kinds of program elements. Use this preferences group to choose label colors.

- ✔ **Label Defaults:** Different types of media and elements are given different colored labels by default. Control those default colors here.

- ✔ **Scratch Disks:** Determine where the video files for your project are stored on your computer. (See the previous section for more on setting up Scratch Disk settings.)

- ✔ **Still Images:** Control the default duration for still images here. Again, you can always change the duration of stills once you've included them in a project, but you may find it handy to change the default duration.

- ✔ **Titler:** Use this preferences group to control which letters appear in style swatches and in the font browser in the Adobe Title Designer.

- ✔ **Trim:** This setting controls the number of frames on the Large Trim Offset buttons in the Trim window.

Customizing Premiere's Windows

As an individual (just like everyone else), you probably like to personalize the software you use to make it better suit your needs. We don't all have the same work habits, and what works for me may not be ideal for you. The programmers at Adobe realized that your idea of the perfect working environment may not be the same as theirs — so they've given you quite a bit of control over some of Premiere's windows. You can even customize some keyboard commands.

Using the Project window

The Project window works kind of like Premiere Pro's filing cabinet. All files that you use in a project are stored in the Project window. By default, files are displayed in a basic list, displaying various details about each file. I usually find this display mode to be the most useful for Premiere, but the Project window also provides an icon view that can be useful too. Icon view (shown in Figure 3-7) displays files and items as icons that help you better visualize the nature of each item. To use icon view, click the Icon button in the lower-left corner of the Project window.

The Project window also contains a menu which lets you further customize the way the window looks. To access this menu, click the tiny right-pointing arrow in the upper-right corner of the Project window (see Figure 3-7). You can activate several useful options from this Project window menu:

✔ Click View⇨Preview Area to turn the preview window at the top of the Project window on or off.

✔ Open the Thumbnails submenu and choose a different size for thumbnail images used in icon view.

✔ Click Edit Columns in the Project window menu to open the Edit Columns dialog box. This dialog box controls which columns appear in list view. Remove any check marks that appear next to columns you don't want to use, or select a column title and click Move Up or Move Down to change the order in which columns appear. Click OK to close the Edit Columns dialog box.

Project window menu

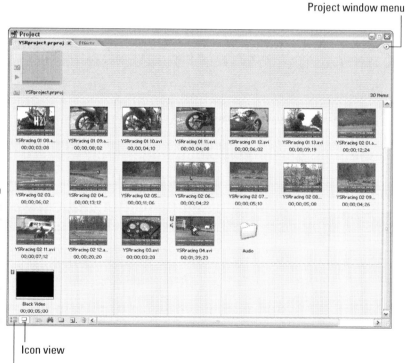

Figure 3-7: Icon view is an alternative way to look at items in the Project window.

Icon view

List view

Modifying the Timeline

Throughout this book, I show the Timeline with default view settings. However, you can adjust some useful view options using a couple of different tools. These tools include

- Click the right-pointing arrow in the upper-right corner of the Timeline to open the Timeline window menu. Here you can click Audio Units to change the timecode to read in audio units rather than video frames (click Audio Units again to switch back to frames) or click Sequence Zero Point to open the Sequence Zero Point dialog box. This dialog box allows you to select a different starting timecode for your current sequence.

- Click the Set Display Style button on the track header for a video track (as in Figure 3-8) and choose a display option from the menu that appears. The default setting is Show Head Only, which means the first frame of the clip appears as a thumbnail at the beginning of the clip. If you choose Show Head and Tail, thumbnail frames appear at the beginning and end of each clip. If you choose Show Frames, a visual progression of frames appears on each clip, as shown in Figure 3-8. If you don't want any thumbnails to appear at all, choose Show Name Only.

- Click the Set Display Style button on the track header for an audio track and choose an option from the menu that appears. Audio-track options are a little more limited. Basically, you tell the Timeline to show just the name of a particular audio clip, or you can tell it to show the *waveform* (a visual representation of the audio levels) of the clip as well.

- Use the Zoom slider at the bottom of the Timeline window to zoom in or out on the Timeline. The plus (+) and minus (–) keys on your keyboard also let you zoom quickly in or out.

Timeline window menu

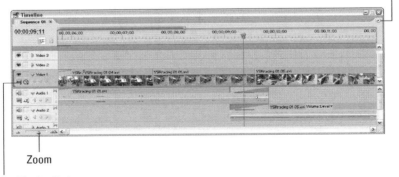

Figure 3-8:
Change the
way clips
appear in
the Timeline
window.

Zoom

Set Display Style

Adjusting the Monitor

No, this section doesn't show you how to use all those little buttons on the front of your computer's monitor (sorry). Instead, I'll show you how to adjust Premiere's Monitor window. To do so, click the little right-pointing arrow in the upper-right corner of the Monitor to open the Monitor window menu. Key options in this menu include

- **New Reference Monitor:** Choose this option to open a new Reference Monitor window. As I show in Chapter 10, a Reference Monitor can be very helpful as you do color correction to your video.

- **Scopes:** A list of all the available scopes (see Chapter 10) can be found in the Monitor window menu. Choose Composite if you just want to see the regular video image.

- **Quality:** Choose whether you want the playback quality in the monitor to be Highest Quality, Draft Quality, or Automatic Quality. The Highest Quality setting may cause playback problems if your computer doesn't meet or exceed the *recommended* system requirements described in Chapter 2. In most cases I recommend using Automatic Quality.

- **Loop:** Choose this option if you want clips in the Monitor to loop over and over when you play them.

- **Audio Units:** Click the Audio Units option to change the timecode display to show audio units rather than video frames.

- **Safe Margins:** Here you can set whether title-safe and action-safe margins appear in the Monitor. If your program will be viewed on broadcast-style TV screens, some action or titles might get cut off at the edge of the screen if they fall outside the title-safe and action-safe margins. The margins are expressed as a percentage of the overall screen area.

- **View Options:** Three general view options for the Monitor window are available: Dual View, Single View, and Trim. The Dual View Monitor appears when you open the Editing workspace (Window⇨Workspace⇨ Editing). The left side is used for source clips; the right side shows the current sequence of clips. (The Single View Monitor shows only the sequence.) When you choose the Trim option, a separate Trim window appears with two panes, as shown in Figure 3-9. This feature helps you perform trim edits more effectively in your projects. (I show you how to make trim edits in Chapter 8.) These settings let you control the appearance of the video image when you're trimming or previewing clips. During some Timeline editing tasks (such as Ripple Edits), you can view the frames affected by your edits in the Monitor in Trim Mode. In the Monitor Window Options dialog box, you can control how the Monitor appears during Trim Mode.

- **Playback Settings:** Click this option to open the DV Playback Settings dialog box. This dialog box (described in greater detail in Chapter 5) helps you control whether and how your work plays on external video hardware.

Figure 3-9:
Open the
Trim
window
from the
Monitor
when you
perform
trim edits.

Mixing up the Audio Mixer

When you're working on a movie project, don't forget about the audio portion of the program. Premiere Pro provides you with a special Audio Mixer window to help you control the levels of the various audio tracks in your project. As with other windows in Premiere, the Audio Mixer can be customized. To see options for the Audio Mixer, click the small right-pointing arrow in the upper-right corner of the Audio Mixer window (see Figure 3-10). In the Audio Mixer window menu that appears, review (and set as needed) the following options:

- ✔ **Master Meters Only:** Normally the Audio Mixer shows controls and meters for each audio track. If you just want to display the Master audio meters for the overall project, choose this option.

- ✔ **Show/Hide Tracks:** Click this option to open the Show/Hide Tracks dialog box and select which audio tracks should appear in the Audio Mixer. You may want to hide tracks that don't contain any audio in the portion of your project on which you're currently working.

- ✔ **Audio Units:** Click this option to display timecode as audio units rather than as video frames.

- ✔ **Loop:** Click this to loop playback over and over.

- ✔ **Switch to Touch after Write:** In Write mode, audio levels are set to the current positions of the audio mixer controls. In Touch mode, changes to audio levels occur only when you actually touch the controls with your mouse pointer. When you release a control while working in Touch mode, it snaps back to the original position. Check the Switch to Touch after Write option if you want the editing mode to switch automatically to Touch after you use Write.

Audio Mixer window menu

Figure 3-10:
Edit audio
using the
Audio Mixer
window.

Customizing keyboard commands

Adobe Premiere Pro follows the same basic design paradigm as most other modern software programs. Premiere's workspace is designed as a GUI (*graphical user interface*, often pronounced "gooey"), which means that program elements are laid out graphically. You navigate program windows and execute editing commands using the mouse to click on buttons, drag-and-drop items, and choose menu items. You can do almost anything in Premiere Pro with a mouse.

Still, don't throw away that keyboard just yet. Many Premiere users find that the mouse just doesn't have enough buttons to quickly perform some important actions. Thankfully, many common commands are accessible by using keys on the keyboard. In fact, Adobe worked hard to ensure that Premiere Pro uses some of the same industry-standard keyboard commands as other professional editing programs. An example is the use of J, K, and L for shuttle control.

To view some of the most common keyboard commands in Premiere Pro, choose Help⇨Keyboard (sorry, you'll have to use the mouse for this one). If you want to customize keyboard commands, choose Edit⇨Keyboard Customization. The Keyboard Customization window appears, as shown in Figure 3-11. This window has two drop-down menus at the top. The first drop-down menu lets you choose a set of keyboard commands. The default set is the Adobe Premiere Pro Factory Defaults (which you can return to at any time by choosing it from the Set menu). The second menu displays different items for which you can set keyboard shortcuts. The choices in this menu are

✔ **Application:** The majority of keyboard commands can be found here. Virtually all Premiere Pro program commands can be found in the Application group.

✔ **Windows:** This group contains commands that are specific to the various windows in Premiere Pro.

✔ **Tools:** Specify keyboard commands for each tool on the Premiere Pro toolbar.

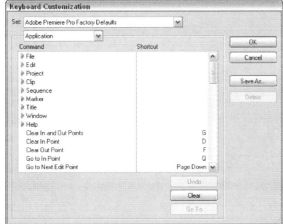

Figure 3-11: Use the Keyboard Customization window to set your own keyboard commands.

Scroll down the lists to see the keyboard shortcuts assigned to each Premiere Pro command. To change a command, click on the shortcut in the Shortcut column, and then type a new shortcut. If your new shortcut is already used by another command, that fact is noted at the bottom of the window.

If you make a lot of changes, I recommend you save your keyboard-command set. To do so, click Save As and give your command set a descriptive name. Afterward, your custom keyboard-command set is available as a choice in the Set menu.

Installing Premiere Plug-Ins

One of the things I really like about Adobe software — from the ubiquitous Acrobat Reader all the way up to Premiere Pro — is that the company designs its programs so capabilities can be added through the use of plug-ins. Some third-party software companies get pretty creative with the features they add. Plug-ins for Premiere Pro can add new effects, transitions, export options, advanced titling options, and more. Chapter 20 highlights several plug-ins for Adobe Premiere. Adobe provides a list of select plug-ins for Premiere online at

```
www.adobe.com/products/plugins/premiere/main.html
```

When you obtain a Premiere Pro plug-in, installation instructions *should* be provided by the publisher. Ideally, the plug-in will come with a setup program or installer that takes care of everything for you. Keep in mind, however, many plug-in publishers assume that you know a thing or two about how Premiere Pro is installed and configured on your system. The main thing to know is that all plug-ins for Adobe programs are stored in a "plug-ins" folder somewhere on your hard drive. When you obtain a new plug-in, often you're expected to copy the plug-in file to that specific folder manually. Of course, it helps to know where the folder *is*. No problem. On a PC running Windows XP, the folder should be right about here:

```
C:\Program Files\Adobe\Premiere Pro\Plug-ins
```

Make sure that Premiere Pro is completely closed *before* you install a new plug-in.

Again, carefully read the documentation that comes with the plug-in (there might be a Readme file) for specific installation instructions. After you place the plug-in file in the folder mentioned here, it should be available the next time you open Premiere Pro. For example, if the plug-in adds a new transition, look for that transition to appear as an option in the Transitions group on the Effects tab when you restart Premiere Pro.

Part II
Gathering Footage

The 5th Wave — By Rich Tennant

In this part . . .

Every journey must have a first step. When your journey involves moviemaking, your first step should be to familiarize yourself with the techniques and concepts of video creation and editing. This part begins by introducing you to the fundamentals of video production, a full understanding of which is crucial to creating successful movies.

After you understand the basics and have shot some video footage, you start working with movie projects in Adobe Premiere Pro — and transfer video from your camcorder into your computer.

Chapter 4

A Crash Course in Video Production

The reels in the Bell & Howell projector began to turn as the bulb blinked on. On the far wall of the darkened living room, the image of a boy appeared. He was holding a shovel, and piles of snow sat all around him. With the rhythmic ticking of the shutter as a soundtrack, the boy silently flung a shovelful of snow. He then looked up and grinned. Suddenly, a reel in the projector jammed and the image froze. For an instant the boy and his shovel were frozen in time, and then just as suddenly the image shriveled away as the bulb's heat melted through the plastic film. "Oops!" exclaimed my grandfather as he switched off the bulb. "Keith, go get me some tape so I can splice this."

A lot has changed since Grandpa filmed Dad shoveling snow in 1959. The movies he shot on his old 8mm film camera had to be processed by a film developer, who wrapped the film around a metal reel and enclosed it in a disk-shaped film can. A special film projector was needed for display, and edits had to be performed with a razor blade and cellophane tape. Shooting the simplest movie was a complicated and expensive undertaking.

The first great revolution in affordable moviemaking equipment was magnetic videotape. Tapes were reusable, they didn't need to be processed like film, and ordinary televisions could be used for playback. High-quality video footage was now easy and affordable, but *editing* that video was still a burdensome process. Thankfully, the second great moviemaking revolution has come in the form of digital video. If you want to make professional-caliber movies, you no longer need years of training and editing equipment costing hundreds of thousands of dollars. Now all you need is a digital camcorder, a modern computer, and an editing program like Adobe Premiere Pro. If you're new to digital video, this chapter introduces you to the technology and shows you how it makes video editing accessible to almost anyone with a computer and a digital camcorder. This chapter also introduces you to video technologies and concepts to help you make more effective use of Adobe Premiere Pro. (If this chapter whets your appetite for information on the basics of digital video and moviemaking, check out my other book, *Digital Video For Dummies, 3rd Edition,* also published by Wiley Publishing, Inc.)

What Is DV?

DV is an abbreviation for *digital video.*

Oh, you want a more detailed explanation? No problem. Computers, as you probably know, aren't very intelligent. They don't understand the serene beauty of a rose garden, the mournful song of a cello, or the graceful motion of an eagle in flight. All computers really understand are ones and zeros. And yet, we force computers to show us pictures, play music, and display moving video. In effect, infinitely variable sounds and pictures must be converted into the language of computers: ones and zeros. This conversion process is called *digitizing.* Digital video is (you guessed it) video that has been digitized.

To fully understand the difference between analog data and digital data, suppose you want to draw the profile of a hill. An analog representation of the profile (as in Figure 4-1) would follow the contour of the hill perfectly because analog values are infinitely variable. However, a digital contour of that same hill would not be able to follow every single detail of the hill because, as shown in Figure 4-2, digital values are made up of specifically defined individual bits of data.

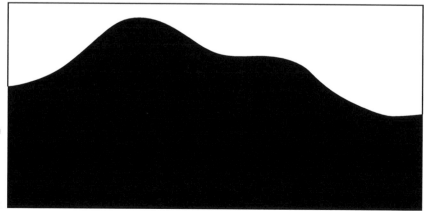

Figure 4-1:
Analog data
is infinitely
variable.

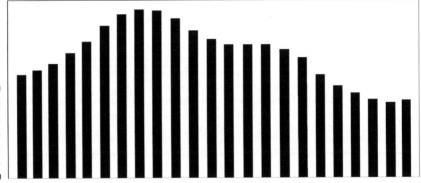

Figure 4-2:
Digital data
contains
specific
values.

Comparing Analog and Digital Video

It could be said that a digital recording will always be theoretically inferior to an analog recording because the analog recording can contain more values. But the truth is that major advances in digital technology mean that this really doesn't matter. Yes, a digital recording must have specific values, but modern recordings have so many unique values packed so closely together that human eyes and ears can barely tell the difference. In fact, casual observation often reveals that digital recordings usually seem to be of higher quality than analog recordings. Why?

One of the problems with analog recordings is that they are highly susceptible to deterioration. Every time analog data is copied, some of the original data is lost. This phenomenon is called *generational loss* and can be observed in that dark, grainy copy of a copy of a copy of a wedding video that was first shot over ten years ago. But digital data doesn't have this problem. A one is always a one, no matter how many times it is copied, and a zero is always a zero. Likewise, analog recordings are more susceptible to deterioration after every playback, which explains why your *Meet the Beatles* LP pops, hisses, and has lost many of its highs and lows over the years.

Whether you're editing analog or digital material, always work from a copy of the master and keep the master safe. When adding analog material to your project, the fewer generations your recording is from the original, the better.

When you consider the implications of generational loss on video editing, you begin to see what a blessing digital video really is. You will constantly be copying, editing, and recopying content as you edit your movie projects — and with digital video, you can edit to your heart's content, confident that the quality won't diminish with each new copy you make.

Understanding Video Fundamentals

Before getting into a detailed description of what video *is,* take a look at what video *is not.* Video is not film. What's the difference? In film, an image is captured when chemicals on the film react with light. In modern video, an image is captured by a *charged coupled device* (CCD) — a sort of electronic eye — and then the image is recorded magnetically on tape. Many films today are actually shot using video, even though they are output to and distributed on film.

How does video work?

Little Jenny picks a dandelion on a sunny afternoon. She brings the fluffy flower to her lips, and with a puff, the seeds flutter gently away on the breeze (they land in the neighbor's immaculate yard and spawn dozens more unappreciated yellow flowers). As this scene unfolds, light photons bounce off Jenny, the dandelion stem, the seeds, and anything else in the shot. Some of those photons pass through the lens of your camcorder. The lens focuses the photons on transistors in the CCD. The transistors get excited, and the CCD converts this excitement into data, which is then magnetically recorded on tape for later playback and editing. This process, shown in Figure 4-3, is repeated approximately 30 times per second.

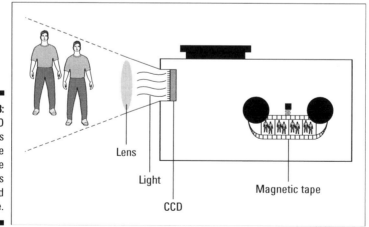

Figure 4-3:
The CCD converts light into the video image that is recorded on tape.

Lens

Light

CCD

Magnetic tape

Many mass-market, consumer-oriented DV camcorders have a single CCD, but higher-quality cameras have three CCDs. In such cameras, individual CCDs capture red, green, and blue light, respectively. Multi-CCD cameras are expensive (most price out on the far side of $2000), but the image produced is near-broadcast quality.

The prehistoric ancestors of camcorders (portable video cameras of about 20 years ago) used video-pickup tubes instead of CCDs. Tubes were inferior to CCDs in many ways, particularly in the way they handled extremes of light. With video-pickup tubes, points of bright light (such as a light bulb or reflection of the sun) bled and streaked across the picture, and low-light situations were simply too dark to shoot.

Decrypting video standards

A lot of new terms have entered the videophile's lexicon in recent years. NTSC. PAL. HDTV. These terms identify broadcast television standards — which are vitally important for anyone who plans to edit video because your cameras, TVs, and tape decks probably conform to only *one* broadcast standard. Which standard is for you? That depends upon where you live:

- **NTSC:** *National Television Standards Committee.* Used primarily in North America, Japan, and the Philippines.

- **PAL:** *Phase-Alternating Line.* Used primarily in Western Europe, Australia, Southeast Asia, and South America.

- **SECAM:** *Sequential Couleur Avec Mémoire.* This category actually covers several similar standards used primarily in France, Russia, Eastern Europe, Central Asia, and most of Africa.

Adobe Premiere Pro supports all three major broadcast formats. When you begin a project, you should always adjust the project settings to the correct format. (See Chapter 5 for more on setting up a new project.)

What you need to know about video standards

The most important thing to know about these three broadcast standards is that they are *not* compatible. In other words, if you try to play an NTSC-format videotape in a PAL video deck, the tape won't work, even if both decks use VHS tapes. This is because VHS is merely a physical *tape* format, not a video format.

Some nice-to-know stuff about video standards

The video standards differ in two primary ways. First, they have different frame rates. The frame rate of video is the number of individual images that appear per second, thus providing the illusion that subjects on the screen are moving. Frame rate is usually abbreviated *fps* (frames per second). Second, the standards use different resolutions. Table 4-1 details the differences.

Table 4-1	Video Standards	
Standard	*Frame Rate*	*Resolution*
NTSC	29.97 fps	525 lines
PAL	25 fps	625 lines
SECAM	25 fps	625 lines

A video picture is usually drawn as a series of horizontal lines. An electron gun at the back of the picture tube draws lines of the video picture back and forth, much like the way the printer head on your printer moves back and forth as it prints words on a page. The resolution of a video image is usually expressed in the number of these horizontal lines that make up the image.

All three video standards listed in Table 4-1 are *interlaced*. This means that the horizontal lines are drawn in two passes rather than one. Every other line is drawn on each consecutive pass, and each of these passes is called a *field*. So on a PAL display, which shows 25 fps, there are actually 50 fields per second.

Noninterlaced displays are also common. Modern computer monitors, for example, are all *noninterlaced,* meaning that all the lines are drawn in a single pass. Some HDTV (High-Definition Television) formats are noninterlaced, whereas others are interlaced. Noninterlaced displays are also sometimes called *progressive scan* displays.

What was that about HDTV?

Speaking of HDTV, a full accounting of all the HDTV formats would almost fill a book by itself. Resolution in HDTV is measured in pixels (like a computer monitor) rather than horizontal lines (like NTSC and PAL). Resolutions for HDTV formats range from as low as 640 x 480 pixels up to 1920 x 1080. Although 640 x 480 may sound low if you have been around computers for a while, it's still pretty good compared to traditional television displays. Frame rates for HDTV range from 24 fps noninterlaced, up to 60 fps (interlaced or not).

With all the uncertainly surrounding HDTV, I recommend against developing video for specific HDTV formats until a single format emerges as a standard in your geographic area or profession. Instead, develop video for your local broadcast format (NTSC, PAL, or SECAM) and assume (hope?) that your audience members have converters on their high-definition TVs.

The many aspects of aspect ratios

Different moving picture displays have different shapes. The screens in movie theaters, for example, look like long rectangles, whereas most TV screens are almost square. The shape of a video display is called the *aspect ratio*. The following two sections look at how aspect ratios affect editing in Adobe Premiere Pro.

Image aspect ratios

The aspect ratio of a typical television screen is 4:3. This means that for any given size, the display is four units wide and three units high. To put this in real numbers, measure the width and height of a TV or computer monitor that you have nearby. If the display is 32 cm wide, for example, you should notice that it's also 24 cm high. If a picture completely fills this display, the picture is also said to have a 4:3 aspect ratio.

Different numbers are sometimes used to describe the same aspect ratio. The 4:3 aspect ratio is sometimes expressed as 1.33:1. Likewise, the 16:9 aspect ratio is sometimes expressed as 1.78:1. But do the math and you'll see that these different numbers still equal the same basic shape.

A lot of movies are distributed on tape and DVD today in *widescreen* format. The aspect ratio of a widescreen picture is usually (but not always) 16:9. If you watch a widescreen movie on a 4:3 TV screen, you will see black bars at the top and bottom of the screen. This format is popular because it more closely matches the aspect ratio of the movie-theater screens for which films are usually shot. Figure 4-4 illustrates the difference between the 4:3 and 16:9 aspect ratios.

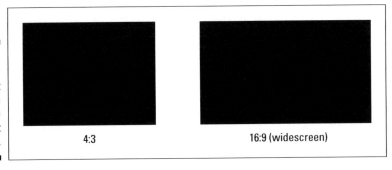

Figure 4-4:
The two most common image aspect ratios.

4:3   16:9 (widescreen)

A common misconception is that 16:9 is the aspect ratio of all big–screen movies. In fact, various aspect ratios for film have been used over the years. Many movies have an aspect ratio of over 2:1 — the image is more than twice as wide as it is high! But for most films, 16:9 is considered close enough. More to the point, it's just right for you because if your digital camcorder has a widescreen mode, its aspect ratio is probably 16:9. Adobe Premiere Pro fully supports 16:9 media, as well as virtually any other film or video format in use today.

Pixel aspect ratios

You may already be familiar with image aspect rations, but did you know that *pixels* can have various aspect ratios too? If you've worked with a drawing or graphics program on a computer, you're probably familiar with pixels. A pixel is the smallest piece of a digital image. Thousands — even millions — of uniquely colored pixels combine in a grid to form an image on a television or computer screen. On computer displays, pixels are square. But in standard video, pixels are *rectangular*. In NTSC video, pixels are taller than they are wide — and in PAL or SECAM, pixels are wider than they are tall.

Pixel aspect ratios become an issue when you start using still computer graphics in projects that also contain standard video. If you don't prepare the still graphic carefully, it could appear distorted when viewed on a TV. For more on preparing still graphics for use in movie projects, see Chapter 6.

Understanding timecode

A video image is actually a series of still frames that flash rapidly on the screen. Every frame is uniquely identified with a number called a *timecode*. The location and duration of all edits that you perform on a movie project use timecodes for reference points, so a basic understanding of timecode is critical. You'll see and use timecode almost every time you work in Adobe Premiere Pro. Timecode is normally expressed like this:

```
hours : minutes : seconds : frames
```

Thus the fourteenth frame of the third second of the twenty-eighth minute of the first hour of video is identified like this:

```
01:28:03:13
```

You already know what hours, minutes, and seconds are. Frames, as stated earlier, are the individual still images that make up video. The frame portion of timecode starts with zero and counts up depending upon the frame rate of the video. In PAL video, frames are counted from 00 to 24 because the frame rate of PAL is 25 fps. In NTSC, frames are counted from 00 to 29.

"Wait!" you exclaim. "Zero to 29 adds up to 30 fps, not 29.97."

You're an observant one, aren't you? As mentioned earlier, the frame rate of NTSC video is 29.97 fps (refer to Table 4-1). NTSC timecode actually skips frame codes 00 and 01 in the first second of every minute — except for every tenth minute. Work it out (let's hear it for calculators!), and you see that this system of reverse leap-frames adds up to 29.97 fps. This is called *drop-frame* timecode. In Premiere Pro and most other video-editing systems, drop-frame timecode is expressed with semicolons (;) instead of colons (:) between the numbers.

Why does NTSC video use drop-frame timecode? Well, back when everything was broadcast in black and white, NTSC video was an even 30 fps. For the conversion to color, more bandwidth was needed in the signal to broadcast color information. Dropping a couple of frames every minute left enough room in the signal to broadcast color information, while at the same time keeping the video signals compatible with older black-and-white TVs. (Clever, those earthlings . . .)

Analyzing DV Tape Formats

Various DV tape formats exist for almost any budget. By far the most common format today is MiniDV, but many others exist. Most alternatives are very expensive, however, and are oriented toward video professionals. I describe the most common formats in the following sections.

MiniDV

MiniDV has become the most popular standard format for digital videotapes. Virtually all consumer and prosumer digital camcorders sold today use MiniDV, which means that blank tapes are now easy to find and reasonably affordable. If you're still shopping for a camcorder and are wondering which format is best for all-around use, let me cut to the chase: MiniDV is it.

MiniDV tapes are small and more compact than even audiocassette tapes. Small is good because smaller tape-drive mechanisms mean smaller, lighter camcorders. Tapes come in a variety of lengths, the most common length being 60 minutes.

All MiniDV devices use the IEEE-1394 FireWire interface to connect to computers, and the DV codec is used to compress and capture video. (*Codecs* are compression schemes — codec is a shortened form of *c*ompression/*dec*ompression.) Codecs are described later in this chapter in the "Understanding Codecs" section. The DV codec is supported by virtually all FireWire hardware and video-editing software, including Adobe Premiere Pro.

Other consumer-grade formats

Not so long ago, MiniDV tapes were expensive and difficult to find. Several manufacturers began to offer alternative formats for digital camcorders, and many of those alternatives are still available. Perhaps the most common alternative to MiniDV is Digital8, created by Sony. Digital8 cameras record DV video on Hi-8 videotapes, which are about the size of audiocassette tapes. Digital8 camcorders are available from both Sony and Hitachi. A 120-minute Hi-8 tape can store 60 minutes of Digital8 video.

Because Hi-8 is a popular format for analog camcorders, Hi-8 tapes have been affordable and widely available for several years. But more recently, the price of MiniDV tapes has come down enough to make Digital8 camcorders less advantageous. Nothing is wrong with Digital8 camcorders; I have an older one (a Sony DCR-TRV103), and it works great. Like MiniDV camcorders, Digital8 camcorders use the DV codec. Plug it into your FireWire port and the computer won't know the difference. It's just that the future of DV recording is MiniDV, not Digital8.

Various other recording formats have appeared on the mass market. Some camcorders use a built-in DVD recorder for storage, but blank DVD media are still relatively expensive and DVD-based camcorders tend to be bulky. Still others use proprietary or built-in recording media. Sony, for example, offers some very small digital camcorders that use a proprietary format called MicroMV. Any common digital format can be used with Premiere Pro, but unless you have a special need, I recommend that you avoid the whiz-bang formats and stick with MiniDV.

Always check the price and availability of blank media before you buy any camcorder. If blanks are unavailable or too expensive, your camcorder could become virtually useless.

Professional-grade formats

Do you have $20,000 burning a hole in your pocket? You could spend that sum very quickly on professional-grade video equipment. Wonderful though MiniDV may be for general-purpose use, it does present some shortcomings when used in a professional environment. Professional-grade formats offer several advantages over MiniDV:

- ✔ Pro-grade tapes are usually more *robust* than MiniDV, which means that they can withstand more shuttling (forwarding and rewinding) and other editing operations.

- ✔ Professional formats usually include outputs that aren't included on many MiniDV camcorders. In addition to the FireWire, S-Video, and composite outputs usually found on MiniDV, pro-equipment often includes component video and Serial Digital Interface (SDI) outputs.

✔ Some newer pro-grade digital cameras can shoot at 24 fps, the frame rate as for film.

✔ Audio-video synchronization is often more precise on professional formats.

Many professional-grade formats are actually derivations of MiniDV. The DVCPro format from Panasonic and the DVCAM format from Sony are both based on the MiniDV format, but they offer more robust assemblies and tracks that are better suited to heavy-duty editing. Sony also offers the Digital Betacam format, which is based on the vaunted Betacam SP analog format. Older pro-digital formats included D1, D2, D3, and D5. These formats also offered robust design, but the video resolutions were lower than the newer MiniDV-based formats.

The bottom line: If you're a video hobbyist, amateur videographer, or corporate video producer on a fixed budget, MiniDV remains a perfectly adequate format, especially if you aren't operating on a professional-grade budget.

Analog formats

Analog video formats have a lot of history, but they're fading quickly from the scene. A major portent of the death of analog came in late 2001, when Sony announced that it would discontinue its beloved Betacam SP format. Betacam SP was long preferred among video professionals, but Sony opted to drop the format because digital equivalents offer virtually the same quality for far less money.

Because analog video has been around for so long, countless formats exist. You've probably seen these formats around, and you may have even owned (or still own) a camcorder that uses one. Besides the generational-loss problems of analog video, analog formats usually provide fewer horizontal lines of resolution. Even the highest-quality analog formats offer only 400 lines of resolution, compared to MiniDV formats, where the cheapest consumer-grade cameras _start_ at 400 resolution lines. Spend a couple thousand dollars and you can get a MiniDV camcorder like the Canon XL1 or Sony DCR-VX2000 that offers over 500 lines. Table 4-2 provides a brief overview of common analog formats.

Table 4-2	Analog Video Formats	
Format	_Resolution Lines_	_Description_
VHS	250	Your basic garden-variety videotape. VHS camcorders are bulky.
S-VHS	400	A higher-quality incarnation of VHS, but the tapes are still big.

(continued)

Table 4-2 *(continued)*

Format	Resolution Lines	Description
VHS-C	250	A compact version of VHS.
8mm	260	Smaller tapes mean smaller camcorders.
Hi-8	400	A higher-quality version of 8mm.
¾ inch Umatic	280	Bulky analog tapes once common in professional analog systems; a higher-quality version offers 340 lines.
Betacam	300	Sony's professional analog format based on Betamax (remember those?).
Betacam-SP	340	A higher-quality version of Betacam.

You can use analog video with Adobe Premiere, but you need a video capture card that can digitize the video. Analog capture devices are discussed in Chapter 2.

Understanding Codecs

A digital video signal contains a lot of data. If you were to copy uncompressed digital video onto your hard drive, it would consume 20MB (megabytes) *for every second of video*. Simple arithmetic tells us that one minute of uncompressed video would use over 1GB (gigabyte). Even with a 60GB hard drive, you would have room for only about 50 minutes of uncompressed video — assuming that big drive was empty to begin with. Dire though these numbers may seem, storage isn't even the biggest problem with uncompressed video. Typical hard-drive busses (and other components in your computer) usually can't handle a transfer rate of 20MB per second; some frames will be dropped from the video.

To deal with the massive bandwidth requirements of video, digital video is compressed using compression schemes called *codecs* (*co*mpressor/*dec*ompressor). The DV codec, used by most digital camcorders, compresses video down to 3.6MB per second. This data rate is far more manageable, and most modern computer hardware can handle it. When you capture DV video from a camcorder using a FireWire interface, a minute of video consumes just over 200MB of hard-drive space. Again, most modern computers can manage that.

Why do codecs matter to you? Adobe Premiere Pro enables you to choose from a variety of codecs when you output the video that you edit. If you capture analog video from a capture card, you'll have to choose a codec for the captured video. Logically enough, the more your video is compressed, the more quality you lose. So consider the following issues when you choose a codec:

- ✔ **Is the movie intended for Internet playback?** Most Internet users still have pretty limited bandwidth. According to Nielsen//NetRatings (www. nielsen-netratings.com), as of mid-2003, only about one-third of Internet users in the United States — the world's largest Internet market — had broadband access. The rest still used dial-up connections with speeds slower than 50 Kbps (kilobits per second). This means that if you're outputting for the Internet and you want your movie to be usable for as many people as possible, you should use higher compression. Alternatively, you may choose to provide several levels of compression for various bandwidths. Provide a bigger, higher-quality version for broadband users— and a smaller, more compressed version for dial-up users.

- ✔ **Is the movie intended for CD-ROM or DVD playback?** Most CD-ROM drives also have serious bandwidth limitations, so you need to use a codec that uses a high compression ratio. If you are outputting for DVD, you need to use the MPEG-2 codec because that's the compression scheme DVD players use.

- ✔ **Are you outputting back to tape?** If so, your own output hardware is your primary concern.

See Chapter 15 for recommendations on specific codecs to use when you're outputting video for various formats.

Comparing Linear and Nonlinear Editing

My grandfather is a tinkerer. Over the years, he has tinkered with wood, old lawn mowers, and even 8mm film. Not content to simply shoot home movies and then watch them as developed, Grandpa would actually edit his source footage into interesting films. He performed edits by cutting the 8mm film with a razor blade and then splicing in new scenes, using cellophane tape (Scotch tape) to hold the splices together.

The process described above is what professional video editors call *linear editing,* and all motion pictures were edited this way in the past. Video, too, was once edited linearly, and until recently, linear editing was the only option available for home video users. Consider the process of dubbing video from a camcorder onto a tape in a VCR. If there is a scene on the camcorder tape that you want to leave off the VHS tape, you might pause recording on the VCR until that scene has passed. This process is another form of linear editing because you perform all of your edits in order from beginning to end.

Linear editing is terribly inefficient. If you dub a program and then decide to perform an additional edit, subsequent video usually has to be redubbed. What is the alternative? *Nonlinear editing,* of course! As the name implies, nonlinear edits can be performed in any order; you don't have to edit material in a specific, one-step-follows-another order. Nonlinear editing is made possible by the miracle of the computer and programs like Adobe Premiere Pro. Suppose (for example) that you have a program in which Scene 1 is followed by Scene 2, but you decide that you want to squeeze in another scene — we'll call it Scene 3 — between Scenes 1 and 2. In Premiere Pro, you simply place Scene 3 in the Timeline between Scenes 1 and 2 (as shown in Figure 4-5), and Premiere automatically moves Scene 2 over to make room for Scene 3 (shown in Figure 4-6). Imagine trying to perform this kind of edit by shuttling tapes in a pair of video decks — take a moment to wince — and you realize what a blessing a nonlinear editor (NLE) like Premiere really is.

Figure 4-5: To insert a scene between two existing scenes, just drop the new scene in the appropriate place on the Timeline.

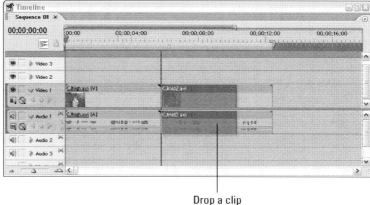

Drop a clip

Figure 4-6: When you perform an insert edit, Premiere automatically shifts subsequent material in the Timeline.

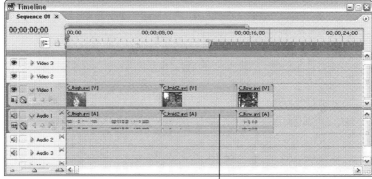

Inserted clip

Shooting Great Video

Throughout the years, editors have been called upon to create movies that are worth watching. But ultimately, a video editor can wield only so much magic. If you want to make a great movie, you need to start with great video footage. And if you don't think "great" video footage is possible (yet) given your equipment and talents, you *can* still improve your techniques enough to make your results a lot more watchable. The following sections give you some simple tips that can help you shoot video like the pros.

Plan the shot

Camcorders are so simple to use these days that they encourage seat-of-the-pants videography. Just grabbing your camcorder and hastily shooting the UFO that happens to be flying overhead is fine, but for most other situations, some careful planning will provide better quality. You can plan many aspects of the shot:

- ✔ **Make a checklist of shots that you need for your project.** While you're at it, make an equipment checklist too.

- ✔ **Survey the shooting location.** Make sure passersby won't trip over your cables or bump the camera.

- ✔ **Talk to property owners or other responsible parties.** Make sure you have permission to shoot; identify potential disruptions (wandering livestock, air traffic if you're near an airport, scheduled mud-wrestling matches, the usual).

- ✔ **Bring more blank tapes and charged batteries than you think you'll need.**

Compose the shot

Like a photograph, a great video image must be thoughtfully composed. Start by evaluating the type of shot you plan to take. Does the shot include people, landscapes, or some other subject? Consider what kind of tone or feel you want to achieve. Figure 4-7 illustrates how different compositions of the same shot can affect the overall tone. In the first shot, the camera looks down on the subject. Children are shot like this much too often, and it makes them look smaller and inferior. The second shot is level with the subject and portrays him more favorably. The third shot looks up at the subject and makes him seem important, almost larger than life.

Figure 4-7:
Composition
greatly
affects
how your
subject is
perceived.

Panning effectively

Another important aspect of composition is *panning,* or moving the camera. A common shooting technique that snapshot enthusiasts use with home camcorders is to pan the camera back-and-forth, up-and-down, either to follow a moving subject or to show a lot of things that don't fit in a single shot. This technique is called *firehosing* and is usually not a good idea. Practice these rules when panning:

- **Pan only once per shot.**

- **Start panning slowly, *gradually* speed up, and slow down again before stopping.**

- **Slow down!** Panning too quickly — say, over a landscape — is a common mistake.

- **If you have a cheap tripod, you may find it difficult to pan smoothly.** Try lubricating the tripod's swivel head. If that doesn't work, limit tripod use to stationary shots. Ideally you should use a higher-quality tripod with a fluid head for smooth panning.

- **Keep the camera level with the horizon.** A tilting horizon is very disorienting.

- **If you're shooting a moving subject, try moving the camera with the subject, rather than panning across a scene.** This reduces out-of-focus issues with the camera lens, and it also helps to keep the subject in frame.

Using (not abusing) the zoom lens

Most camcorders have a handy zoom feature. A *zoom lens* is basically a lens with an adjustable focal length. A longer lens — also called a *telephoto lens* — makes faraway subjects appear closer. A shorter lens — also called a *wide-angle* lens — allows more of a scene to fit in the shot. Zoom lenses allow you to adjust between wide-angle and telephoto views.

Because the zoom feature is easy to use and fun to play with, amateur videographers tend to zoom in and out a lot. I recommend that you avoid zooming during a shot as much as possible. Overuse of the zoom lens disorients the viewer, and it creates focal and light problems whether you're focusing the camera manually or using auto focus. Some zoom-lens tips include the following:

- ✔ **Avoid zooming whenever possible.**

- ✔ **If you must zoom while recording, zoom slowly.** You may need to practice a bit to get a feel for your camera's zoom control.

- ✔ **Consider repositioning the camera instead of using the zoom lens to compose the shot.** Wide-angle lenses have greater *depth of field*. This means that more of the shot is in focus if you're zoomed out. If you shoot subjects by zooming in on them from across a room, they may move in and out of focus. But if you move the camera in and zoom the lens out, focus will be less of a problem.

Light the shot

Light can be subdivided into two basic categories: good light and bad light. Good light allows you to see your subject, and it flatters your subject by exposing details that you want shown. Shadows aren't completely eliminated, but the shadows don't dominate large portions of the subject either. Bad light, on the other hand, washes out color and creates lens flares — the reflections and bright spots that show up when the sun shines across the lens — and other undesired effects. Consider Figure 4-8. The right side of the subject's face is a featureless white glow because it's washed out by intense sunlight. Meanwhile, the left side of the face is obscured in shadow. Not good.

Figure 4-8:
Improper
lighting
spoils this
shot.

How do you light your shots effectively? Remain ever aware of both the good light and the bad. If you don't have control over lighting in a location, try to compose the shot to best take advantage of the lighting that is available. Here are some more lighting tips that may come in handy:

✓ **Bounce intense lights off a reflective surface.** Light reflecting from a surface, such as a white sheet or foil screen, is more diffused, providing more flattering lighting than shining bright light directly on the subject.

✓ **Use multiple light sources of varying intensity.** Light on the front of the subject brings out facial details, while light from above and behind high-lights the subject relative to the background.

✓ **Watch for backlight situations like the one shown in Figure 4-9.** Try to put extra light on the foreground subject, avoid bright backgrounds, or increase the camera's exposure control. Some cameras have an auto-matic backlight compensation feature, though as you can see on the right side of Figure 4-9, sometimes the result isn't much better.

✓ **Shield your lens from bright light sources, particularly the sun.** Intense light can reflect on the lens glass and cause flares that only show up later on video. If your camera lens doesn't have a black hood, you can use your hand or black tape to make a temporary shield (check the viewfinder to ensure that your shield doesn't appear in the shot).

✓ **Check your camera's documentation.** Your camcorder might include built-in features to help you deal with special lighting situations, such as sporting events or a sun-washed beach.

✓ **Use lens filters.** A neutral-density filter, for example, reduces light in bright outdoor settings and makes colors appear more vivid. A polariz-ing filter controls how reflective surfaces (like water or glass) appear.

Figure 4-9: Egad, who is that shadowy figure on the left? Oh, there he is, horribly over-exposed on the right.

Shoot the shot

Perhaps the most important tip I can give you before you shoot your video is this: *Know your camera.* Even the least-expensive digital camcorders available currently are packed with features that were wildly advanced (and expensive) just a few years ago. Most digital camcorders include image stabilization, in-camera effects, and the ability to record 16-bit stereo audio. But these advanced features won't do you much good if they aren't turned on or configured properly. Spend a few hours reviewing the manual that came with your camcorder and practice using every feature and setting.

Keep the camcorder manual in your gear bag when you hit the road. It may prove an invaluable reference when you're shooting on location. Also, review the manual from time to time; no doubt some useful or cool features are lurking that you forgot all about. If you've lost your manual, check the manufacturer's Web site. You might be able to download a replacement manual.

Virtually all modern camcorders include automatic exposure and focus control. But no matter how advanced this automation may seem, it's not perfect. Get friendly with the manual exposure and focus controls on your camera (if it has them) and practice using them. If you always rely on autofocus, inevitably your video will show the queasy effects of the lens "hunting" for the right setting during some shots — especially if you shoot moving subjects or in poor light. If your camera has a manual focus mode, you can avoid focus hunting by turning off auto focus. Also, getting handy with the manual exposure control (also called the *iris*) will ultimately give you more control over light exposure in your video.

Chapter 5

Starting and Managing Your Movie Projects

In This Chapter

▶ Getting your project started

▶ Tweaking the project settings

▶ Collecting information about a project

Software companies like to create names for program elements that are meant to be analogous to something in "real" life. For example, if you want to delete a file on a Windows PC, you put it in the *Recycle Bin*. When you want to check your e-mail, you look in your *Inbox*. Sometimes the names they choose work, and sometimes they don't. I used to have an Internet service that had pages named *Runway* and *Boardwalk*. One of them was a page of search engines, and the other a Web directory. Which was which? I forgot all the time.

Adobe probably could have gotten more creative with the names given to parts of Premiere Pro. Thankfully, they picked a few words that worked and stuck with them. When you work on a movie project, for instance, that project is called a (drum roll, please) *project*. It doesn't get much simpler than that, folks. This chapter is all about projects in Adobe Premiere Pro. I show you how to create new projects, modify existing projects, and manage the various projects you have.

Starting Your Project

When you first launch Adobe Premiere Pro, you probably see a welcome screen similar to Figure 5-1. The screen gives you quick access to several important commands:

✔ **Recent Projects:** A list of projects that you have recently worked on appears under Recent Projects. Click the name of a project to open it.

✔ **New Project:** No big surprises here! If you're starting a new project, click the New Project icon.

✔ **Open Project:** Have to open an older project that doesn't appear in your list of recent projects? Click the Open Project icon and browse to the desired project file.

✔ **Help:** The Help icon is for people who don't have a book like this one.

Figure 5-1:
This friendly
welcome
screen
appears
whenever
you launch
Premiere
Pro.

You'll also notice a button called "Exit" at the bottom of the welcome screen. Don't click this button; all it does is close Premiere. Instead, click the New Project icon. This will open the New Project window shown in Figure 5-2. The New Project window also appears if you choose File⇨New⇨Project while you're using Premiere Pro.

The New Project window (Figure 5-2) has two tabs. The Load Preset tab allows you to create a new project using a *preset.* A preset is basically just a collection of project settings that specify the size and shape of the video image, the audio format, and other important details. Premiere Pro comes with several different presets to match the most common types of video. If none of the presets seem to match your needs, you can create a custom project using the other tab in this window, the Custom Settings tab.

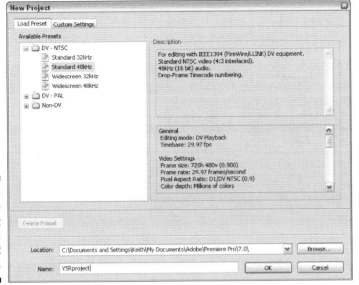

Figure 5-2:
Begin a new
project
using the
New Project
dialog box.

Using project presets

As you look at the list of presets on the Load Preset tab of the New Project
window, you're probably wondering, "Which preset should I choose?" This
depends on the type of video that you're working with. The presets found on
the Load Preset tab of the New Project window are divided into three basic
categories:

- **DV-NTSC:** If you're working with video from a digital camcorder that
  uses the NTSC broadcast standard (the video standard used in North
  America), use one of these presets. I recommend 48 kHz sound unless
  your camcorder was set to record 32 kHz (12-bit) sound. Only choose
  the Widescreen setting if you shot the material using your camcorder's
  widescreen (16:9 aspect ratio) feature.

- **DV-PAL:** These presets are used just like the DV-NTSC presets, except
  that they are designed for use with video equipment that uses the PAL
  broadcast standard (used in Europe, South America, and elsewhere).

- **Non-DV:** Only use one of these presets if you know that you're not working with DV-format video. The Full Screen No DV presets are designed
  mainly for video that is captured from an analog video source. The
  Quarter Screen presets are for small-size video images and are really

only suitable for making movies for the Web. Use the Square-Pixel presets only if you're working from video imported from another computer-based source (such as a CD-ROM or online movie).

When you click a preset in the list on the left, you'll notice that details about that preset appear in the Description menus on the right. Here you can review all the gory details about each preset. To start a new project using one of the presets, simply choose the desired preset from the list, type a name for your project in the Name field at the bottom of the New Project window, and click OK. A new project will be created for you and the standard Premiere Pro workspace will appear.

If you plan to work primarily with standard-shape (not widescreen) video that you've shot using a digital camcorder, the preset to use is Standard 48 kHz, under either of two video standards — DV-NTSC or DV-PAL. See Chapter 4 if you're not sure whether you use NTSC or PAL video equipment.

Choosing custom project settings

The Custom Settings tab of the New Project window (shown in Figure 5-3) allows you to specify many unique details about your project. In most cases I recommend you create a new project using a preset from the Load Preset tab, but if you know you need some custom settings, the Custom Settings tab is the place you want to be. This tab offers four categories of options. Click one of the categories in the list and then adjust settings on the right. Settings in each of the four categories are detailed in the next few sections.

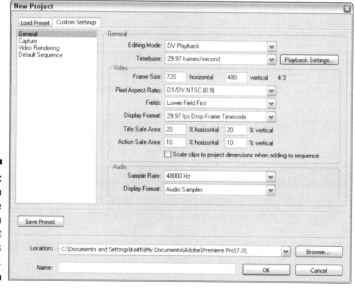

Figure 5-3:
You can choose custom project settings here.

It's important to choose proper settings when you first start a project, especially settings that control the audio and video quality of the project. However, you can change some project settings later if you wish. To adjust settings for a project on which you're currently working, choose Project↷Project Settings and then choose a category of settings that you want to adjust. You'll notice the window that appears looks suspiciously similar to the Custom Settings tab of the New Project window shown in Figure 5-3. Notice, however, that once the project is created, some settings cannot be changed. The next few sections tell you which settings are set in stone once the project is created.

General settings

General project settings in the New Project window determine the basic audio and video format for your project. Important General settings include

- ✔ **Editing Mode:** If you're working with DV-format video, choose DV Playback from this menu. Use Video for Windows if you're working with video from another source, such as an analog camcorder. This setting cannot be changed once the project is created.

- ✔ **Timebase:** This menu controls the frame rate of your project. Choose the frame rate that matches the video you'll be importing and editing. For example, the timebase for NTSC video is 29.97 frames per second (fps). Like the Editing Mode, you cannot change the timebase once the project has been created.

- ✔ **Playback Settings:** Click this button to open the DV Playback Settings dialog box as shown in Figure 5-4. If you have a DV device (such as a digital camcorder), the settings in this dialog box control how your media play (and what media play) on the device as you work in Premiere. Playback settings are divided into four basic categories:

  - **Video Playback:** As you edit your video you will constantly be playing it back to see how your edits look. If you enable the Play Video on DV Hardware option, video from your project will play both in the Premiere Pro window and on your DV device, if the DV device happens to be connected to your computer and turned on. In Chapter 15, I explain the benefits of previewing video on an external monitor.

  - **Audio Playback:** Just like video, audio can also be played through your external DV device. If your external DV device is just a camcorder, however, you will probably find that playback from the camcorder's built-in speaker is pretty pathetic. I usually choose the Play Audio on Audio Hardware option, which means the audio plays through my computer's sound card and speakers. If you don't like the way audio fragments sound as you move slowly back and forth through video clips, disable the Play Audio on Audio Hardware while Scrubbing option.

  - **Real-Time Effects:** Unlike many older editing programs, Adobe Premiere Pro allows you to preview special effects and other advanced edits in real time. You no longer have to wait for render files to be created. Real-time previews require a very powerful computer, however, and you may find that your computer isn't able to play those effects both on your computer screen and on an external DV device. If you encounter jerky playback or other problems with real-time previews, choose the Playback on Desktop Only option.

- **Export to Tape:** When you want to export a finished movie to the tape in your DV device, it's usually important to export audio along with the video. Choose Play Audio on Audio Hardware only if you just want to export video to tape, but not audio.

✔ **Frame Size:** Adjust the height and width of your video in pixels. The aspect ratio of your current frame size is also displayed. The frame size cannot be changed once the project is created.

✔ **Pixel Aspect Ratio:** Choose a setting from the menu that matches your video. Choose Square Pixels only if you're working with video imported from a computer source like a CD-ROM or the Internet. Choose carefully; this is another one of those settings that you can't adjust later on.

✔ **Fields:** As explained in Chapter 4, video images are typically made up of two interlacing sets of horizontal lines called *fields*. This menu controls which field is drawn first. PAL video usually draws the upper field first; NTSC video usually draws the lower field first. Only choose No Fields if you're working with media from a computer source.

✔ **Display Format (under Video):** This menu controls how timecode is displayed while you work in your project. (See Chapter 4 for a detailed explanation of timecode.)

✔ **Title Safe Area:** As I describe in Chapter 14, most TVs cut off portions of a video image at the edges of the screen. This problem is called *overscan*. To make sure that titles don't get cut off by overscan, Premiere can temporarily display Title Safe margins as a visual guide to potential overscan on the video image. You can adjust the size of the Title Safe Area if you wish.

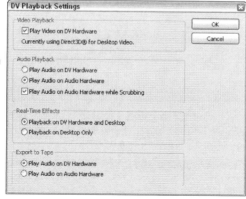

Figure 5-4:
This dialog box controls how your project is played back on external hardware.

✔ **Action Safe Area:** This is similar to the Title Safe Area, and is designed to ensure that important action on the screen isn't cut off by overscan. The Action Safe Area is usually a little closer to the edges of the screen than the Title Safe Area.

✔ **Scale clips to project dimensions when adding to sequence:** When this option is checked, clips that have a different size or shape will automatically be scaled up or down to match the project settings. If the clip has a different aspect ratio — for example, you place a 16:9 widescreen clip in a 4:3 fullscreen sequence — the inserted clip will be resized without affecting the aspect ratio. This will create a letterbox effect for the inserted clip.

✔ **Sample Rate:** This menu sets the audio sample rate for your project (see Chapter 13 for more on sample rates and working with audio). Higher sample rates usually mean better quality audio. The sample rate cannot be changed after the project is created.

✔ **Display Format (under Audio):** Control how audio is expressed on-screen using this menu. I find that displaying Audio Samples is easiest to work with.

Capture settings

Capture settings control the default source from which you will capture video. The choices available here depend on what hardware is installed on your system. If you plan to capture video from a digital camcorder connected to your FireWire (IEEE-1394) port, you'll want to choose DV/IEEE 1394 Capture in the Capture Format menu. If you have an analog capture card or a secondary camera (such as a USB Web cam), it may be available in the menu.

If your camcorder (or other DV source) is currently connected to your FireWire port and is turned on, you will also see a DV Settings button in the Capture settings screen. Click this button if you see it. In the DV Capture Options dialog box that appears (Figure 5-5), you can control whether audio or video plays on your computer during capture. If you have a computer that is on the low-end of the system requirements scale for Adobe Premiere Pro (see Chapter 2), you may want to remove the check marks next to both of the options under During Capture. This can prevent dropped frames (where some frames of video don't get captured, resulting in flawed playback quality) during video capture on slower computers.

Figure 5-5:
Uncheck the bottom two options if you have a slower computer.

Video Rendering settings

As you edit a project and add transitions and effects to your video, Premiere Pro must apply your edits using a process called *rendering* (building preview files for video). When Premiere renders your work, it creates temporary files on your hard drive that allow your edits to plan properly. Video Rendering settings control the format of these *render files*. Choose a Compressor that matches your video format, such as DV (NTSC) or DV (PAL). You can also specify a color depth, but I recommend that you keep this setting as high as possible.

The Video Rendering options also contain a check box called Optimize Stills. If your project has a lot of still images, choose this option to reduce rendering time. Optimizing stills could cause some playback problems, however. If you encounter glitches or other problems when the stills play, disable optimization.

Default Sequence settings

The Default Sequence settings control how Premiere Pro sets up your workspace when your project first opens. The Video Tracks option allows you to specify the number of tracks in the Timeline when you first open the program (you'll find out how to use tracks in Chapter 8).

The Audio section of Default Sequence settings has a few more options. The Master menu specifies whether the audio format for your project will be Mono, Stereo, or 5.1. The 5.1 option, new in Premiere Pro, allows you to tailor your soundtrack for surround-sound playback. Below the Master menu, you can specify the number of audio tracks — for each format — that you want to appear.

Don't worry too much about the number of audio or video tracks you specify in the Default Sequence options. All these settings do is set how many tracks you start out with; you can easily add more tracks later if you want.

Creating your own presets

Although the built-in presets that come with Premiere Pro are pretty versatile, they must appeal to a broad range of users. This means that while one of the preset groups of settings might come close to meeting your needs, there may still be some settings that you change. Rather than manually changing all these settings every time you start a new project, Premiere Pro lets you save your own presets for future use.

When you have your project settings the way you like them, simply click the Save Preset button at the bottom of the Custom Settings tab. In the Save Project Settings dialog box, type a helpful name and description for your preset, such as "XL1 Widescreen" or "Intel Web cam." Click OK to close the dialog box. From now on, your custom preset will appear in the list on the Load Preset tab of the New Project window.

Saving a Project

Saving a project in Premiere Pro is pretty straightforward. Just choose File ⇨ Save from the menu bar and you're done. If you want to save the project with a different name, choose File ⇨ Save As, and if you want to save a copy, choose File ⇨ Save a Copy.

You probably could have figured out how to save a project on your own, so why this section? One of the interesting things about Premiere Pro is that although video files tend to be very large, project files are actually quite small. Indeed, the project file for a 30-minute movie may be smaller than 50 kilobytes (KB). This is because the project file doesn't contain any actual audio or video. But the project file *does* contain

 ✔ Edit points and keyframes that you create

 ✔ Pointers to the original source clips

 ✔ Information about effects that are applied to the project

 ✔ The layout of Premiere windows and palettes from the last time you worked on the project

Because Premiere project files are so small, it's a good idea to frequently save backup copies of a project. This way, you can easily go back to an earlier version of your project if you don't like some of the changes that you've made. You can tell Premiere to save a new version of your project automatically, while archiving old versions, every few minutes or so.

So where *are* all the big files? Not only do the source files for your audio and video take up a lot of disk space, but whenever you render some of your work for playback or output, huge render files are created as well (as mentioned in the previous section). All these big files live on your *scratch disk*. Your scratch disk might simply be your main hard drive, or you may have a hard drive dedicated solely to video storage. (See Chapter 3 for more information about scratch disks.) On a Windows XP system, the default scratch disk for audio and video that you capture is

```
C:\Documents and Settings\YourUserName\My
            Documents\Adobe\Premiere Pro\7.0\
```

Before you start deleting files from the scratch-disk folder, make sure you don't need those files anymore. If (for example) you delete a video file from the scratch disk, any projects that use that file become incomplete. And if you delete preview files, you have to spend long minutes (or hours) re-rendering those previews if you ever need them again.

Opening an existing project

Premiere gives you a lot of ways to open a project that you've been working on. Premiere Pro works like most other Windows programs, which means you can use any of the following standard methods to open a project:

- ✔ Launch Premiere Pro and choose a project from the Recent Projects list in the Premiere Pro welcome screen (see Figure 5-1).

- ✔ In Premiere Pro, choose File➪Open Recent Project➪and choose a project from the submenu that appears.

- ✔ In Premiere Pro, choose File➪Open Project and browse to the project file.

- ✔ Drag a project file and drop it on the Premiere Pro program window (Premiere must already be open for this to work).

- ✔ In Windows, choose Start➪My Recent Documents and select a Premiere project from the list (if the one you want appears in the list).

Chapter 6

Capturing, Importing, and Managing Media

In This Chapter

▶ Capturing media to edit

▶ Importing media from other sources

▶ Organizing media into the stuff of movies

*I*f you think Adobe Premiere Pro is fun now, just wait until you actually have some material to edit in this amazing program. Actually, don't wait. Let's start gathering some media into Premiere right now, shall we? No time like the present, I always say.

This chapter guides you through the process of capturing audio and video using Premiere, whether you're capturing video from a digital camcorder, analog camcorder, or another source. This chapter also shows you how to import various types of media, and you get some help with the task of organizing your media.

Capturing Media

Most of my movies begin life as concepts floating around in the gray matter of my brain. A cartoonish light bulb appears overhead, and before I know it I'm shooting video, editing it in Premiere, and sharing my grand production with anyone fortunate enough to be in the room at that moment. That "editing it in Premiere" step can be broken down into three basic phases:

✔ Import

✔ Edit

✔ Output

Obviously, before you can edit your project, you need something to edit. You can get source material into Premiere by importing existing files or by capturing media from an external source (the most common example of which is a digital camcorder). The following sections show you how to capture audio and video in Premiere Pro. (We cover importation of video files, still graphics, music, and other media later in the chapter.)

Setting up your hardware

This is the part of the book where I'm supposed to show you a simple diagram of a camcorder connected to a computer by a cable. If only it were that easy. Preparing your computer for video capture can actually be a complicated process, and you must approach this process carefully to achieve success.

The next couple of sections describe a lot of ways to make your computer perform better during capture. These same techniques can also be used to increase performance during editing, rendering, and output too!

The first thing to go is memory . . .

Whether you're capturing DV video using FireWire or analog video using a video-capture card, video capture puts very high demands on your computer. The processor, RAM, and hard drive in particular must be able to work fast to capture video without *dropping frames* (failing to capture some frames of video because the computer can't keep up with the video stream) or causing other problems. As you prepare to capture video, follow these basic guidelines:

- ✔ **Close all applications except Premiere Pro.** This includes utility programs and even antivirus programs. Temporarily disabling antivirus programs greatly increases the performance of your system.

- ✔ **Defragment your hard drive.** Years ago, it was vitally important to regularly defragment the hard drive on a Windows PC. Today, many PC experts would tell you that disk defragging isn't very important anymore — but they probably don't do any video editing! Editing video is one of the most hard-drive-intensive things you will ever do on a computer, and it's critically important that your disk be optimized for best possible performance. To defragment your hard disk using Windows XP, choose Start⟹ All Programs⟹Accessories⟹System Tools⟹Disk Defragmenter.

- ✔ **Disable your screen saver if you have one, as well as those fancy desktop-beautification schemes.**

- ✔ **Take control of virtual memory.** In Windows, manually configure virtual memory to be twice the size of physical RAM. This process can be complicated, so before you adjust memory settings, I recommend that you pick up a book that provides memory-management procedures for your particular operating system. I recommend *Windows XP Bible* by Alan Simpson and Brian Underdahl (Wiley Publishing, Inc.).

✔ **Adjust your power-management settings so your monitor and hard disks won't shut down in the middle of a long capture job.** Use the Power Options icon in your Windows Control Panel to adjust power-management settings.

✔ **Temporarily disable unneeded memory-resident items that are not directly related to video capture or vital operating system functions.** Unneeded items include antivirus programs, Internet programs, and system monitors. In Windows, memory-resident programs can often be disabled using System Tray icons, as shown in Figure 6-1. Right-click each icon and choose Close or Disable for as many of them as possible.

Figure 6-1:
You can usually close memory-resident programs using System Tray icons.

If your computer matches the system requirements outlined in Chapter 2, chances are you won't have any trouble with video capture. But if you do encounter capture troubles, the above ideas should help you out. Some of the measures I mentioned can be complicated, however. In particular, controlling the way Windows manages memory is an advanced topic that I can't fully cover here. I strongly urge you to pick up a book that covers your operating system in detail, such as the aforementioned *Windows XP Bible*, or *Windows XP For Dummies,* by Andy Rathbone, both published by Wiley Publishing, Inc.

Configuring DV hardware

Configuring your computer for video capture may not be easy, but at least configuring DV hardware is. Along with high video quality, simplicity is one of the main strengths of DV. The most common way to capture video from a DV camcorder or video deck is to use a FireWire (IEEE-1394) port on your computer. You should also tell Premiere Pro what specific piece of DV hardware you're using. Follow these steps:

1. **Connect your DV camcorder or deck to your FireWire port using an appropriate cable.**

2. **Turn on the device.**

If you're capturing from a camcorder, turn it on to VTR (video tape recorder) mode, not camera mode. If Windows displays a message saying that a DV device was detected, choose Take No Action and click OK.

 3. **Launch Premiere Pro.**

If Premiere was already open, in some rare cases you may need to quit and then restart the program to ensure that the program recognizes your DV hardware.

 4. **Create a new project and choose a DV preset that matches the type of video you plan to capture.**

See Chapter 5 for more on choosing a good preset for your project.

 5. **In Premiere Pro, choose Edit⇨Preferences⇨Device Control.**

The Preferences dialog box appears with the Device Control options displayed.

 6. **Click Options.**

The DV Device Controls Options dialog box appears as shown in Figure 6-2.

 7. **Choose your video standard (NTSC or PAL) from the Video Standard drop-down list.**

See Chapter 4 for more on video standards.

 8. **Choose the brand of your camcorder or DV device from the Device Brand menu.**

 9. **Choose a type or model number from the Device Type menu.**

If your DV device doesn't seem to be listed, click Go Online for Device Info. Premiere Pro checks Adobe's online hardware database and update as necessary.

 10. **Choose a format from the Timecode Format menu.**

Generally speaking, NTSC-format video uses Drop-Frame timecode, and everything else uses Non Drop-Frame timecode.

 11. **If you see "Offline" next to the Check Status button, click Check Status to see if Premiere can detect your camera.**

If it still says Offline, make sure that the camera is turned on to VTR mode, the battery is charged, and your FireWire cable is properly connected.

 12. **Click OK twice to close the dialog boxes when you're done.**

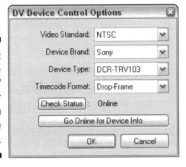

Figure 6-2:
Configure
your DV
device for
use with
Premiere
Pro.

If you got hung up on step number 11, there is probably something wrong
with your DV device, your computer, or both. This is especially true if you
were able to locate the brand and model of your device in the menus. If your
device wasn't specifically listed, it simply may not be supported by Premiere
Pro. Check the documentation that came with the device (or the manufacturer's Web site), and find out what the recommended procedure is for capturing video. If your device was listed and still registers as offline, follow
these troubleshooting tips:

✔ **Close and restart Adobe Premiere Pro.** While you're at it, go ahead and
restart your computer too. Make sure that the camcorder's power is
turned on *before* you restart Premiere.

✔ **Double-check the physical connection to your computer.** Is the
FireWire cable properly installed and secure?

✔ **Check to see whether any device drivers need to be installed.** The
device manufacturer's documentation may provide information about
this. In Windows, open the System icon in the Control Panel, click the
Hardware tab, and then click Device Manager. (DV devices are most
often listed under Imaging Device, as shown in Figure 6-3.) If the power is
on, the device is connected, and you can't find it in the Device Manager,
then the software device driver is not properly installed or there is a
physical problem with a component.

**While you're in the Device Manager, make sure that your 1394 Bus
Controller (your FireWire port) is OHCI-compliant and configured
properly.** A yellow exclamation mark means the item is *not* configured
properly on your system. To correct this problem, consult the documentation or technical support that came with the FireWire controller card
or your computer. If you're not sure whether your 1394 Bus Controller is
OHCI-compliant, check the controller's documentation. Usually the
Device Manager listing for your 1394 Bus Controller will say something
about being OHCI-compliant, like the one shown in Figure 6-3.

FireWire interface

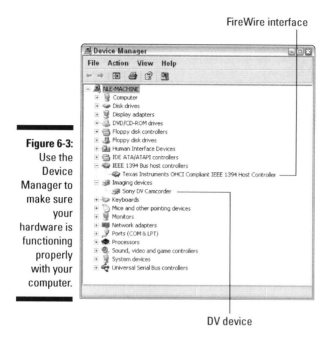

Figure 6-3:
Use the
Device
Manager to
make sure
your
hardware is
functioning
properly
with your
computer.

DV device

> ✔ **Be sure that the DV device recognizes the FireWire connection.** The display on your camcorder or DV deck may show an indication such as "DV IN" if the connection is detected.

Configuring analog hardware

Although digital video seems to be the wave of the future, there are still a lot of great analog video devices out there. To capture analog video, you must have a device that can digitize analog video into a digital format for computer editing. This device may be a video capture card that is installed in your computer, or it may be an external device called a video converter, which connects to your computer using a FireWire or SCSI interface. (Chapter 2 recommends some analog capture cards, and I feature some video converters in Chapter 21.)

Before you do anything else, read the documentation that came with your capture hardware. That documentation no doubt contains specific instructions for capturing video. In fact, there's a good chance that your capture card came with its own software utility for capturing video. That utility may include features that help you adjust color and video quality during capture. If your card came with its own capture software, you may want to use it for video capture rather than Premiere Pro — especially if you have trouble capturing with Premiere. Just make sure that the captured video is of a quality and format that you can use in Premiere.

Before you use Adobe Premiere to capture analog video, configure your hardware as follows:

1. **Connect your analog camcorder or deck to your capture device.**

   Connect all cables as described in the documentation.

2. **Turn on the device. If you're capturing from a camcorder, turn it on to VTR mode, not camera mode.**

3. **Launch Premiere.**

   If Premiere was already open, you may have to quit and then restart the program to ensure that the program recognizes your capture hardware.

4. **Choose a preset that matches the type of video you plan to capture.**

   For analog video, your best choice is most likely Full Screen No DV (NTSC or PAL as appropriate) from the Non-DV group of presets. (For more on choosing a good preset for your project, see "Starting Your Project" in Chapter 5).

5. **In Premiere, choose Project➪Project Settings➪Capture.**

   The Capture panel of the Project Settings dialog box appears. Review the settings listed here and adjust them in accordance with the documentation for your capture hardware. Each capture card is different, so reviewing the documentation that came with the card — and following the instructions found there — is critical. If you're capturing analog video, you will usually be able to specify quality settings. Remember, higher quality will place higher demands on the storage and processing capabilities of your computer.

6. **Click OK to close the Project Settings dialog box.**

Capturing video

It's hard to believe that we are this many pages into a chapter titled "Capturing, Importing, and Managing Media" and so far we haven't captured, imported, or managed any media at all. The only thing we have managed to do is get ready for capture. Getting ready for capture is no small matter, though. In fact, *preparing* to capture is the most challenging part of the process.

If you have jumped ahead and plan to just plug in your camcorder and start capturing without much preparation, you may experience troubles — particularly dropped frames. If you experience trouble during capture, check out the preceding pages of this chapter. (I won't tell a soul.)

Understanding device control

Remember that movie *Back to the Future,* where Christopher Lloyd's character controlled a toaster, a coffeepot, a dog-food dispenser, and various other appliances with his computer? Yes, it really has been two decades since that movie came out, and no, we still don't control our coffee machines or refrigerators with computers. However, thanks to a technology called *device control,* we can control camcorders and video decks with our computers. (It's a start.)

Device control is one of the most accurately named technologies to come along in quite some time. It allows you to control your devices using a computer. For example, if your DV camcorder is connected to your FireWire port, you can start playing the tape in that camcorder by clicking the Play button in Adobe Premiere Pro. Cool, huh?

Not only is device control cool, it's useful. When you capture video, synchronization between the computer and the videotape player is crucial — Premiere Pro has to access and use the timecode recorded on the tape. Device control is (therefore) especially important if you plan to capture batches of video. *Batch captures* use timecode to identify where to start and stop, and thanks to device control, Premiere's batch-capture feature can automatically play, fast forward, rewind, and stop the tape as needed to capture the desired batches of video.

Most DV camcorders and decks allow device control. Commands for device control are shared through the FireWire cable. Some professional-grade analog decks also offer device control, but it usually requires a separate serial cable connected between the computer and the playback device. Device control also requires a deck that accurately records and uses timecode.

Okay, McFly, now that you understand device control, let's start capturing some video!

After your hardware is configured and ready for capture, follow these steps to identify video that you want to capture and then capture it:

1. **Connect all the necessary cables, turn on your hardware, launch Premiere, choose a preset, and perform all the other preparatory steps described earlier in this chapter.**

2. **In Premiere, choose File⇨Capture.**

   The Capture window appears.

3. **Click the Settings tab.**

   On the Settings tab (shown in Figure 6-4), review the capture settings, locations, and Device Control settings and adjust as necessary (again, these subjects are covered earlier in this chapter).

   In the Device Control section, you will notice settings for Preroll Time and Timecode Offset. When you start to capture a clip of video, Preroll Time controls how far the start of the clip the tape rewinds before it starts to play. It's usually a good idea to set three to five seconds of preroll, just to make sure that the tape drive in your DV device gets up to proper speed before the capture begins. Of course, keep in mind that this means you won't be able to capture video from the first few seconds of a tape. Some devices may also have poorly synchronized timecode, in which case you may need to set a *timecode offset* to compensate. Leave this setting at zero unless you notice a difference between the timecode displayed in your camcorder or DV device and the timecode shown in Premiere's Capture window.

4. **Click the Logging tab on the right side of the Movie Capture window to bring the tab to the front.**

5. **If you have device control, click Play in the capture window. If you don't have device control, press the Play button on your playback device. The video should play in the viewer window.**

   If you don't have device control, skip Steps 6, 7, 8, and 9 in this section.

6. **Use the controls located beneath the viewer section of the Capture window to review the tape.**

   To identify the exact frame at which you want to start and finish capturing, use the left and right arrow keys on your keyboard (or click the Step Back and Step Forward buttons in the Capture window) to move back or forward a single frame at a time. Figure 6-5 details the various playback controls.

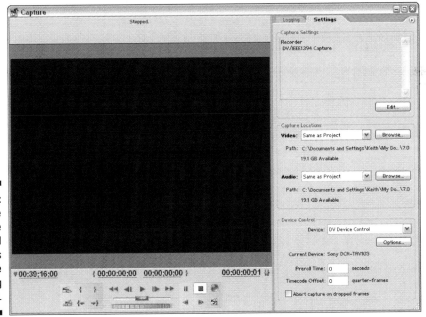

Figure 6-4:
Review the capture settings and preferences before capturing your video.

Figure 6-5:
Use
playback
controls to
identify In
and Out
points.

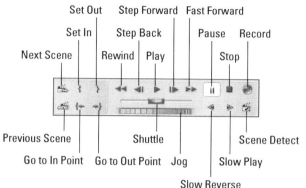

One of the handiest new features in Adobe Premiere Pro is scene detection. If you know that you want to capture an entire scene on the tape, click the Previous Scene button in the preview window. Premiere Pro automatically rewinds the tape and detects the beginning of the scene, and automatically pauses the tape at the first frame of that scene. To detect the end of the scene, click Next Scene. Premiere plays the tape forward to the end of the scene and stops the tape on the first frame of the next scene.

7. **When you find the spot where you want to start capturing, click the Set In button — located beneath the viewer of the Movie Capture window — to set an In point (you can also click the Set In button on the Logging tab).**

   The timecode listed next to the Set In button on the Logging tab should now match the timecode shown under the left corner of the viewer window.

8. **Locate the place where you want to stop capturing, and then click the Set Out button, either under the viewer or on the Logging tab.**

   The timecode next to Out on the Logging tab should match the timecode under the right corner of the viewer (as in Figure 6-6).

9. **Note the duration of your capture.**

   As you can see in Figure 6-6, the duration of my capture is nine seconds and 19 frames.

10. **If you have device control and you want to capture the video right now, click In/Out under Capture on the Logging tab.**

    Device control rewinds the tape in your playback device as needed and capture the video. If you have set up Premiere so that video and audio are not played on the computer during capture, the viewer screen is black during capture. An indicator at the top of the viewer window tells you how many frames have been captured, as well as how many frames have been dropped (with any luck, the dropped-frames figure remains at zero).

If you don't have device control, rewind the tape to just slightly before the point at which you want to begin capture. Click the Record button beneath the viewer in the Movie Capture window and then press the Play button on your playback device. When you want to stop capturing, click the Stop button in the Movie Capture window and then press Stop on your playback device.

When the capture job is done, a dialog box asks you to name the clip and provide a description if desired. Once saved, the clip appears in Premiere's Project window. If you expand the Project window so it looks like the one shown in Figure 6-7 (or just scroll using the scroll bar at the bottom of the window), you can read a lot of information about your clip, including image size, audio quality, timecode from the source tape, and more.

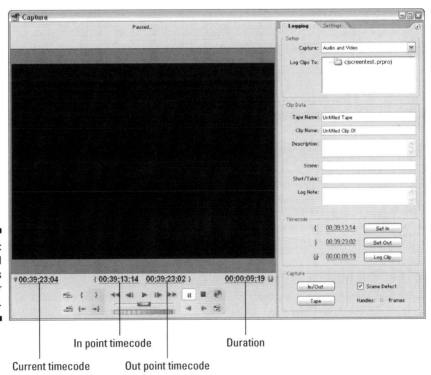

Figure 6-6:
Mark In and Out points for your capture.

In point timecode

Duration

Current timecode

Out point timecode

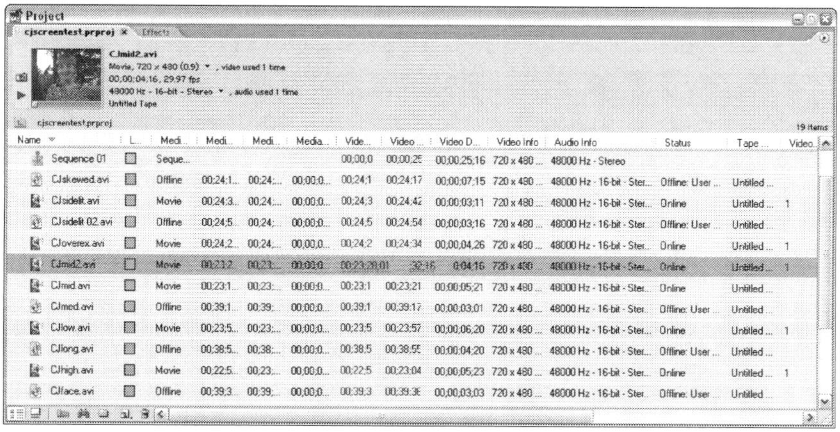

Figure 6-7:
Captured
clips appear
in the
Project
window.

(Project window screenshot showing captured clips)

Eek! I dropped a frame!

Of all the capture problems you may encounter, by far the most common —
as well as the hardest to troubleshoot — is dropped frames. If you're capturing NTSC video from a DV camcorder, for example, Premiere captures 29.97
frames per second (fps). If something in the computer gets choked up, it may
miss, or *drop,* one or more frames during capture. Dropped frames create
unacceptable quality problems for captured clips in Premiere Pro.

If you finish capturing a clip and a Properties dialog box appears, that is a
bad sign. Review the statistics in this dialog box. If you see a line that says,
`This movie appears to have DROPPED FRAMES`, you almost certainly
have dropped frames during capture — and that usually means redoing
the capture.

Timecode breaks on the tape can confuse Premiere Pro into thinking it
dropped frames when it really didn't. Timecode breaks often occur when you
reuse tapes by recording new footage over old. When the end of the new
footage is reached, the timecode may change and thus confuse Premiere. If
you have been reusing tapes — not something I recommend — you might
want to consider this as a possible cause of dropped frames reports.

Determining the cause of dropped frames can be challenging; however, I have
found that the most common cause is that the hard disk couldn't maintain
the required data rate during capture. Usually this isn't a problem on computers that match even the minimum system requirements for Adobe Premiere
Pro, but it is not beyond the realm of possibility either. If you have captured a
clip that has dropped frames, right-click that clip in the Project window and
choose Properties. For DV-format video, the Average Data Rate *should* read

about 3.6MB per second. If the Average Data Rate is lower, or if the Date Rate/Sec graph is not a perfectly straight line (like the one in Figure 6-8), your hard drive couldn't keep up with the data stream. Common causes include

✔ Programs other than Adobe Premiere Pro were open during capture.

✔ The hard drive has not been defragmented recently.

✔ Another computer was trying to access the hard drive over your network (if you have one) during capture.

If your Date Rate/Sec graph is a straight line but you still dropped frames, the cause is more likely your DV device or the tape. But if your hard disk does appear to be the culprit, you can try to correct the problem by methodically re-preparing your computer for capture as described earlier in this chapter. Close unneeded programs, defragment your hard drive, buy more RAM, or consider upgrading your drives. If your capture card came with its own capture software, you may want to try using that software to capture, and then import the captured clips into Premiere for editing.

Average Data Rate

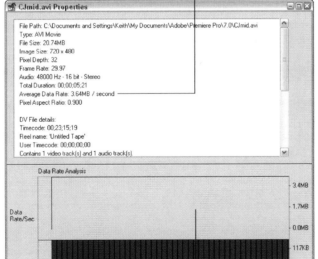

Figure 6-8:
Use the
Properties
dialog box
to determine
possible
causes of
dropped
frames.

Data Rate/Sec graph

Detecting scenes

If you have a videotape full of video, chances are that tape actually contains many different scenes. A scene usually begins when you press Record and ends when you stop recording. Dividing your video into scenes is useful not only because it saves tape, but it also makes editing easier when you're working with that video later in Premiere. Over the past few years, many video-editing programs have provided a useful feature called *scene detection*. As you captured video with such simple programs as Apple iMovie or Windows Movie Maker, the software automatically detected breaks between scenes. When all the video was captured, you had a bin full of usefully organized video clips, each one containing a handy, easy-to-work-with scene.

Surprisingly, although scene detection has been common in cheap (or even free) low-end editing programs, many high-end, pro-oriented programs like Adobe Premiere lacked this useful feature. Thankfully, Adobe has incorporated scene detection into Adobe Premiere Pro, making the process of capturing video clips much, much easier. To use Premiere Pro's scene-detection feature during capture, follow these steps:

1. **Open Premiere Pro and choose File⇨Capture.**

2. **In the Capture window, set In and Out points as described earlier in this chapter for a portion of video that you want to capture.**

   The space between the In point and Out point may contain many different scenes on the tape.

3. **Enter a name for the clips in the Clip Name field on the Logging tab.**

4. **Place a check mark next to Scene Detect under Capture.**

5. **Click In/Out under Capture to capture the video.**

   Premiere Pro captures all of the video between the In point and Out point. Each time Premiere detects a new scene, a new clip is created.

When all of the scenes between the In point and Out point have been detected and captured, close the Capture window. Each scene that was captured now appears as a separate clip in the Project window, as shown in Figure 6-9. As you can see in the figure, Premiere Pro automatically gives each clip the name you specified in Step 3, and an ascending number is tacked on to the end of each scene name.

Scene detection works by using the clock that is built into your camcorder. Virtually any modern camcorder has a built-in clock and calendar; the date and time of each recording is recorded onto the videotape along with audio, video, and timecode. Because there will always be a time gap between scenes (that gap may be seconds, minutes, hours, or even days), Premiere Pro can use those gaps to identify the beginning of each new scene.

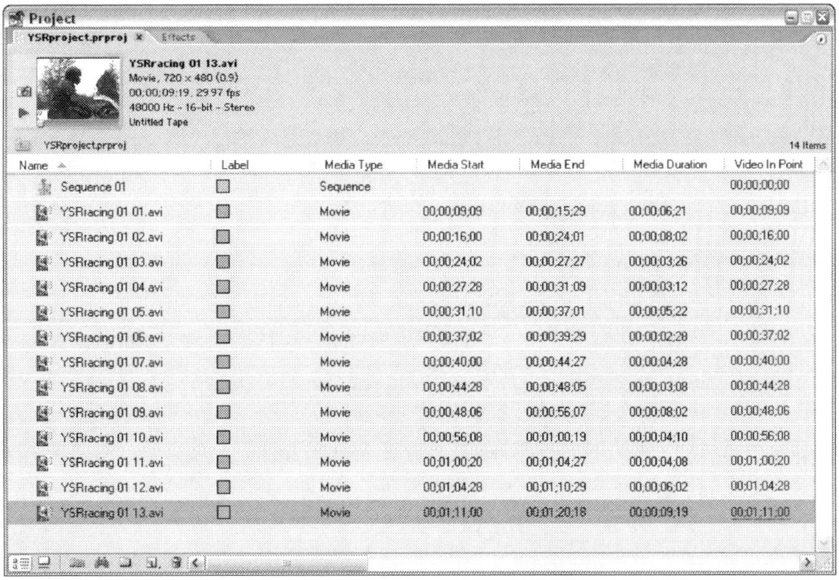

Figure 6-9:
Premiere
Pro
detected
and
captured 13
different
scenes in
my captured
video.

Doing batch captures

Capturing video into logical, useful clips on your hard drive has always been a time-consuming process, but it was even more so before Premiere incorporated scene detection (described in the previous section). One timesaving feature that Adobe Premiere *has* had for a long time is called *batch capture*. With batch capture, you can create a log of clips that you want to capture before you actually capture them. Later on you can tell Premiere to go back and automatically capture all the different clips in your log while you take a coffee break.

But why bother creating a log of desirable clips? Why not just capture the whole tape? Any given tape will contain some portions of video that you want to use, and some that you don't. For example, you probably want to use that clip that just happens to show a UFO zooming by in the background, but you probably don't want to use the five minutes of video you "shot" when you forgot to turn the camcorder off before sticking it in your camera bag (don't feel bad, it happens to everyone eventually). Aside from the problem of eating up valuable hard-drive real estate with undesirable video, working with one giant clip that contains all the video on a 60-minute tape can be clumsy and inefficient.

Even with scene detection, batch capture remains a useful feature. Just keep in mind that scene detection doesn't work with batch capture, so if you want to create a separate clip for each scene, you'll need to log each scene individually. The next few sections show you how to use Premiere's batch capture feature.

To perform batch captures, you must have a capture device with device control. This is because Premiere Pro must be able to operate the playback controls on the device during batch capture, and Premiere must be able to accurately read the timecode from the tape.

Logging clips

The first step in performing batch captures is to log the clips that you actually want to capture. To log clips, follow these steps:

1. **Open the Capture window by choosing File⇨Capture.**

2. **Use the playback controls under the viewer in the Capture window to identify a clip that you want to capture. Move to the exact frame at which you want to begin.**

3. **On the Logging tab, click Set In.**

   The current timecode should now appear in both the In and Out boxes.

4. **Use the playback controls to move to the exact frame at which you want to stop capture and click Set Out.**

   The timecode for the Out point should now appear in the Out box. The duration of the capture is also noted.

5. **Click Log Clip.**

   A Log Clip dialog box appears, as shown in Figure 6-10.

6. **Enter a file name.**

   You may also enter a description, scene name, or other information if desired.

7. **Click OK when you're done.**

   The logged clip is added to a batch list for your project.

8. **Repeat steps 3 through 7 for each clip on the tape that you want to log.**

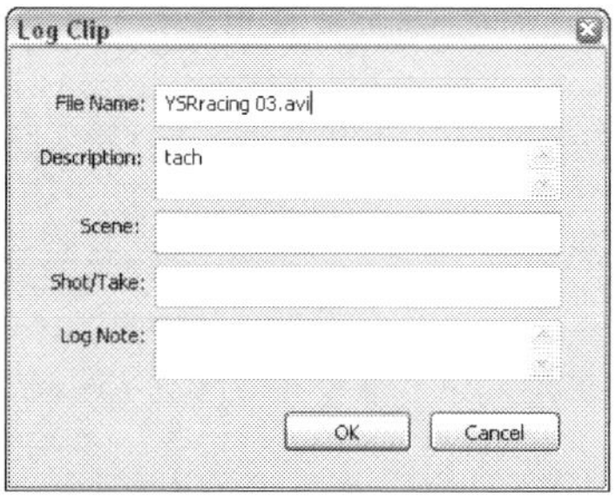

Figure 6-10:
Provide a file name and other information for the logged clip.

Log Clip	
File Name:	YSRracing 03.avi
Description:	tach
Scene:	
Shot/Take:	
Log Note:	
	OK Cancel

Capturing logged clips

After you have logged some clips that you want to capture, the logged clips appear in your Project window, labeled Offline in the Media Type column. As you can see in Figure 6-11, the bottom two clips in my Project window are logged but they have not yet been captured. To capture logged clips, follow these steps:

1. **Hold down the Ctrl key on your keyboard and click once on each offline clip in the Project window that you want to capture.**

2. **When you have selected each clip that you want to capture, choose File⫇Batch Capture.**

   The Batch Capture window appears.

3. **Click OK to close the Batch Capture window.**

   The Capture window appears and asks you to insert the tape containing the offline clips.

4. **Click OK when the correct tape has been inserted into your camcorder or video deck.**

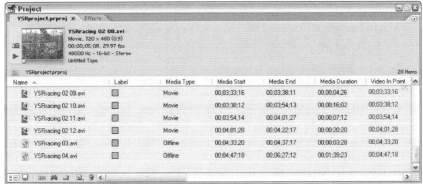

Figure 6-11: The bottom two clips are labeled "Offline" in the Media Type column.

Premiere Pro shuttles your tape to the correct location and captures your logged clips. When batch capture is complete, a message appears, telling you that batch capture is finished. Click OK to close this message. Your clips should now be available as Movie clips in the Project window.

Importing Media

There is no doubt in my mind that all the video you record with your camcorder is indescribably perfect just the way it is. But, if I may be so bold, wouldn't it be *even better* if you enhanced it a bit with some music, or perhaps some illustrative stills? Good, I'm glad you agree. Premiere can import all kinds of media, even video produced by another application. Supported formats include

- AI: Adobe Illustrator graphic
- AIFF: Audio Interchange File Format
- ASF: Microsoft Advanced Streaming Format
- AVI: Audio/Video Interleave, also called Video for Windows
- BMP: Bitmap still graphic
- DV: Digital video format
- FLC/FLI: Autodesk Animator animation
- FLM: FilmStrip
- GIF: Graphics Interchange Format image
- JPEG: Joint Photographic Experts Group image
- MPEG: Motion Picture Experts Group movie
- MP3: MPEG Layer-3 audio
- MOV: QuickTime movie
- PICS: Pixar animation
- PICT: Macintosh image format
- PCX: PC Paintbrush image
- PSD: Adobe Photoshop document
- Sound Designer I/II: An audio composition and editing tool
- TGA: Targa bitmap graphic
- TIFF: Tagged Image File Format
- WAV: Windows sound format
- WMA: Windows Media Audio
- WMV: Windows Media Video

Any of the formats in this list can be imported into Premiere Pro and used in your projects. Of all these formats, you may find that still graphics and audio files are among the most common. The next section shows you how to import audio from an audio CD or another source. Next I show you how to prepare still graphics for use in Premiere Pro. After you've done that, you can move to the last section, which describes how to actually import files (stills or not).

Capturing audio

Up to this point, I've talked primarily about capturing video, as well as the audio recorded along with most video. You can also capture audio all by itself if you want — whether it's just the audio recorded on your videotape, or music from an audio CD in your CD-ROM drive.

The method you use depends on the audio source and your computer. If you're capturing audio from a videotape in your camcorder or video deck, follow the instructions given earlier in this chapter for capturing video. However, in the Capture window, choose Audio from the Capture menu in the upper-right corner of the Logging tab (normally this menu is set to Audio and Video). Doing so results in only audio being captured.

If you want to use audio from an audio CD, first record the track(s) you wan onto your hard drive, using third-party recording software. Adobe Premiere Pro can import MP3 files, as well as Windows Media Audio (WMA) files. The ability to import WMA files is handy because you can record audio from any CD to your hard disk in WMA format using Windows Media Player, which comes with Windows XP. To copy music using Windows Media Player:

1. **Place an Audio CD in your CD-ROM drive and launch Windows Media Player by choosing Start⇨All Programs⇨Windows Media Player.**

2. **In Windows Media Player, click Copy from CD.**

   A list of tracks on the current audio CD should appear. Usually Windows Media Player automatically identifies the album, songs, and artist using an online music database, but if not you can manually enter song names, the name of the artist, and other information about the song if you wish. To manually enter a song or artist name, click once on the field, wait for a second, and then click again. You should then be able to type a name. Entering a descriptive name and artist name for the song helps you find it later.

3. **Use the playback controls to play the tracks and identify songs that you want to copy.**

4. **Place check marks next to each song that you want to copy.**

5. **Click Copy Music at the top of the Windows Media Player window.**

   Windows Media Player shows the copying in progress. When the desired files are copied to your hard disk (Windows Media Player displays the message, `Copied to Library`), go ahead and close Windows Media Player.

6. **In Premiere Pro, choose File⇨Import.**

7. **Browse to the folder containing the song that you copied.**

   Unless you've changed Windows Media Player's default settings, the copied songs appear in the My Music folder of your My Documents folder. Folders are automatically created to organize music by artist and album.

8. **Choose the song you want to import and click Open.**

   The imported song now appears in your project window.

Preparing stills for your movie

You're probably pretty accustomed to seeing images that have a 4:3 aspect ratio. Your computer's monitor most likely has a 4:3 aspect ratio. Most still photos that you take have a 4:3 aspect ratio. And of course, most TVs have a 4:3 aspect ratio. So dropping a 4:3 digital photo into a DV-based video project should be easy, right? Not really.

If you don't know the answer to the above question, I suggest that you spend some time in Chapter 4. There you'll find some important fundamentals about working with video, including screen and pixel aspect ratios.

Before you insert a still image into a video project, you must also consider pixel aspect ratio. Digital graphics usually have square pixels; video usually has rectangular pixels. The frame size of NTSC video is usually 720 x 480 pixels. Do the math and you'll find that this does *not* work out to 4:3 (it's actually 3:2). However, it still *appears* to have a 4:3 aspect ratio because NTSC video pixels are slightly taller than they are wide. To account for this, adjust the image size of your stills before you import them into Premiere. For NTSC video, your images should be 720 x 534 pixels before importing them into Premiere. For PAL video, the images should be 768 x 576 pixels before you import. To adjust the size of an image using Adobe Photoshop (a typical and excellent image-editing program), follow these steps:

1. **Open the image and save it as a Photoshop document (PSD) before performing any edits.**

   Photoshop documents can be imported directly into Premiere.

2. **In Photoshop, choose Image⇨Image Size.**

   The Image Size dialog box appears.

3. **In the Image Size dialog box, remove the check mark next to Constrain Proportions, as shown in Figure 6-12.**

4. **In the Pixel Dimensions section of the Image Size dialog box, enter 720 (NTSC) or 768 (PAL) in the Width field and 534 (NTSC) or 576 (PAL) in the Height field. For both fields, choose Pixels from the accompanying drop-down menus.**

Don't concern yourself with the Print Size section. You only use that when printing still graphics out on paper.

5. **Click OK, and then save and close the image.**

   After you click OK in the Image Size dialog box, your still image probably looks somewhat distorted. Don't worry; after the image is imported into an NTSC or PAL video program, it will look right.

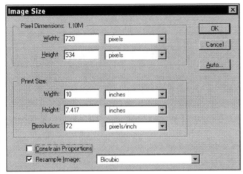

Figure 6-12:
Adjust the size of your still before importing it into a video project.

Importing stills and other fun stuff

Importing still graphics, audio files, and other neat things into Premiere is really easy. If you're importing a still image into a project that is based on NTSC or PAL video, first adjust the image size as described in the previous section. Then follow these steps:

1. **In Premiere, choose File⇨Import.**

   You can also import an entire folder if you wish, or a Premiere project.

2. **Browse to the file that you want to import.**

   Note that All Format Types is selected in the Files of Type menu by default. If you want to search for files of only a certain type, choose the desired type from this menu.

3. **Click Open.**

   The imported file appears in your Project window.

If the file you want to import doesn't show up in the Import window — and you're certain that you're looking in the correct folder —the file may be of a type that isn't supported by Premiere. (To double-check, see my list of supported file types earlier in this chapter.)

Organizing Your Media

When most people think of Adobe Premiere Pro, they think mainly of video, but this is truly a multimedia-rich program. You'll no doubt work with many different kinds of media in Premiere — audio, video, still graphics, or even text. You'll wind up using files from all over your computer, and possibly even your network. Keeping track of all this media stuff can be a challenge, but Premiere can help. This section shows you how to manage your media.

Managing source clips

Premiere does its best to make efficient use of your disk space. For example, suppose you import a video clip into three different projects. Does this mean you have three separate copies of that clip on your hard drive? No, in all three projects Premiere Pro points to the same source file. Although this is an efficient way to do business, it also means you must be careful about moving or deleting source files. If you move or delete a source file, any projects that point to that source file can't access it. Inaccessible files are also called *offline* files in Premiere Pro.

Where does Premiere store all your source files? They are stored on your scratch disk, which can be a separate hard drive or a specific folder on your main hard drive. To determine the location of your scratch disk, choose Edit⇨Preferences⇨Scratch Disks. The Scratch Disks section of the Preferences dialog box appears as shown in Figure 6-13. Paths are given for your scratch disks for captures and previews for both audio and video, as well as con-formed audio. *Conformed audio* files are basically copies of audio files that have been conformed to your project, incorporating your various edits. (For more on working with audio, see Chapter 13.)

Using Scratch Disk information in the Preferences dialog box, you can browse your hard drive (using Windows Explorer or My Computer) and identify large source files that are taking up a lot of disk space. In particular, check for the following suspects:

- **Adobe Premiere Pro Auto-Save folder:** This folder contains archived back-up copies of project files (.PRPROJ). These usually don't take up much space, but you can safely delete archives for older projects. Before deleting archives, make sure that the original project files are backed up on a CD-R or other safe place.

- **Adobe Premiere Pro Preview Files folder:** This folder is located in your scratch disk folder for Video Previews. Rendered preview files are stored here, subdivided into folders labeled by project. If you see a folder for an old project that you're not working on anymore, you can probably save a lot of disk space by deleting that folder. Just keep in mind that if you ever want to work on that project again, you may have to sit through the rendering process all over again as the preview files are recreated.

- ✔ **Capture files:** When you capture media, it ends up as files on your scratch disk. Some of those files, particularly video files, take up a lot of space. You can save a lot of that space by deleting old AVI video files, but make absolutely certain that none of the files you delete are needed by current projects. Projects always link back to the original source file, so if you delete a source file, any projects that used it now have offline media. Make sure that you still have the original source tapes for those media in a safe place.

- ✔ **Conformed Audio Files folder:** Some of the conformed audio files in this folder get surprisingly big. If you see any files in here that you know are for old projects, you can delete them. Deleting conformed audio doesn't have any affect on the original source file for the audio. Conformed audio files are discussed in Chapter 13.

- ✔ **Project files and batch lists:** These files don't use up much space, and I generally recommend against deleting them. One simple way to "back up" batch lists is to simply print them out. Double-click a Batch Capture Log file on your scratch disk to open it in a text editor like Notepad, and then choose File⇨Print. I usually print out batch lists, fold them into little squares (batch list origami can be a great way to express yourself), and then stick them in the plastic tape case with the original source tape to which the batch list corresponds.

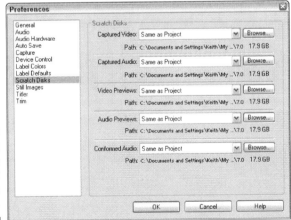

Figure 6-13: Review the location of your scratch disk here.

For more on using and configuring scratch disks, see "Setting Up Your Scratch Disks" in Chapter 3.

Using the Project window

As you work in a project, any media that you import or capture is added to your Project window. The Project window is usually pretty small, but if you expand the window, as shown in Figure 6-14, you'll see a lot more information about your clips. (You can expand the Project window by clicking-and-dragging on the lower-right corner of the window.) Key functions you can perform in the Project window include

- **Using bins to organize material.** Bins work like folders on your hard drive, and you can create your own bins by clicking the Bin button. Click-and-drag items to move them into bins.

- **Clicking New Item to quickly create a title, black video, bars and tone, or other video element.**

- **In List view, clicking a column head to sort clips by that heading.**

- **Clicking an item to view it in the preview area of the Project window.** Click Play next to the preview area to play audio or video clips.

Preview clips   Use bins to organize material.

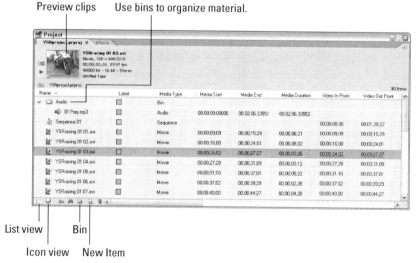

Figure 6-14:
Use the Project window to manage media in Premiere.

List view   Bin

Icon view   New Item

Use the view controls to switch between List view and Icon view. As you can see in Figure 6-15, Icon view can help you better visualize the content of each clip. The picture shown on the icon for each video clip is called the *poster* frame, and usually the poster frame is simply the first frame of the clip. In some cases, however, you may find it helpful to use a poster frame from a different part of the clip. To set a new poster frame for a clip, here's the drill:

1. **Click a clip once in the Project window.**

   The clip should now be active in the preview area in the upper left corner of the Project window.

2. **Click Play next to the preview area to start playing the clip.**

   The Play button turns into the Stop button once the clip starts to play.

3. **Click Stop when you see the frame that you want to use as the new poster frame.**

   You'll need to be quick with the mouse button because the Project window's little preview area won't let you move back and forth through a clip frame-by-frame.

4. **With the desired frame showing in the preview area, click the Poster Frame button.**

   The Poster Frame button is located just above the Play button. The new poster frame should now appear on the clip.

Figure 6-15:
Icon view can help you better visualize the contents of each clip.

Part III
Editing in Premiere Pro

The 5th Wave   By Rich Tennant

"Would it ruin the online video concert experience
if I vacuumed the mosh pit between songs?"

In this part . . .

With Adobe Premiere Pro, you have chosen one of the world's greatest video-editing programs. Just a couple of years ago, the editing capabilities offered in Premiere Pro were only available on professional-grade systems that cost hundreds of thousands of dollars.

Part III explores Premiere Pro's editing capabilities. You get a chance to edit clips, assemble them into a project using the Timeline, and then add some transitions, special effects, audio, and other special movie elements.

Chapter 7

Editing Clips

● ●

● ●

*I*n the American economy, the basic currency is the dollar. The light-year is used to express interstellar distances, and in video editing, the basic unit of measure is the clip. Chunks of audio, video, or even still graphics are all referred to as *clips* when you work in a nonlinear video-editing program. Of course, unlike dollars or light-years, there is no specific standard which defines a clip, but short or long, clips are your basic unit of measure when working in Adobe Premiere Pro. This chapter introduces you to the details of your clips and shows you how to work with them in your projects.

Getting to Know Your Clips

Clips that you capture or import into Premiere Pro all wind up in the Project window (see Chapter 6 for more on capturing and importing clips). Clips come in many shapes and sizes, so to speak. Types of clips include

  ✔ Video clips

  ✔ Audio clips

  ✔ Still graphics

  ✔ Titles

  ✔ Color mattes (a solid-colored clip)

  ✔ Black video

  ✔ Bars and tones (used to calibrate sound and color on video equipment)

  ✔ Universal counting leaders (a countdown that helps synchronize audio and video)

You can generate any of the last five items in this list by clicking the New Item button at the bottom of the Project window. (For more on working with titles, see Chapter 14. See Chapter 15 for information on when and how to use bars and tone, black video, and counting leaders.)

Analyzing clip details

You can learn a lot about a clip in the Project window. To view a brief summary, click a clip. The clip is loaded into the preview area in the upper-left corner of the Project window, as shown in Figure 7-1. You'll also see a summary of the clip's length, frame size, and audio quality as appropriate. This summary appears just to the right of the preview window.

If you require even more information about a clip, right-click it in the Project window and choose Properties from the menu that appears. A Properties dialog box opens, containing more detailed information than you likely need to know about the clip. These details can help you troubleshoot problems that you may be experiencing with that clip.

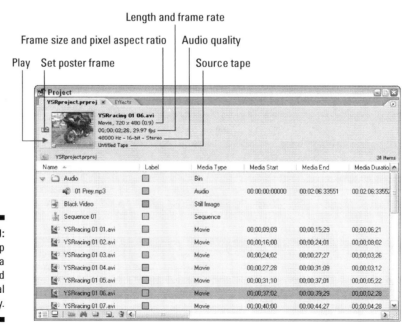

Figure 7-1: Select a clip to view a preview and statistical summary.

Playing clips

When you select a clip in the Project window, a preview of it appears in the tiny preview window in the upper-left corner. If the clip is audio or video, you can play it by clicking the Play button just to the left of the preview window. You can move to specific parts of the clip using the slider underneath the preview window.

As you can see, the clip previews provided in the Project window are pretty small. If you get tired of squinting, you may want to load the clip into the Monitor window to preview it. Besides giving you a bigger window in which to preview the clip, the Monitor is also where you will pare the clip down to just the portion you want to use in your movie. Follow these steps to play your clip in the Monitor window:

1. **Switch to the Editing workspace mode by choosing Window⇨ Workspace⇨Editing.**

   The Monitor window appears and switches to Dual View, if it wasn't like that already.

2. **Click-and-drag a clip from the Project window and drop it in the left pane of the Monitor window.**

   The clip will now appear in the left pane of the Monitor window, as shown in Figure 7-2.

3. **Use the playback controls at the bottom of the Monitor window (as in Figure 7-3) to preview the clip.**

Figure 7-2: A clip has been loaded into the Monitor from the Project window.

The Monitor window offers buttons and tools for controlling playback and various other editing actions. Some of these controls may be entirely new to you, especially if you are new to video editing. Figure 7-3 details the Monitor's playback controls.

Some of the controls shown in Figure 7-3 are described throughout this chapter and in Chapter 8. Take a close look at the playback controls right now by loading a clip into the Monitor and clicking the Play button. Somewhere in the middle of the clip, click the Stop button (the Play button turns into the Stop button after you click Play). Now you can play with some controls that help you identify specific frames in a clip:

✔ **Click the Step Forward button.** The clip moves forward by one frame. You can also press the right-arrow key on your keyboard to move forward one frame at a time.

✔ **Click the Step Back button.** The clip moves back a frame. You can also control the Step Back function by pressing the left-arrow key.

✔ **If you want to remember a certain spot in the clip, move to the spot and click the Set Marker button.** This places a marker at the current location in the clip. A marker is kind of like a virtual sticky note. Use the Go To Previous Marker and Go To Next Marker buttons to quickly jump from marker to marker. I'll show you more about using markers later in this chapter.

✔ **Place the mouse pointer directly on the Shuttle control.** Click-and-drag it to the right. Notice that as you drag the Shuttle farther to the right, the clip advances forward at an increasing rate. Drag the Shuttle left to play the clip backward. Let go of the Shuttle by releasing the mouse button. The Shuttle snaps back to the middle and the clip stops playing. Shuttle controls have been common on professional video equipment for years because they provide quick yet precise control over playback.

✔ **Place the mouse pointer directly on the Jog control.** Click-and-drag the jog control back and forth. The clip rolls frame by frame as you move the jog. Jog controls are also a legacy of professional video equipment.

✔ **As a clip plays, notice that a blue indicator moves to show you your current location in a clip.** This blue indicator is often called the CTI, short for *current time indicator*. In some other editing programs, the CTI is also called the *playhead*.

In addition to the Monitor window controls, Adobe Premiere Pro allows you to rely heavily on keyboard buttons as well. Premiere Pro uses the industry-standard key combination of J-K-L to control shuttle operation in the Monitor window. Press J to shuttle back, L to shuttle forward, and K to stop. Notice that the J, K, and L keys are conveniently located right next to each other on your keyboard.

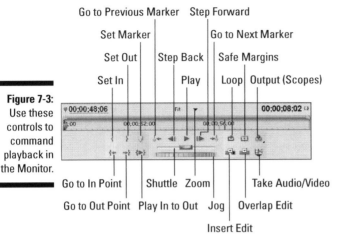

Go to Previous Marker   Step Forward

Set Marker   Go to Next Marker

Set Out   Step Back   Safe Margins

Set In   Play   Loop| Output (Scopes)

Figure 7-3:
Use these
controls to
command
playback in
the Monitor.

Go to In Point   Shuttle Zoom   Take Audio/Video

Go to Out Point Play In to Out Jog   Overlap Edit

Insert Edit

If you don't like using the mouse-button controls *or* the keyboard, you may want to invest in a multimedia controller such as the Contour A/V Solutions ShuttlePRO. A multimedia controller connects to your computer and has special buttons and knobs to make moving about and controlling playback easier. The ShuttlePRO's ergonomic design and dial control for shuttling and frame jogging ultimately save me time, frustration, and wrist movement. I feature this useful device in Chapter 21.

The Ins and Outs of In and Out Points

In a perfect universe, there would be peace on Earth, we'd all be drinking free Bubble-Up and eating rainbow stew, and every clip of video would start and end at exactly the right time. Alas, this world is not quite perfect just yet. But at least in the case of video, you can provide the illusion of perfection by using *In points* and *Out points*. In and Out points are critical in video editing because they let you control which portions of a clip appear in the video program and which portions don't appear. So get your silver spoon ready because the following sections serve up steps for perfecting your clips by using In points, Out points, and other markers.

Setting In and Out points

Setting In points and Out points on a clip is pretty easy, and Premiere Pro gives you several different methods to choose from. I strongly recommend that you set In and Out points on a clip *before* you insert it into a sequence in your project's Timeline. For this process, I recommend using the Editing workspace (Window➪Workspace➪Editing) because it provides a dual-pane Monitor window that I find easier to work with.

The In point is the spot where the clip begins playing in the project. In general, you should not set the In point at the very beginning of the clip if you can avoid it. The main reason for not doing so is to facilitate transitions. Suppose (for example) you want to apply a Cross Dissolve transition to the beginning of a clip, and you set it to last for one second — during this one-second period, the previous clip fades out and the new clip fades in. To facilitate such a transition, Premiere normally uses the "extra" material just beyond the In and Out points of the adjacent clips.

An Out point is, of course, the spot where you want to stop using the clip. As with In points, Out points should not be set at the very end of a clip if you can possibly avoid it. (Keep in mind that transitions need leeway.)

After you have used the Monitor controls to position the CTI where you want to set an In or Out point, Premiere Pro provides a couple of methods for setting these points (refer to Figure 7-3 for control locations):

  ✔ In the Monitor, click the Set In Point or Set Out Point buttons.

  ✔ Press I (In point) or O (Out point) on your keyboard.

After you've marked In and Out points on a clip, the duration of your marked clip portion appears to the upper-right of the Monitor window controls. As you can see in Figure 7-4, I have set In and Out points to select exactly five seconds of this clip.

Using other markers

In points and Out points usually get all the attention in books like this, but you can use many other markers in your clips as well. To set a marker at the current position in the clip, right-click the CTI (see Figure 7-4) and choose Set Clip Marker from the menu that appears. A submenu offering several different kinds of markers appears. Different kinds of markers include

  ✔ **In, Out:** These are your basic In points and Out points, as described in the previous section.

  ✔ **Video In/Out, Audio In/Out:** Use these if you want audio and video to go in or out separately. Figure 7-5 shows that I edited a clip into the Timeline so the Audio In point starts well before the Video In point.

  ✔ **Unnumbered:** If you want to mark only a single spot in the clip, add an unnumbered marker. I like to use these to mark the location of visual events, which I later match with an audio soundtrack.

✔ **Next Available Numbered, Other Numbered:** Use numbered markers if
you want to set more than one marker in the same clip. Choose Next
Available Numbered if you just want Premiere Pro to select a number
automatically. Choose Other Numbered if you want to set a specific
number yourself.

Figure 7-4:
Mark In and
Out points
on your clip
before
editing it
into the
Timeline.

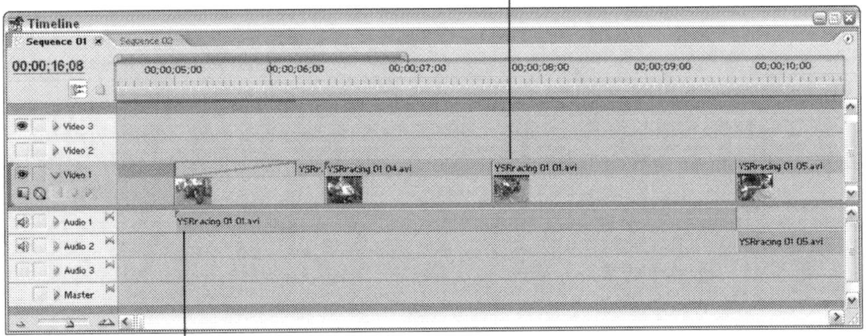

CTI   Duration of marked clip

Video In point

Figure 7-5:
In and Out
points can
be marked
separately
for audio
and video.

Audio In point

When you right-click the CTI, you'll notice that besides Set Clip Marker there are two other options. You can choose Go to Clip Marker or Clear Clip Marker. Choose Go to Clip Marker to open a submenu of markers that you have already set. Click one of the markers to jump directly to that location.

If you want to delete a marker, right-click the CTI and choose Clear Clip Marker. Select an option from the submenu that appears. As you can see, you can clear the current marker, all markers, In points and Out points, or specific numbered markers.

Modifying Clips

What *is* a clip, really? When you see a list of clips in the Project window, you're looking at references to actual files on your hard disk. When you set markers on clips or perform edits, you're actually editing the references in Premiere Pro, and not the original source file. This is important because it leaves the original source file undisturbed for future use. It also saves storage space because you don't have multiple copies of the same material all over your hard drive.

You can even duplicate clips without eating up extra disk space. Duplicate clips come in handy when you have a really long clip containing a lot of material, some of which you might use in different parts of your project. To duplicate a clip, right-click it in the Project window and choose Duplicate. A copy of the clip will now appear in the Project window. If you want to give the copy a more useful name, right-click it and choose Rename.

The next few sections show you how to make some basic modifications to your clips before inserting them into a sequence in your movie project.

Controlling a clip's duration

The duration of a clip is determined by the length of time between the In and Out points for the clip. For audio or video clips, I recommend that in most cases, you only adjust the duration of the clip by setting In and Out points. However, you can change the duration by entering a numeric value as well. Although this normally isn't a good idea for video, you often set a numeric duration value for still clips. The duration of a still clip determines how long it plays when inserted in a movie. To adjust the duration of a clip, follow these steps:

1. **Select a clip in the Project window.**

2. **Choose Clip⇨Speed/Duration.**

The Clip Speed/Duration dialog box appears. In Figure 7-6, I am adjusting the duration of a still clip. Because it's a still clip, options that only pertain to audio and video clips (Speed, Reverse, Audio Pitch) are unavailable.

3. **Enter a new duration for the clip in the Duration field.**

   Clip duration is expressed in the same format as timecode, so it should be read as

   ```
   hours:minutes:seconds:frames
   ```

   To enter a new duration, either type a new number or click-and-drag left or right on the blue timecode number. As you drag the mouse pointer left, the duration decreases. As you drag the mouse pointer right, the duration increases.

   These click-and-draggable timecodes were first seen in some parts of Adobe Premiere 6.5, and they are fully implemented throughout Adobe Premiere Pro. As you will see as you click-and-drag on timecodes, you can move the mouse as far across your desk as you like, and when you release the mouse button, the pointer will reappear on-screen right where it started (as opposed to being somewhere off the edge of the screen). Timecode adjustments have never been easier!

4. **Click OK when you're done.**

The clip in Figure 7-6 is set to play for exactly five seconds.

Figure 7-6:
Set the duration of your clip using timecode.

You can also adjust a clip's duration in the Timeline. See Chapter 8 for more on working with clips in the Timeline.

Speeding up (or slowing down) your clips

Besides adjusting the duration of a clip, you can also adjust the speed at which it plays. Speed adjustments can give you a fast motion or slo-mo effect. Before you dismiss speed adjustment as gimmicky, consider some useful applications of this feature:

✔ You can adjust the length of the clip without reshooting it. If you have a specific period of time in your project that a clip must fill, but the clip is shorter than the gap, slow the clip down slightly.

✔ You can use speed adjustments to correct too slow or too fast shots. If you're not happy with the speed at which the camera pans across a scene — say, across a landscape — adjust the speed of the clip to speed up or slow down the pan as desired.

✔ You can use speed adjustments to change the mood or feel of a shot. If an action scene doesn't seem quite as exciting as you would like, speed it up just a bit. Conversely, if two lovers are running across a grassy field at sunset toward each other's embrace, slow the speed down a bit to increase the drama.

✔ You can create interesting voice effects by adjusting playback speed of audio clips. A faster speed makes the voice sound small and wacky (like Alvin and the Chipmunks), and a slower speed makes the voice sound large and ominous (like Darth Vader).

Just be aware of the potential negative effects of speed adjustment. While moderate speed adjustments to video may be imperceptible to the eyes of most viewers, even slight speed adjustments to audio tracks will be immediately obvious.

Also, you may find that your video doesn't seem to play smoothly when you slow it down or speed it up. When you slow down a clip, Premiere Pro must duplicate some frames so the clip still fills the required duration. When you speed up a clip, some frames are removed. Choose your speed-change percentage carefully to ensure that frames are added or removed evenly. Table 7-1 lists percentages that will give reasonably smooth speed changes in Premiere Pro. If you plan to change the speed of a clip, use one of these percentages for the smoothest possible playback.

Table 7-1	Safe Speed-Change Percentages for Video Clips
Safe Slow-Motion Speeds	*Safe Fast-Motion Speeds*
50%	100%
33.33%	200%
25%	300%
20%	400%
16.67%	500%

"I feel like I keep making the same edits over and over . . . "

Do you ever feel like you keep repeating yourself? Do you find yourself performing the same redundant tasks? Do you often feel like you do the same thing over and over? Before you form any habits that might lead to a repetitive stress injury, you may want to see if you can adjust a setting in Adobe Premiere Pro that might save you a lot of repeated effort.

Take still graphics, for example. If you use a lot of stills in your movie projects, you may find that you adjust the duration repeatedly for each still — by the same amount almost every single time. Premiere has a default duration for still graphics, and you can adjust that default if you want. To do so, choose Edit⇨Preferences⇨ Still Image. The default duration for a still image is 150 frames, which works out to about five seconds in NTSC video, or six seconds in PAL video. Simply enter a new number in the Default Duration box, remembering the frame rate of the video that you work with.

If you do a little math, you'll see a pattern in the speed-change percentages in Table 7-1. If you turn all of the Safe Slow Motion percentages into ratios, you would see that they all start with the number one. The 50% speed gives a ratio of 1:2, which means that every single frame will be turned into *two* frames when Premiere Pro adjusts the speed. With a speed change of 25% (1:4), each frame becomes four frames. Likewise, all of the Safe Fast-Motion percentages end with 1when converted to ratios. The 200% speed gives a ratio of 2:1, and the 300% speed gives a ratio of 3:1.

Adjusting the speed of a clip in Premiere Pro is pretty easy:

1. **Select a clip on which you want to adjust the speed.**

   You can choose a clip in the Project window, or one that has already been edited into the Monitor. I recommend that you work with a duplicate of the original.

2. **Choose Clip⇨Speed/Duration.**

   The Clip Speed/Duration dialog box appears, as shown in Figure 7-7.

3. **Enter a new percentage number in the Speed field.**

   To make the clip play at double its original speed, enter **200** percent. To make the clip play at half its original speed, enter **50** percent. The duration of the clip is adjusted automatically, based on your percentage change. Again, I strongly recommend that you use a percentage from Table 7-1.

4. **If you want the clip to play in reverse, place a check mark next to the Reverse Speed option.**

   This option can be handy if you're going for a "fast rewind" look for the clip.

5. **Place a check mark next to Maintain Audio Pitch to, er, maintain the audio pitch of the clip.**

   This is another one of those really cool new features of Adobe Premiere Pro. If you maintain the audio pitch, you can make speed adjustments to video without making the accompanying audio sound like Alvin and the Chipmunks or Darth Vader (see my earlier comment on this subject). This feature is especially handy if you want to maintain ambient sound effects with a clip. Experiment with this setting, trying the clip with and without the Maintain Audio Pitch setting enabled. Play the clip each way and see how this option affects the audio.

6. **Click OK to close the Clip Speed/Duration dialog box.**

7. **Play the clip to preview your speed changes.**

Figure 7-7:
Adjusting
the speed of
your clips
can be more
than just a
gimmick.

"Oops!" Undoing Mistakes

Don't feel bad; everyone makes a mistake once in a while. For some of us, making mistakes is a way of life! Adobe Premiere understands that you might make a goof occasionally — and like any good computer program, it's forgiving. Premiere Pro incorporates the Undo feature beloved by computer users the world over. If you make a mistake, you can quickly undo it by choosing Edit➪Undo. The Edit menu lists the last action that was performed next to Undo so you know exactly what it is you're undoing. If you don't like using the Edit menu, you can also quickly undo an action using the keyboard shortcut Ctrl+Z.

Did you change your mind again? Perhaps that "mistake" wasn't such a bad thing after all. If you want to redo the mistake that you just undid, choose Edit➪Redo (or press Ctrl+Shift+Z).

One of the things I really like about the interface design in Adobe software is the use of floating palettes. Palettes provide quick access to powerful features, yet they're easy to show or hide as needed. One of the more useful palettes in Premiere Pro is the History palette, shown in Figure 7-8. The History palette appears by default when you use the Editing workspace (Window⇨Workspace⇨Editing), or you can display the History palette at any time by choosing Window⇨History.

The Premiere Pro History palette shows you a list of the edits you've made, in order — the last 100 actions you performed, with the most recent edit at the bottom of the list. To move back in history, simply click an item in the list and then click the Trash bin icon at the bottom of the palette. When you click OK to confirm the action, you undo the selected item — *and all actions following it.* If you want to clear the history, click the right-facing arrow in the upper-right corner of the History palette and then choose Clear History.

Figure 7-8:
Use the
History
palette to
review your
recent edits
and go back
in time if
needed.

Chapter 8

Working with the Timeline

*H*ungry? Me too. Let's visit your favorite restaurant, shall we?

```
[transit to restaurant]
```

Hey, nice place. What is it you like best about this restaurant, anyway? Sure, the location is good, the atmosphere is pleasing, and the staff is cordial, but ultimately it's what goes on back in the kitchen that determines how favorable your dining experience is.

You can think of the Timeline as Adobe Premiere Pro's "kitchen" — you carefully choose ingredients for your project and then blend them together in the Timeline until you've cooked up a movie worth serving to your audience. How effectively you use the Timeline determines whether your productions are fine video delicacies or half-baked episodes. This chapter shows you how to use Premiere Pro's Timeline for editing your movie projects. Put on your apron and let's get cooking!

Understanding the Timeline

The Timeline is where the various elements of your movie are assembled. As I mention in Chapter 3, video is considered a *linear* medium because when you watch video, one sequence follows another from start to finish. You can think of a movie as being laid out along a line through time. When you create a movie in Adobe Premiere Pro, you lay out all the different scenes and portions of the movie along a Timeline (as shown in Figure 8-1).

Current timecode

Additional sequences   CTI   Ruler   Video tracks

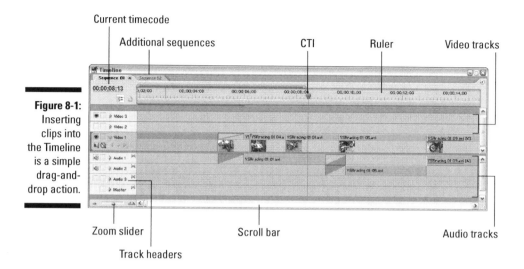

Figure 8-1:
Inserting
clips into
the Timeline
is a simple
drag-and-
drop action.

Zoom slider   Scroll bar   Audio tracks

Track headers

One of the most significant improvements to Adobe Premiere Pro is that it can now create multiple sequences in the Timeline. Each sequence behaves like a separate, individual Timeline. In previous versions of Premiere, you were limited to just one Timeline per project. (I'll show you how to work with multiple sequences later in this chapter.)

As you can see in Figure 8-1, the Timeline shows a lot of useful information and is easy to navigate. Key features of the Premiere Pro Timeline include

✓ **Track headers:** Each video and audio track has a header on the left side of the Timeline. The track headers remain visible even as you scroll the Timeline. Track headers contain important controls (described in the following section).

✓ **Ruler, timecode, and CTI:** Your current location in the Timeline is indicated by the timecode (shown in the upper-left corner), ruler, and CTI (Current Timecode Indicator). When you play the Timeline, the CTI moves to show your exact location.

✓ **Zoom and scroll controls:** Use the zoom slider in the lower-left corner of the Timeline to zoom the view in or out. You can also use the plus (+) and minus (–) keys to zoom in or out. Use the slider at the bottom of the Timeline to scroll left or right.

Working with tracks in the Timeline

By now you've probably noticed all those different audio and video tracks in the Timeline. Tracks are perhaps the most important feature of the Premiere Pro Timeline because they allow tremendous versatility and control over the sound and pictures in your project. For example, one audio track might contain the sound that goes with a certain video clip, whereas a second audio track contains voice-over narration and a third track provides background music. With multiple video tracks, you can perform special compositing effects, picture-in-picture effects, overlay titles, and more. Adobe Premiere Pro allows you to have up to 99 separate video tracks, as well as 99 audio tracks. The next couple of sections show you how to keep track of your Timeline tracks when you work in Premiere.

Adjusting track views

Tracks have a variety of important view settings and controls that you can set. Some of these controls are shown all the time, whereas others only appear when you expand the view of the track. Track controls (shown in Figure 8-2) include

- **Track Output:** Click this button to effectively "hide" the track from the project. When an eye (video tracks) or speaker (audio tracks) appears in this button, the track is active in the project.

- **Lock Track:** Click here to place a padlock in the button and lock the track. A locked track cannot be edited. Video Track 2 is locked in Figure 8-2. Click the Lock Track button again to unlock the track.

- **Expand Track:** Click this arrow to spin it down and expand the view of the track. Expanding the track reveals the Set Display Style and Keyframe controls.

- **Set Display Style:** Click-and-hold this button to open a submenu of options. The menu options control how clips appear in the Timeline. For video tracks you can specify whether a thumbnail image of the clip appears at the clip's head, tail, both, or neither (Show Names Only). For audio tracks, you can specify whether or not waveforms appear.

- **Show Keyframes:** Keyframes are crucial tools for controlling transparency and video effects in a clip because they serve as landmarks within the clip. Audio keyframes allow you to precisely control audio volume. Chapters 11 and 12 show you more about working with video keyframes. Chapter 13 describes audio keyframes. Use the Add/Remove Keyframe button to (surprise!) add or remove keyframes, and use the Next and Previous Keyframe buttons to navigate from one keyframe to the next.

Adding and renaming tracks

You can put as many as 99 video tracks and 99 audio tracks into the Adobe Premiere Pro Timeline, although it is difficult to imagine what one might do with that many. When it comes to Timeline tracks, however, having too many is better than not having enough, so I'm certainly not complaining. If you need more tracks in your Timeline than those already present, you can add them by following these steps:

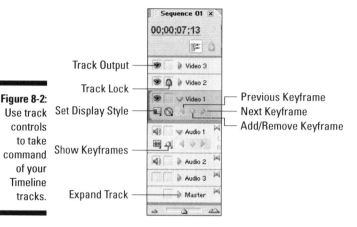

Figure 8-2:
Use track
controls
to take
command
of your
Timeline
tracks.

1. **Choose Sequence⇨Add Tracks.**

   The Add Tracks dialog box opens as shown in Figure 8-3.

2. **Enter the number of tracks you want to add next to Video Tracks, Audio Tracks, or Audio Submix Tracks (as appropriate).**

3. **Choose an option from the Placement menu.**

   In most cases you'll want to just stick with After Last Track.

4. **If you are adding audio or audio submix tracks, choose an option from the Track Type menu.**

   Track Type options include Mono, Stereo, or 5.1.

5. **Click OK to close the dialog box and add your tracks.**

You can also add, delete, or rename tracks by right-clicking a blank area of any track header in the Timeline. You may find it handy to give some tracks more descriptive names, to better reflect what you put in that track. Track names won't appear in the final movie, so you can choose any name that you find useful as you edit.

Using the Premiere Pro toolbar

Somewhere in a garage, closet, basement, or shed, you probably have a toolbox full of tools. Toolboxes are great for organizing screwdrivers, hammers, wrenches, and various other implements of destruction. Software programs typically have many different tools as well, and those tools are usually organized on toolbars. Adobe Premiere Pro provides a floating toolbar that usually appears in the lower-left portion of the screen.

If you don't see a toolbar like the one shown in Figure 8-4, choose Window↩
Tools. The Premiere Pro toolbar should appear. To use a tool, simply click it
in the toolbar or press its keyboard shortcut. When you move the mouse
pointer over the Timeline, the pointer image looks like the selected tool.
Table 8-1 lists the tools in the Premiere Pro toolbar, along with the keyboard
shortcut and function for each.

Table 8-1	Premiere Pro Toolbar Tools	
Tool	*Keyboard Shortcut*	*Function*
Selection Tool	V	Use the Selection tool, the most commonly used tool, to select clips for click-and-drag edits.
Track Select Tool	M	When you use this tool to click a clip, the clip and all subsequent clips in the same track are selected.
Ripple Edit Tool	B	Use this tool to perform a ripple edit. Ripple edits are described later in this chapter.
Rolling Edit Tool	N	Use this to perform a roll edit (also described later in this chapter).
Rate Stretch Tool	X	This tool can change the playback speed of a clip. See the section on changing clip speed later in this chapter.

(continued)

Table 8-1 *(continued)*

Tool	Keyboard Shortcut	Function
Razor Tool	C	As the name implies, this tool works like a razor blade. Use it to split clips when you click them.
Slip Tool	Y	Perform slip edits with this tool. (You guessed it: I describe slip edits later in this chapter.)
Slide Tool	U	Another type of edit described in this chapter — the slide edit — is performed using this tool.
Pen Tool	P	Use the Pen tool to adjust keyframes for audio levels (see Chapter 13), video clip opacity (Chapter 11), and other effects (Chapter 12).
Hand Tool	H	Click-and-drag the Timeline to scroll back and forth.
Zoom Tool	Z	Use this tool to zoom in on the Timeline. Hold down the Alt key while clicking with the Zoom tool to zoom out.

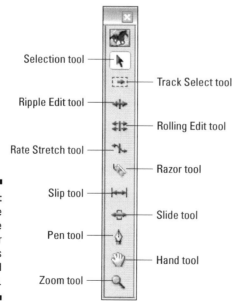

Figure 8-4:
The Premiere Pro toolbar contains many useful tools.

Selection tool — Track Select tool

Ripple Edit tool — Rolling Edit tool

Rate Stretch tool — Razor tool

Slip tool — Slide tool

Pen tool — Hand tool

Zoom tool

Editing Clips into the Timeline

Before you start assembling stuff into the Timeline to make your movie, make sure you've used the Monitor window to edit clips and mark In points and Out points (Chapter 7 explains how). After you've completed that process, you can start editing your marked clips into the Timeline where your project is actually assembled. The following sections show you how to edit clips into the Timeline and then help you figure out what to do with those clips once they're there.

Editing clips into the Timeline is easiest when you work in the Editing workspace. Workspaces are covered in more detail in Chapter 3, but to open this workspace, choose Window➪Workspace➪Editing.

Inserting clips

You've probably already discovered that a lot of work in Adobe Premiere Pro is performed by simply dragging –and dropping items onto new locations. And so it is when editing clips into the Timeline. After you have set In and Out points for a clip in the Monitor window, the easiest way to add that clip to the Timeline is to simply drag and drop it on your sequence. You can drag clips from the Monitor window or the Project window directly into the Timeline. As you can see in Figure 8-5, I am dragging a clip to the Timeline after marking In and Out points in the Monitor.

Premiere Pro provides two other methods for placing a clip in the Timeline as well. These editing methods — called *insert* and *overlay* — are usually more precise and efficient ways to place clips in the Timeline at exactly the desired location. Each type of edit is a little different:

- ✔ **Insert Edit:** The incoming clip is inserted at the current location of the CTI (current time indicator). Clips that fall after the CTI are moved over to make room. Figure 8-6 shows an insert edit.

- ✔ **Overlay Edit:** The incoming clip is inserted at the current location of the CTI, but rather than moving subsequent material over the incoming clip simply replaces it. Figure 8-7 shows an overlay edit.

To perform an insert or overlay edit, follow these steps:

1. **Use the Monitor window to set In and Out points for a clip (as described in Chapter 7).**

2. **Place the Timeline CTI at the exact location where you want the incoming clip to start.**

   Use the left- and right-arrow keys to fine-tune the location of the CTI, one frame at a time.

Insert edit ⌐Overlay edit

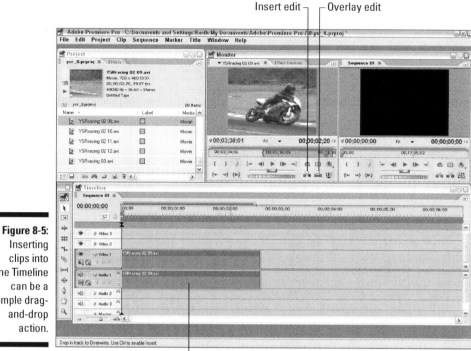

Figure 8-5:
Inserting
clips into
the Timeline
can be a
simple drag-
and-drop
action.

Drag-and-drop clips to the Timeline

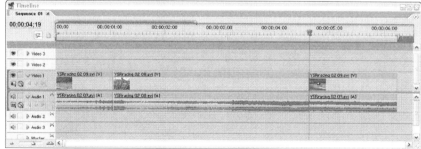

Figure 8-6:
An insert
edit inserts
the clip and
shifts
subsequent
material
over to
make room.

3. **Click the track header for the track where you want to place the incoming clip.**

The selected track is sometimes called the *target track*. Choosing a target track is fairly important. Figure 8-8 shows basically the same exact overlay edit as Figure 8-7, except that I have chosen Video 2 as my target track instead of Video 1. Because the video in Video 2 is layered over the top of Video 1, the remainder of the clip in Video 1 is replaced when the CTI gets to the beginning of the clip in Video 2.

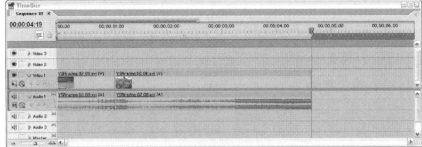

Figure 8-7:
An overlay edit inserts the clip in place of subsequent material.

4. **Click the Insert Edit or Overlay Edit button (Figure 8-5) in the Monitor to perform an insert or overlay edit.**

The clip now appears in the Timeline. Using this method of placing clips in the Timeline is usually more precise than dragging and dropping because you can pick an exact location for the edit using the CTI. Dragging and dropping clips can seem downright clumsy by comparison.

Figure 8-8:
Here I have performed an overlay edit into the Video 2 track instead of Video 1.

Overlay edits are used in a variety of situations. Here are some common uses for overlay edits:

✔ If you want titles to appear over a video image, you overlay a title clip over a video clip. (I show you how to create and add titles in Chapter 14.)

✔ If you want to briefly show a clip in the middle of another longer clip, you can overlay it and switch back and forth between clips. For example, the long clip might show a figure skater gliding across an ice rink while the short overlaid clip provides a close-up of the skater's face.

✔ Combine multiple clips into one scene in a process called *compositing*. Compositing is often seen on TV when a meteorologist appears to stand in front of a moving weather map. The meteorologist is actually standing in front of a blue or green screen, and the weather map is composited in with special editing equipment. In Chapter 11, I'll show you how to do compositing in Adobe Premiere Pro.

Moving clips

After you have some clips in the Timeline, it's time to actually do something with them. Probably one of the most common things you'll do is simply move clips around. Moving a clip is so easy that you've probably already figured out how: You simply click-and-drag clips to new locations. You can drag clips back and forth in a track, or drag them to a different track altogether.

If you're trying to move a clip at very small increments, you may get frustrated by the tendency of clips to snap to the nearest adjacent clip edge when you get close. Click the Snap button under the timecode indicator in the upper-left corner of the Timeline (the Snap button looks like a magnet). This disables the snap-to-edges feature. Click the Snap button again to enable snap-to-edges.

Other methods for "moving" a clip exist. Some clip movements can affect the In and Out points of clips, tweak adjacent clips, or change the duration of the program in the Timeline. Table 8-2 outlines the four basic types of edits.

Table 8-2	Edit Types		
Edit Type	*Description*	*Clip Duration*	*Program Duration*
Roll edit	Drag the edit line between two clips to change the Out point of one and the In point of another.	Changed	Not changed
Ripple edit	Drag the edit line to change the In or Out point on one clip without affecting other clips.	Changed	Changed
Slip edit	Drag the clip to change the In and Out points of that clip.	Not changed	Not changed
Slide edit	Drag a clip to change the In and Out points of adjacent clips.	Not changed	Not changed

Each of the edits described in Table 8-2 is easy to perform and is described in the following sections. To select one edit type or another, first click the appropriate tool in the Premiere Pro toolbar (as in Figure 8-4).

Performing roll edits

No, this isn't the sort of edit you do while attempting aerobatics in a plane. As mentioned in Table 8-2, a *roll edit* adjusts the Out point of one clip and the In point of the adjacent clip. You make this change by clicking and dragging the edit line between two clips. The duration of each clip is changed, but the duration of the overall program stays the same. Figure 8-9 illustrates a roll edit. This edit is rolling the Out point of Clip A and the In point of Clip B.

Figure 8-9: A roll edit changes the duration of adjacent clips without affecting the overall program.

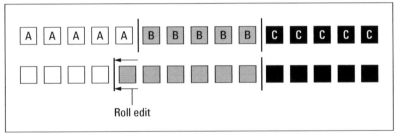

Roll edit

When you perform a roll edit, remember that the amount you "roll" the edit line is limited by the amount of source material still available for the clip that is being lengthened. To perform a roll edit, follow these steps:

1. **Choose the Rolling Edit tool in the Premiere Pro toolbar.**

2. **Hover the mouse pointer over the edit point between the clips you want to roll.**

   The mouse pointer changes to a vertical line with arrows pointing both left and right.

3. **Click-and-drag the edit point.**

   The Monitor window changes to show you the new In and Out points of the rolled clips, as shown in Figure 8-10.

Performing ripple edits

No hip waders required. Honest. A *ripple edit* differs from a roll edit by modifying only one clip instead of two adjacent clips. The result of editing the In or Out point on only one clip is that you change the length of the whole program. In Figure 8-11, the Out point for Clip B has been rippled left, thereby shortening Clip B *and the whole program.*

A ripple edit relies on extra material in the source clip only if your ripple edit extends the clip. To perform a ripple edit, follow these steps:

1. **Choose the Ripple Edit tool in the Premiere Pro toolbar.**

2. **Hover the mouse pointer over the edit point of the clip you want to ripple.**

   The mouse pointer changes to a bracket facing toward the affected clip.

3. **Click-and-drag the edit point.**

   The Monitor window changes to show you the new In or Out point of the rippled clip.

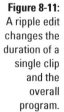

Figure 8-10:
The Monitor displays your new In and Out points as you perform a roll edit.

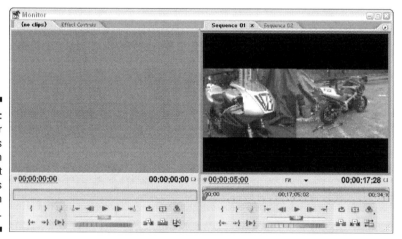

Figure 8-11:
A ripple edit changes the duration of a single clip and the overall program.

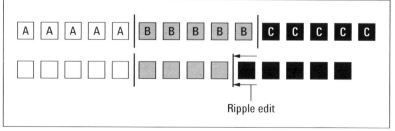

Ripple edit

Deleting blank space with Ripple Delete

It's virtually inevitable that you'll wind up deleting a clip from the Timeline. When you do so, a gaping hole is left in the Timeline where that clip used to be. You could fill in the space by dragging each subsequent item in the Timeline over, but this can be time-consuming, and if you've done a lot of advanced edits, you could make a mistake. Another solution might be to find an alternate clip that can be used to fill the vacancy left in the Timeline. If all else fails, you could insert a black matte with the word "Intermission" splashed across it. Then your audience thinks you meant to leave the space blank. (Yeah, it's so crazy it might just work. . . .)

The only problem with an "Intermission" placard is that really good intermission music can be difficult to choose. Better yet, use a ripple edit to automatically delete the blank space left over in the Timeline — and automatically shift all subsequent material over. To do so, simply click the undesired void to select it and then choose Edit➪Ripple Delete. You can also right-click the void and choose Ripple Delete from the menu that appears.

Performing slip edits

No, this isn't where you put in a banana peel and a pratfall. A *slip edit* simply slips the In and Out points of a clip to a different place on the Timeline, without changing the duration between those points. Adjacent clips aren't affected, nor is the duration of the overall program. To perform a slip edit, follow these steps:

1. **Choose the Slip tool in the Premiere Pro toolbar.**

2. **Hover the mouse pointer over the clip you want to slip.**

   The mouse pointer changes to a double-headed arrow between two vertical lines.

3. **Click-and-drag the clip.**

   As you can see in Figure 8-12, the Monitor window changes so that four frames are shown. The left frame shows the Out point of the previous clip, the right frame shows the In point of the following clip, and the two middle frames show the new In and Out points of the clip you're slipping.

Performing slide edits

No trombone required. A *slide edit* is, in fact, the opposite of a slip edit. As you slide a clip back and forth, its In and Out points remain unchanged, but the In and Out points of *adjacent* clips change to accommodate the clip you're sliding. As you can see in Figure 8-13, as Clip B slides to the right, Clip A lengthens, Clip C shortens, and the overall duration of the program is unchanged.

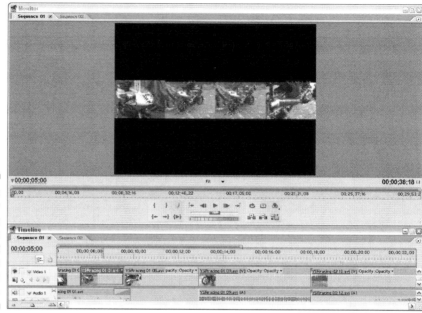

Figure 8-12:
The Monitor shows you the new In and Out points as you perform a slip edit.

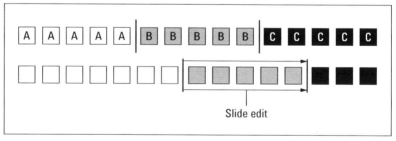

Figure 8-13:
A slide edit changes the duration of adjacent clips.

Slide edit

As with roll edits, a slide edit requires that extra source material be available on the clip that is being lengthened. To perform a slide edit, follow these steps:

1. **Choose the Slide tool in the Premiere Pro toolbar.**

2. **Hover the mouse pointer over the clip you want to slide.**

   The mouse pointer changes to a double-headed arrow that crosses two vertical lines.

3. **Click-and-drag the clip.**

The Monitor window changes so that four frames are shown similar to the slip edit shown in Figure 8-12. However, during a slide edit, the center two frames remain static, the left frame shows the new Out point of the previous clip, and the right frame shows the new In point of the following clip.

Replacing frames with three- and four-point edits

Another edit technique that I haven't talked about yet also exists: a replace. "Replace" is a common editing technique in various computer programs. In word-processing programs, for example, you can choose Edit⇨Replace and replace an old text string with a new one. Premiere Pro also allows you to replace material, and you do it using traditional video-editing techniques called *three-* and *four-point edits*. Suppose you want to replace some frames in your Timeline with a few new frames from a new source. To do that, you need at least three pieces of information:

✔ The In point on the source clip for the new material.

✔ The In point for the spot in the Timeline where you want to start replacing material.

✔ An Out point on either the source clip or Timeline so the length of the replacement is defined.

If you perform an edit using these three bits of information, each one corresponding to an In point or an Out point, you perform a *three-point edit*. Premiere Pro automatically figures out where a fourth Out point should be, based on the duration given by the one Out point you've already defined (either on the Timeline or in the source clip).

You can, of course, define all four points if you want — thus making it a *four-point edit* — and if the marked durations on the source clip and Timeline don't match, Premiere Pro helps you resolve the difference. (More about that in a minute.)

For the moment, sticking to three points is a good idea. To perform a three-point edit, follow these steps:

1. **Switch the Monitor window to Dual view if it isn't there already (click the tiny right-pointing arrow in the upper-right corner of the Monitor and choose Dual View) so that the current sequence is shown on the right side and the source is shown on the left.**

Remember, the source side of the Monitor shows the source clip that you are getting ready to add to the Timeline (but haven't added yet); the sequence side of the Monitor shows the actual program that is already assembled in the Timeline.

2. **Drag a clip from the Project window and drop it on the source side of the Monitor to load the new source clip.**

3. **Mark In points for the source clip and the sequence using the marker controls at the bottom of each side of the Monitor window.**

4. **Mark an Out point on either the source clip or the sequence.**

   If you have a specific portion of the Timeline that you want to replace, mark the Out point on the sequence. If you have a specific portion of the source clip that you want to edit in, mark the Out point on the source.

5. **Click a track header in the Timeline to specify a target track for the incoming clip.**

6. **Click the Overlay button on the source side of the Monitor.**

If you do a four-point edit and the durations don't match, you'll see the Fit Clip dialog box, as shown in Figure 8-14. If you see this dialog box, you have several options:

- ✔ **Change Clip Speed:** The speed of the source clip is adjusted to fit the marked duration on the Timeline.

- ✔ **Trim Clip's Head or Tail:** The In (Head) or Out (Tail) point of the source clip is adjusted so the durations match. These options are only available if the marked source clip is longer than the marked duration in the Timeline.

- ✔ **Ignore Sequence In or Out Point:** Choose one of these options to basically turn the edit into a three-point edit.

- ✔ **Cancel:** Yes, that Cancel button over to the right of the Fit Clip dialog box is an option to consider. Click this if you want to go back and change the In and Out points you marked.

Figure 8-14:
This dialog box appears if the durations don't match during a four-point edit.

Selecting clips

If you've been following along with this chapter from the beginning, you've probably noticed that we've been working with only one clip at a time. You can, however, select and work with multiple clips in the Timeline, portions of clips, portions of multiple clips, multiple portions of clips, select clipped portions of multiple selected clipped clips . . . er, ah, well, you get the idea.

The Premiere Pro toolbar (shown in Figure 8-4) includes two basic selection tools. They are

✔ **Selection Tool:** Use this tool for 99% of your clip-selection needs. Click a clip once to select it. Hold down the Shift key and click multiple clips to select them. Click-and-drag a box around a range of clips to select all of them.

✔ **Track Select Tool:** When you click a clip, that clip is selected — along with all subsequent clips in that track. Track contents that precede the clip on which you click are not selected. Hold down the Shift key while clicking a clip to select all clips in all tracks following the one you click.

Freezing frames

At the risk of getting an old J. Geils Band song stuck in your head, consider the freeze frame. You can actually "freeze" video so that the video stops and a single frame appears on-screen. Adobe Premiere Pro allows you to freeze frames of video and keep them on screen. Here's how:

1. **Move the CTI in the Timeline to the exact frame you want to freeze.**

   You may need to use Step Forward and Step Back buttons at the bottom of the Monitor window to find the exact frame that you want to freeze.

   An even easier way to move forward or back one frame at a time is to use the left- and right-arrow keys on your keyboard. Press the left arrow to move one frame back, and press the right arrow to move forward a frame.

2. **Click the clip to make sure it is selected and choose Marker⊳Set Clip Marker⊳Other Numbered.**

   The Set Numbered Marker dialog box appears.

3. **Enter 0 (zero) in the Set Numbered Marker field and click OK.**

   A small clip-marker icon should now appear on the clip in the Timeline.

4. **Choose Clip⊳Video Options⊳Frame Hold.**

   The Frame Hold Options dialog box appears.

5. **Place a check mark next to Hold On and choose "Marker 0" from the menu.**

   Note that you can freeze a clip on the In point or Out point as well.

6. **If the frame comes from interlaced video (NTSC or PAL DV video *is* interlaced) place a check mark next to the Deinterlace option.**

   This prevents flickering when the frame appears on-screen and is most useful if the frame comes from a portion of the clip that contains fast motion or action.

7. **Click OK to close the dialog box.**

The entire clip now consists of a single frame, held static on-screen. Play your sequence to see what it looks like.

Changing the speed of clips

If you watched much TV in the 1970s, you probably remember a series called *The Six Million Dollar Man.* It revolved around a former test pilot named Steve Austin (Lee Majors) who, after a horrific plane crash, was rebuilt using cybernetic enhancements (we assume that those enhancements cost about $6 million, including installation). The cybernetics gave Steve super strength and speed, abilities he used to fight crime and battle the forces of evil. Several times each episode, Steve Austin would run somewhere. In order to show that Steve was actually running inhumanly fast, we would see the hero running . . . in slow motion. (I guess it made sense to someone.)

Video technology has progressed a great deal since the '70s, but few computer-generated effects would provide the same dramatic effect as slo-mo video and some well-crafted music. Changing the speed of your own clips in Adobe Premiere Pro is an effective (yet often overlooked) visual effect you can apply to video. You can adjust the speed of clips in the Timeline to create your own fast- or slow-motion effects. To adjust the speed of a clip in the Timeline, follow these steps:

1. **Select a clip in the Timeline for which you want to adjust the playback speed.**

2. **Choose Clip⇨Speed/Duration.**

   The Clip Speed/Duration dialog box appears as shown in Figure 8-15.

3. **Enter a new percentage in the Speed field.**

   If you want to slow the clip down, enter a rate that is below 100%. If you want to speed it up, enter a rate above 100%. Leave the New Duration field alone for now.

4. **Click OK.**

Slicing and dicing with the Razor tool

In Chapter 7, I compared clips to currency because a clip is the basic unit of measure in Adobe Premiere Pro. Something you often need to do with currency is change it into smaller denominations. For example, if you want to buy a soft drink from a vending machine, a $20 bill is probably too large. Likewise, you'll sometimes find that you need to make change (so to speak) with clips in Premiere. Premiere Pro gives you a simple little tool that lets you quickly turn one large clip in the Timeline into many smaller ones. This tool is called the Razor and is located in the Premiere Pro toolbar.

The Razor tool comes in handy more often than you might think. For example, suppose you want a clip to freeze in the middle of playback. You can set a poster frame and then choose Clip⇨ Video Options⇨Frame Hold to freeze the clip, but this freezes the entire clip (see the section titled "Freezing Frames" earlier in this chapter).

What if you want the clip to play normally up until the point where it reaches the desired frame? The solution is to slice the clip in two at the point where you want to freeze playback. Start by placing the CTI on the exact frame where you want to freeze the frame. Next, click the Razor tool in the Premiere Pro toolbar to select it. When you hover the mouse pointer over a clip, the pointer turns into a razor blade. Hover the mouse pointer directly over the CTI so that the vertical line in the Razor tool icon matches up perfectly with the CTI. Now click the mouse button to razor the clip in two at this spot. This gives you two clips instead of just one. Leave the first clip — the one before the CTI — alone so that it plays normally. On the second clip — the one that comes after the CTI — adjust the Frame Hold settings so that the clip holds on the In Point. Now your video plays normally until it gets to that frame, at which time it freezes.

You may need to experiment a bit with the rate that you choose. In Figure 8-15, I have cut the speed of the clip in half to 50%. You may find that some speed changes result in rough or jerky playback. (See Table 7-1 in Chapter 7 for specific recommendations on speed changes that should provide smoother playback.)

Figure 8-15: Adjust the playback rate of the clip to change its playback speed.

Using Markers in the Timeline

Markers can be extremely helpful as you work in the Timeline. You can use markers as reference points for key events, visual indicators as you edit, or cues for events such as Web links or DVD chapter references. Any markers that were added to a source clip before it was added to the Timeline also appear in the Timeline (see Chapter 7 for more on working with clip markers). Markers that are added only to a sequence in the Timeline, however, are not added to the source clips. Timeline markers — called *sequence markers* in Premiere Pro — appear on the Timeline ruler, as shown in Figure 8-16.

Sequence marker

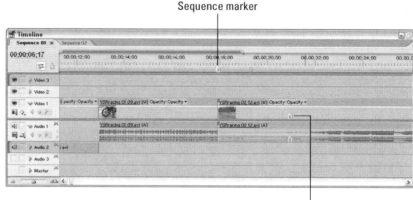

Figure 8-16:
Timeline
markers
appear on
the Timeline
ruler.

Clip marker

Adding markers to the Timeline

Markers can serve various purposes. In Figure 8-16, I have added markers to indicate where specific visual events occur. I used those markers as references when I later edited in some audio that needed to align with those visual events. To add a marker to a sequence in the Timeline:

1. **Move the CTI to the exact location where you want to place a marker. If necessary, use the left- and right-arrow keys on your keyboard to move frame by frame to the correct location.**

2. **Choose Marker⇨Set Sequence Marker and choose a marker from the submenu that appears.**

The marker now appears on the Timeline ruler. Pretty easy, huh? If you ever want to get rid of a marker, simply choose Marker⇨Clear Sequence Marker and choose an option from the submenu to sentence a marker to the electronic ether.

Using sequence markers as chapter references

DVDs represent the most important multimedia revolution of recent years. The Digital Versatile Disc has become *the* standard for mass-market video distribution. In June 2003, the video rental industry reported that DVD rentals exceeded VHS tape rentals for the first time ever. After a few minutes spent watching a movie on DVD, it's easy to see why so many folks are eager to abandon their rattling old VHS tapes.

A popular DVD feature is its capability to quickly jump from scene to scene with the click of a button. No longer must you wait for a tape to cue forward or back when you want to skip to a specific scene. But when you click a remote control button for your DVD player, how does the player know where the next scene is? Simple: Someone who helped prepare that movie for DVD spent some time creating chapter references at key intervals in the program. Premiere Pro lets you create your own chapter references in your projects. Chapter references are incredibly useful, not only if you decide to output your movie to DVD, but also if you're distributing it online in QuickTime format. (The Apple QuickTime Player supports chapter references as well.)

To create chapter references for your movie, first create sequence markers at the desired locations for the references. Then double-click a marker. When the Marker dialog box appears, enter a name and/or number for the chapter reference in the Chapter field. Click OK when you're done.

Moving around with markers

Moving around in the Timeline is perhaps my favorite use of sequence markers. As I'm working through a project I often say to myself, "I'll probably want to come back to this point." That's my cue to create a marker. Eventually I have a collection of markers that I can use to quickly jump back and forth in the project. There are several methods for moving around in the Timeline using markers:

- ✔ Choose Marker⇨Go to Sequence Marker and then choose an option from the submenu.

- ✔ On the keyboard, press Ctrl+Right Arrow to move to the next sequence marker. Press Ctrl+Left Arrow to move to the previous sequence marker.

- ✔ Right-click the Timeline ruler, choose Go to Sequence Marker⇨and select an option from the submenu.

Working with Multiple Sequences

One of the most important new features in Adobe Premiere Pro is the Timeline's capability to accommodate multiple sequences. Each sequence works like a separate, individual Timeline. Multiple sequences can serve a variety of purposes. For example, you can

✔ **Create multiple versions of the same project.** Creative vision is a wonderful thing, but whenever there is more than one person working on a project, creative visions can butt heads. Even if you're working alone, you may have a tough time deciding exactly how a project should flow. You could create a separate sequence for each "creative vision" that you (or someone) has for a project. Later, when you preview the project to other editors or co-producers, you can quickly show each version of the project simply by playing one sequence and then the other.

You can also use multiple sequences to test how certain settings affect your movie. Make duplicates of a sequence and apply different settings or effects to each one to see how the changes look.

✔ **Break up a single project into smaller, more manageable sequences.** If you're working on a very long project, you may find it useful to separate different parts of the project into separate sequences. You can safely make radical changes to one sequence without affecting the other sequences. Separate sequences can later be linked together — or nested — to create the big final project.

✔ **Create picture-in-picture effects.** A simple way to create picture-in-picture or split-screen effects is to create a separate sequence for each picture and then nest one sequence within the other.

✔ **Reuse complex sequences.** If you have an opening logo with credits or some other complex scene that gets used many times in a movie, create a separate sequence for it. That sequence can then be reused or nested as many times as you like.

Of course, there are many possible uses for multiple sequences. Consider this just another tool that Premiere Pro gives you for your creative toolbox!

Adding sequences to your project

Multiple sequences appear in Adobe Premiere Pro as tabs in the Timeline window. Sequences are also listed in the Project window, right alongside video clips, audio clips, still graphics, and other objects. The project shown in Figure 8-17 has two sequences. To add a sequence to your project, simply choose File⟹New⟹Sequence. The New Sequence dialog box appears. Enter a name for the sequence, specify the number of video and audio tracks you want it to have, and click OK. Your new sequence is now listed in the Project window and as a tab in the Timeline window.

Don't worry too much about how many audio and video tracks you specify for a sequence. You can always add tracks to the sequence later. Chapter 3 shows you how to add tracks to the Timeline.

Sequence tabs

Sequences

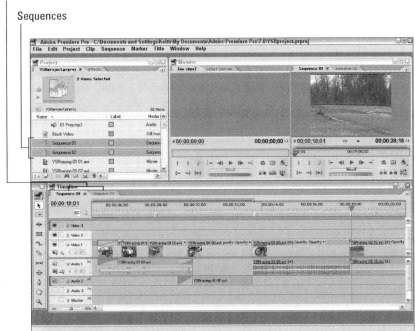

Figure 8-17:
Premiere
Pro allows
you to have
multiple
sequences
in your
projects.

You've probably noticed that sequence tabs in the Timeline have little close (X) buttons on them when that sequence is active. If you click the close button, that sequence disappears. Don't worry! You haven't deleted anything. You'll notice that the closed sequence is still listed in the Project window. Just double-click the sequence in the Project window to re-open it in the Timeline.

If you don't like switching back and forth between tabs in the Timeline window, you can also open a sequence in its own separate Timeline window. To do so, simply click-and-drag a sequence tab from the Timeline window and drop it on an empty part of the Premiere Pro screen. The result (with some rearranging) looks something like Figure 8-18.

Nesting sequences

The best thing about being able to have multiple sequences in Premiere Pro is that you can link those sequences together. The process of linking sequences is called *nesting*. A nested sequence plays just like any other clip in the Timeline. Consider the Timeline shown in Figure 8-19, where I have nested a sequence called Sequence 2 by placing it in Sequence 1. When the clip "YSRracing 01 09.avi" is finished playing, Sequence 2 starts to play, just as if it were any other clip. I can even create a transition to the sequence or apply other effects if I wish.

Nesting a sequence is pretty simple: Just drag-and-drop it from the Project window to the Timeline, just as you would a video clip. In Figure 8-19, I have added a sequence to the Video 1 track, but you can nest a sequence on any track you wish. (In Chapter 19, I show you how to create a picture-in-a-picture effect by using a nested sequence in an overlay track.)

If you want to nest only part of a sequence, first drag the sequence from the Project window to the source (left) side of the Monitor window. Set an In point and Out point for the sequence, and then edit it into the Timeline (as described earlier in this chapter) for video clips.

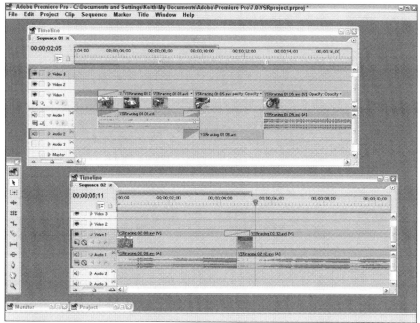

Figure 8-18:
Sequences can be opened in their own Timeline windows.

Figure 8-19:
Sequences
can be
opened in
their own
Timeline
windows.

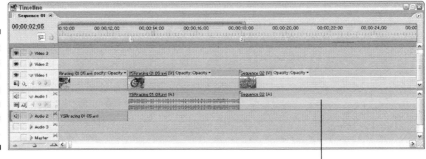

Nested sequence

Chapter 9

Transitioning Between Clips

In This Chapter

▶ Choosing the right transition

▶ Using transitions in your projects

▶ Customizing transitions

Movie editing per se is nothing special, really; anyone with two VCRs and a cable can dub desirable bits of video from one tape to another. But fine-tuning your edits frame by frame, applying your own soundtrack, and adding special effects — now, *that* is special. Adobe Premiere Pro gives you the capability to do all that and more. If you've followed along in previous chapters — capturing video onto your computer's hard drive, sorting through clips, picking out the parts you want to use, and assembling those clips in the Timeline — you're ready for the next step in your video-editing adventure.

One of the first things you'll probably want to do to dress up your project is to add some fancy transitions between scenes. Premiere Pro's transitions can be used to make scenes fade in or out, pull open like a stage curtain, spiral down into a vortex, and more. Transitions provide visual breaks between scenes that help the viewer understand that the setting or mood of the movie is changing. This chapter shows you how to choose, apply, and customize transitions in your projects.

Choosing Effective Transitions

One of the trickiest aspects of movie editing (for me, anyway) is making clean transitions between clips. Sometimes the best transition is a simple, straight cut from one clip to the next. Other times you need a fancy transition — say, one that rotates the image from the old clip in an ever-decreasing radius, like a vortex spinning, spinning towards the center, until — a tiny black dot at the center of the screen — it disappears entirely. Most of your transitions probably fall somewhere in between.

Adobe Premiere Pro comes with 73 unique video transitions that you can use in your projects. You can add additional transitions to Premiere using third-party plug-ins (see Chapter 20 for more on Premiere Pro plug-ins). But for now, focus on the 73 standard video transitions. They are divided into ten categories:

- **3D Motion:** This is a group of ten transitions that apply various kinds of motion to one clip as it disappears to reveal the next one. Most of the transitions here involve getting the exiting clip to swing like a door or spin in a spiral.

- **Dissolve:** My favorite transition, the Cross Dissolve, can be found here. It's my favorite not because it is fancy but because it's *not*. The Cross Dissolve is subtle; one clip blends smoothly into the next. It's softer than a straight cut — and if I want the program to be about what's in the clips (and not about fancy transitions), this is the one I choose. Cross Dissolve is just one of five Dissolve transitions available with Premiere Pro.

- **Iris:** The seven Iris transitions are all variations on a theme of one clip starting as a point in the middle and growing to fill the screen. Different Iris patterns include circles, squares, stars, diamonds (I know, it's starting to sound like a breakfast cereal!), and more.

- **Map:** The Channel Map and Luminance Map remap colors to create a transition.

- **Page Peel:** The five Page Peel transitions simulate the turning of a page. Use these to make the transition from your "Once upon a time . . ." screen to the story!

- **Slide:** This descriptively named group contains 12 transitions, all variations on sliding a clip one way or the other. These subtle transitions are also among my favorites.

- **Special Effect:** This group contains six advanced and varied transitions that apply various combinations of color masks and distortions while moving from one clip to the next.

- **Stretch:** The five Stretch transitions are pretty cool, even though technically some of them *squeeze* rather than stretch the clip image during transition.

- **Wipe:** Wipes are a general style of transition that has been around for a while: One clip appears from the edge of the screen and appears to wipe over the previous clip like a squeegee. Premiere includes no less than 17 different Wipe transitions.

- **Zoom:** There are four Zoom transitions, and as you would imagine, they all simulate different camera zooms.

With so many unique transitions to choose from, selecting just the right one can be challenging. When you consider that most transitions can also be fine-tuned and customized, the endless possibilities can make one's head spin. So how do you choose? Because video production is such a creative and personal endeavor, I couldn't possibly recommend a perfect transition for every situation. I do, however, have a few basic transition rules that I like to follow:

- ✔ **Use transitions sparingly.** You don't need to apply a transition between every single clip and the one that follows. That's too much. I try to save transitions for changes of scene. Simple camera angle or position changes in the same scene (for example) usually don't warrant a transition. Watch a typical feature-length movie and you'll probably see just a small handful of simple transitions, even though the movie may be a couple of hours long.

- ✔ **Keep 'em short.** Later in this chapter, I show you how to control the length of a transition. Most transitions should be short, usually one second or less.

- ✔ **It's all about the pictures.** Editing can help shape the mood and flow of a movie, but ultimately the focus of your project is the video content. The desire to show off your editing skills with fancy transitions can be tempting — but generally speaking, transitions should complement and enhance the video images, not overpower them.

- ✔ **Follow your inspiration.** You should be familiar with the various transition styles that are available in Premiere Pro, even the ones you seldom if ever use. In a moment of late-night, caffeine-induced inspiration it might come to you: "*This* is the spot for that fancy, spinning, 3D transition!"

Premiere Pro also has a couple of audio transitions. In this chapter, I mainly want to talk about video transitions, so for more on working with audio transitions, slide, peel, or dissolve your way over to Chapter 13.

Using Transitions in the Timeline

Adding transitions to a movie project in Adobe Premiere Pro is pretty easy. The tricky part, in my opinion, is choosing a transition that looks good without detracting from the overall flow of the project. In the previous section, I talk about choosing an effective transition. Now let's actually put some transitions to use.

Using the Transitions palette

If you're new to video, you may be surprised by how many different transitions are possible between two clips. As mentioned previously in this Chapter, Adobe Premiere Pro comes with 73 transitions already built in, and you can add even more by using third-party plug-ins.

Premiere stores all its transitions on the Effects tab of the Project window. Click that tab to reveal it. If the Effects tab isn't visible, choose Window↔ Effects to open the Effects tab in its own window (as shown in Figure 9-1). Transitions are divvied up into ten subfolders, which you can reveal by clicking the arrow next to Video Transitions. Click an arrow next to a subfolder to see a list of transitions. In Figure 9-1, you can see that five transitions are listed in the Dissolve subfolder.

Adding a transition to your project

The software designers at Adobe must really like drag-and-drop because, as with so many other editing actions in Premiere, drag-and-drop is the best way to apply a transition. Simply choose a transition and drag it directly from the Effects tab to the desired spot on the Timeline, as shown in Figure 9-2.

When you add a transition to the Timeline, the In and Out points of adjacent clips are automatically extended to facilitate the transition. Thus each clip needs some unused frames that were trimmed off when you edited the clip into the Timeline. Thus, if a transition lasts one second, the preceding clip must have at least one half-second of trailing material, and the following clip must have one half-second of leading material. Keep this in mind when you set In and Out points as you edit clips into the Timeline (see Chapter 7 for more on setting In and Out points).

Figure 9-1: Premiere Pro organizes transitions into subfolders.

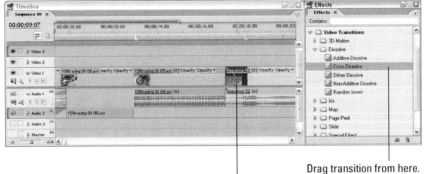

Figure 9-2:
Drag
transitions
to the edit
point
between
clips in the
Timeline.

Drag transition from here.

Drop transition here.

If the clips lack sufficient leading or trailing material, you'll see a warning message like the one shown in Figure 9-3. The warning message means that Premiere Pro duplicates some frames to make enough leading and/or trailing material, and this duplication usually looks pretty bad. If you see this warning, click OK and then play the transition to see what I mean. A couple of solutions to this problem are possible:

✔ **Shorten the length of the transition.** If the clips have *some* leading and trailing material, but not quite enough for the current transition length, you might be able to make the transition work if it's shorter. I show you how to adjust transition duration later in this chapter, in the section called "Controlling transitions."

✔ **Ripple-edit the clips.** Choose the Ripple Edit Tool in the Premiere Pro toolbar (see Chapter 8 for more on ripple edits) and drag the edges of the leading and trailing clips until you've trimmed about half a second from each clip. Because a ripple edit basically trims material off the clip and changes the In and Out points, this should create enough leading and trailing time to facilitate the transition.

Figure 9-3:
You'll need
to make
some clip
changes if
you see this
warning.

If you want to apply a transition between two clips, those clips must be in the same Timeline track. Fortunately, one of the most welcome new changes with Adobe Premiere Pro is the ability to use transitions in any video track. Previous versions of Premiere only allowed you to use transitions in the Video 1 track.

Controlling transitions

More often than not, you'll probably just plop a transition down on the Timeline and use it as it sits. Sometimes, however, you may want to fine-tune the transition. For example, you can change the length of a transition by clicking-and-dragging on either side of the transition. To do so, first click the Selection tool in the Premiere Pro toolbar (the Selection tool is at the top of the toolbar and looks like a single large arrow) and then click-and-drag one side of a transition to lengthen or shorten it.

You can also modify the duration of a clip using the Effect Controls tab of the Monitor window. Click a transition in the Timeline to select it, and then click the Effect Controls tab in the left pane of the Monitor. Controls for the transition appear as shown in Figure 9-4. If you don't see the Effect Controls tab in your Monitor, choose Window➪Effect Controls or double-click the transition in the Timeline. The controls open in a new window, as shown in Figure 9-5.

The default duration for most clips is one second, but you can make the transition as short or long as your source clips and common sense allow. To adjust the duration of a transition using the Effect Controls, enter a new number in the Duration field. You can also click-and-drag left or right on the Duration field to adjust the time. In Figure 9-5, I have changed the duration of the transition to just 25 frames.

The Effect Controls window includes a number of different controls, as you can see in Figure 9-5. Some key settings and features include

   ✔ **Split-track Timeline:** The right side of the Effect Controls window contains a small Timeline window showing just the current track. If you've used previous versions of Premiere, you may notice that this looks similar to the split-track Timeline that was used in the old A/B Editing workspace, part of Adobe Premiere 6.5 and earlier. The split-track Timeline is useful here because it shows how much leading and trailing material is available for each clip, as shown in Figure 9-5. You can roll edit the transition in this Timeline by dragging it back and forth (see Chapter 8 for more on roll edits).

Duration

Effect Controls tab

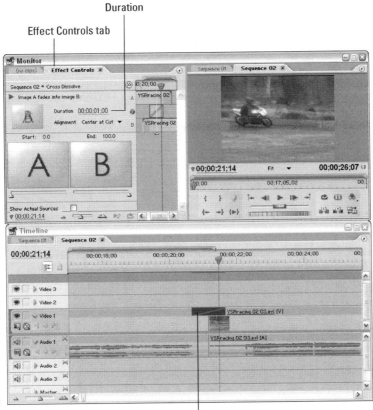

Figure 9-4:
Use the
Effect
Controls tab
to fine-
tune your
transitions.

Click transition to select it.

✔ **Alignment:** Use the Alignment menu under the Duration field to control alignment of the transition. Normally a transition uses the Center at Cut setting, but you can also make the transition start or end at the location of the original cut between clips.

✔ **Preview window:** Click the Play button above the preview window (in the upper-left corner) to see a visual representation of the transition. Some transitions (like the Cube Spin transition shown in Figure 9-5) allow you to change direction. You can usually do this by clicking the arrows around the edges of the preview window.

✓ **Start/End controls:** The Start and End boxes (you can't miss them; the Start box has a giant "A" in it, and the End box has a giant "B") represent the outgoing clip (A) and the incoming clip (B). Use the slider controls underneath these boxes to change where the transition starts or ends.

✓ **Show Actual Sources:** The giant "A" and "B" are meant to represent clips in your movie. But if these alphabetic metaphors aren't working for you, click the Show Actual Sources option. The actual video clips appear instead of the letters.

✓ **Reverse:** Enabling the Reverse option can reverse the direction of many transitions.

✓ **Other options:** Some transitions have additional options. The transition controls in Figure 9-5 include options for a border and anti-aliasing. Anti-aliasing smoothes the edges of the transition. Experiment with other options to customize the appearance and function of your transitions.

Preview window   Available trailing material

Available leading material   Transition

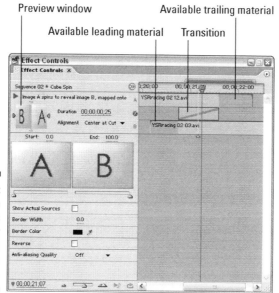

Figure 9-5:
Transition
controls
vary
depending
on the type
of transition.

Remember, more than 70 different transitions come with Premiere Pro, all with different settings to adjust, so your dialog box may not look like Figures 9-4 or 9-5. Play around a bit to find the transitions and combinations of settings that work best for you!

Some transition options allow you to specify a color for a border or other transition element. To choose a color, click the color swatch to open the Color Picker window. When you choose a color in the Color Picker, watch out for a yellow triangle with an exclamation point in the upper-right corner of the window. If you see the warning icon, it means that the color you chose won't appear properly on video equipment in your area (NTSC or PAL). In that case, your best option is to choose a different color.

Using a default transition

Premiere Pro knows that a lot of people have one type of transition that they use most of the time. It just so happens that my favorite transition — the Cross Dissolve — is the default transition in Premiere Pro. (Sorry — it's just so useful I can't resist it.) The default transition is especially handy if you want to quickly apply a transition without having to open the Transitions palette. The default transition can be used in several ways:

- ✔ Move the edit line in the Timeline to where you want to apply the default transition. Click the track header for the track that contains the clips between which you want to apply the transition, and then choose Sequence➪Apply Video Transition.

- ✔ In the Project window, you can select all the clips you want to edit into the Timeline, and then choose Project➪Automate to Sequence (or click the Automate to Sequence button at the bottom of the Project window). Place a check mark next to the Apply Default Video Transition option in the dialog box that appears, and then click OK.

You can change the default transition if you want. To set a new default transition, follow these steps:

1. **Open the Effects tab in the Project window, or choose Window➪Effects.**

2. **On the Effects tab, expand the Video Transitions folder.**

3. **Locate the transition that you want to use as your default transition and click the transition once to select it.**

4. **Click the small, right-pointing arrow in the upper-right corner of the Effects tab and then choose Set Default Transition in the menu that appears, as shown in Figure 9-6.**

You can also change the default transition duration using the Effects tab menu. When you choose the Default Transition Duration option from the menu, the Preferences dialog box appears with the General options group displayed. The default duration for video transitions is 30 frames, but you can change it to any length you want. This default duration applies to all transitions, not just the default transition.

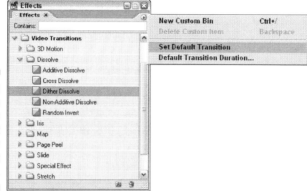

Figure 9-6:
Use the
Effects tab
menu to set
a new
default
transition.

Previewing transitions

Transitions add a great deal of complexity to a video image; for this reason, a transition must usually be rendered before export, and sometimes you may even need to render a transition to preview it properly. When you place a transition on the Timeline, a red bar appears above it on the Timeline. If you try to preview the transition without rendering it, the transition will probably play just fine. If it doesn't play acceptably, you may want to try rendering the transition. There are two ways to render a transition:

 ✔ Select the sequence you want to render, and then choose
  Sequence➪Render Work Area.

 ✔ Select the sequence that you want to render, and then press the Enter
  key on your keyboard.

When you choose to render the work area, Premiere Pro renders the *whole* work area. A lot of your Timeline probably doesn't need to be rendered, but any unrendered areas are rendered when you choose this command. If all you need to render in the work area is a single transition, the process takes mere seconds. If long clips with effects or speed changes need to be rendered, you could be waiting a few minutes. In that case, a progress bar appears on-screen to tell you how many frames must be rendered — and approximately how long it will take.

Chapter 10

Improving Your Video Images

*P*erfection. We dream of it, yearn for it, strive toward it, but seldom achieve it. When you shoot video, you take time to make sure that the lighting, shadows, and colors in the shot are as favorable as possible, but the video you shoot (or anybody shoots, for that matter) is seldom truly perfect.

Fortunately, Adobe Premiere Pro includes powerful new color-correction tools to help you improve and modify the appearance of your video images. These tools include an advanced Color Corrector filter, a Color Match filter, and broadcast-style video scopes to help you analyze your video. This chapter helps you understand and use Adobe Premiere Pro's color-correction tools on your movie projects.

Understanding the Color Corrector

Video editors are often left with the task of perfecting — or at least improving — imperfect video. Adobe Premiere Pro has joined the ranks of advanced nonlinear editing programs that provide advanced color-correction tools to help video look better. The Color Corrector is easily one of the most important — and welcome — new features of Adobe Premiere Pro. Premiere's color-correction tools can help you

✔ Improve and enhance color for better overall appearance.

✔ Identify and remove out-of-gamut or "illegal" colors for footage destined for broadcast.

✔ Change the look or mood of a project by modifying the use of color. Consider films like *The Matrix* or *Batman,* where colors are carefully manipulated to give the movie a particular mood.

The Color Corrector filter is the Big Kahuna of the color-correction tools provided in Premiere Pro. You can access this filter from the Effects tab in the Project window (or choose Window⇨Effects). The Color Corrector is located in the Image Control bin inside the Video Effects bin, as shown in Figure 10-1. The Premiere Pro Color Corrector makes color correction, easier, more precise, and more predictable. Changes that the Color Corrector makes to a video image are applied in the following order:

1. Black/white balance

2. HSL (hue-saturation-lightness) hue offsets

3. HSL controls

4. RGB controls

5. Curves

6. Video limiter

When you adjust controls in the Color Corrector, you'll see settings listed in roughly this order. The processing order listed above is the order in which Premiere Pro actually applies changes to a video clip. If you change a setting in the RGB controls, for example, the whole filter is reapplied to the clip, in the processing order just given. Although you can make changes in any order you wish, I strongly recommend that you work through the Color Corrector's settings in order. Doing so will give more predictable results because you won't be undoing your own work.

If you're working with video that you plan to output to DVD or videotape, remember: The way a TV shows colors is different from the way a computer monitor accomplishes the same task. Bottom line: Your computer monitor may not be the best place to preview color changes, especially if your audience will view the finished movie on a TV screen. (See Chapter 15 for more on previewing your video using an external TV monitor.)

Using the Video Scopes

How do you measure color? Most people can tell the different between yellow and blue just by looking at them — but how do you know that what you perceive as blue is *truly* blue? Color perception is a problem that video editors have had to wrestle with for decades, especially when working with video monitors that all vary slightly in the way they show color. Special scopes were developed to measure the values of light and color in video images, and traditionally these scopes have been used to calibrate monitors, video decks, and other video equipment.

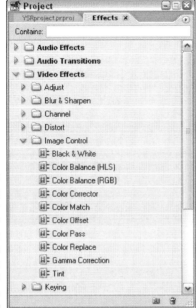

Figure 10-1:
The Color
Corrector
resides in
the Image
Control bin
under Video
Effects.

Premiere Pro now includes some professional-style video scopes built in to the program. Although you can't use these scopes to calibrate your video monitors or tape decks, you can use them to evaluate and measure the light and color in your video images. Among other things, you can use Premiere's scopes to identify colors and light that exceed broadcast-video standards. The scopes also provide an objective measure of your video images that doesn't depend on your eyes having perfect color perception or your video monitor reproducing perfect color. The scopes include

- ✔ Vectorscope: Measures color

- ✔ Waveform monitor: Measures light

- ✔ YCbCr Parade: Measures light and color levels for YUV color, the type of color used by TVs

- ✔ RGB Parade: Measures RGB color levels, the type of color used on computer monitors

To display a scope, click the Scopes button as shown in Figure 10-2 and choose a scope from the menu that appears. Notice that some of the choices in the Scopes menu are actually combinations of scopes. For example, the Vect/Wave/YCbCr Parade option displays the Vectorscope, Waveform monitor, and YCbCr Parade. If you just want to see the regular video image again, choose Composite from the Scopes menu. To better understand the scopes, create a new project consisting of color bars by following these steps:

1. **Choose File⇨New⇨Project to create a new project.**

2. **Choose a standard DV-NTSC or DV-PAL preset and name your project "colorbars" or something similar.**

   See Chapter 5 for more on presets.

3. **Click OK to close the New Project dialog box and create your new project.**

4. **In the new project, choose File⇨New⇨Bars and Tone.**

   You now have an item called Bars and Tone in the Project window.

5. **Click-and-drag the Bars and Tone item to the Video 1 track in your Timeline window.**

You should now see color bars in your Monitor window. The next few sections show you how to read and understand Premiere Pro's scopes.

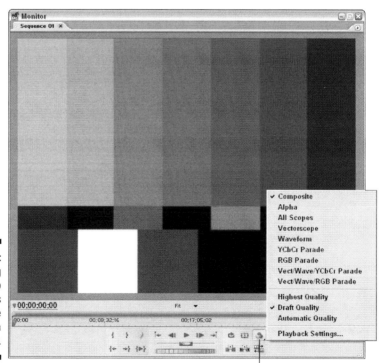

Figure 10-2:
Previewing video images makes title creation a lot easier.

Click to bring up the Scopes menu.

Viewing the Vectorscope

Vectorscopes have long been used to measure colors (called *chroma* in video geek speak) that appear in a video signal. Video-production facilities use analog Vectorscopes to measure video signals and calibrate their equipment. A Vectorscope is round like the one shown in Figure 10-3. Within the scope, you see six boxes. These boxes are called *targets* and each target represents a different color. If you're viewing the Vectorscope on color bars (as I am in Figure 10-3), you notice that the scope shows a few little dots — almost all of them right in the middle their respective targets.

Each pixel of color in a video image is represented by a dot on the Vectorscope. Color bars only show up as dots right in the middle of the various targets because color bars show only calibrated "perfect" colors. Video production facilities use these targets to calibrate their equipment using color bars, but Premiere Pro doesn't have anything to calibrate, so the Vectorscope targets are rather pointless.

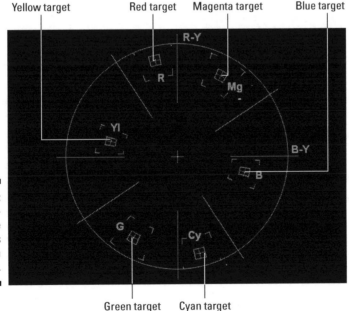

Yellow target   Red target   Magenta target   Blue target

Green target   Cyan target

Figure 10-3:
The Vector-
scope
measures
color in a
video image.

So what good is the Vectorscope? You can use the Vectorscope to determine how saturated the colors are in your video images. Consider the Vectorscope in Figure 10-4, which is measuring a *real* video image. Each dot on the Vectorscope at left represents a pixel of color from the video image at right. Dots closer to the center represent less-saturated colors; dots farther out represent more-saturated colors. This Vectorscope indicates that the video image has a lot of deeply saturated red color. Dots that fall outside the ring at the edge of the Vectorscope represent colors that are probably not broadcast-legal for my local video standard; I should probably reduce red saturation in this image. (I show you how to adjust saturation later in this chapter.)

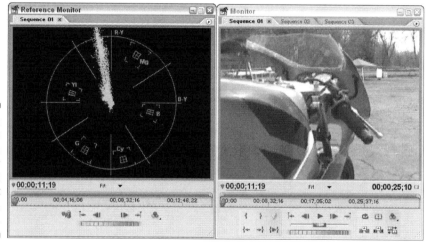

Figure 10-4: This video image has a lot of deeply saturated red (just trust me, okay?).

Illuminating the Waveform monitor

Waveform monitors measure the light (called *luminance* by the video pros) in video images. Like analog Waveform monitors, the Premiere Pro Waveform monitor measures light in IREs. *IRE* stands for *Institute of Radio Engineers* and IRE is the basic unit of measure for light in video. Figure 10-5 shows what the Premiere Pro Waveform monitor looks like when it's measuring the light in color bars.

Want to *really* sound like a video geek? Refer to the IRE scale on the left side of a Waveform monitor as a *graticule* (a fancy word for "scale").

As with the Vectorscope, each dot on a Waveform monitor represents a pixel of light in the video image. Whiter light falls near the top of the Waveform, and darker light falls near the bottom of the Waveform. If you are preparing video for broadcast, light levels above 100 IRE or below 7.5 IRE on the

Waveform monitor might exceed your local broadcast standards. In North America, the allowable range usually falls between 110 IRE and –20 IRE, but you should consult your local broadcast house for the exact standards that apply to you. Most modern DV camcorders can record light that exceeds these values, so if you're working on a project destined for broadcast, you'll need to pay special attention to the Waveform monitor.

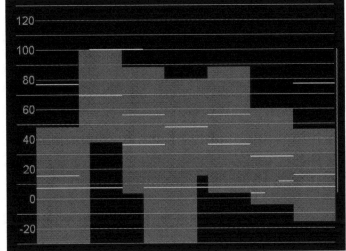

Figure 10-5:
The Waveform monitor measures light in a video image.

Even if you aren't working on a project for broadcast, the Waveform monitor can tell you a couple of important things about your video images. Consider the Waveform monitor on the left side of Figure 10-6, which is measuring the video image on the right. This Waveform tells us that the video image has an abundance of extreme light and dark values. The concentrations at the top and bottom of the monitor indicate a problem called *luma clamping*. The white and black areas of the image exceeded the capabilities of the camera, meaning that some colors and details are lost. White areas that suffer from luma clamping appear chalky and washed out. Use the HSL controls and Video Limiter controls to resolve luma clamping and other light issues.

I hate to sound too critical, but another great way to avoid luma clamping is to not shoot overexposed video in the first place. Pay careful attention to exposure settings on your camcorder (see Chapter 4) when you shoot video. Some camcorders can show a zebra-stripe pattern in the viewfinder on over-exposed areas of the image. If you see this pattern, your image is probably overexposed.

IRE scale. Some light areas suffer from luma clamping.

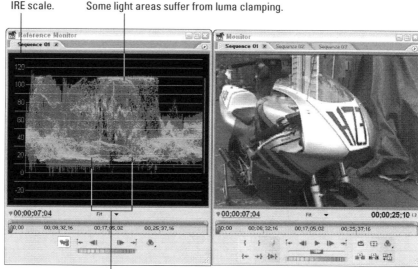

Figure 10-6:
This video
image
suffers
from luma
clamping.

Luma clamping affects dark areas, too.

Saluting the YCbCr and RGB Parades

Everyone loves a parade, even video editors. The Scopes menu in Premiere Pro includes a couple of parades, and although you may be disappointed to learn that they do not involve marching bands or Shriners buzzing about in little go-karts, they do provide some information about your video images.

The YCbCr Parade measures the color (chroma) and light (luma) values in a video image using the YUV color space (YUV is the color format for TVs; see Chapter 4 for more on color spaces). As you can see in Figure 10-7, the YCbCr Parade is divided into three parts:

- ✔ **Luminance:** This portion of the YCbCr Parade is basically just a scrunched up Waveform monitor. It measures luminance values, a.k.a. *light.* The video image in Figure 10-7 does have slight luma clamping, as indicated by the concentration of light near the top of the monitor.

- ✔ **B-Y chroma:** This measures the color levels in the blue minus luminance portion of the video signal.

- ✔ **R-Y chroma:** This measures the color levels in the red minus luminance portion of the video signal. The scale in Figure 10-7 indicates that this image has an abundance of saturated red color.

If you're familiar with component video (again, see Chapter 4), you'll notice that the three parts of the YCbCr Parade mirror the three signals in component video.

Luminance   B-Y chroma   R-Y chroma

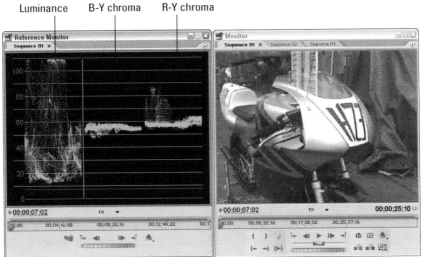

Figure 10-7:
"I love a
YCbCr
Parade!"

The RGB Parade is also divided into three sections. The sections measure levels of red, green, and blue colors, respectively. Either Parade scope works well if you want a quick reference to color or light levels in a video image. The YCbCr Parade basically provides all the same information as the Waveform monitor and Vectorscope, but in a single display. The RGB Parade is useful because you can identify whether certain color levels are too high in the video image. If you see lines near the top of the scale similar to the signs of luma clamping shown in Figure 10-6, you may have *chroma clamping*. Reduce color levels as needed.

Correcting Colors

Correcting and changing colors in video is much more art than science. Every video camera has different characteristics, every scene is lit differently, and every project has different color needs. I guess this is my way of saying that you won't find a magic formula here to help you make each and every video clip look perfect. When you want to adjust video colors, trial-and-error is an inevitable part of the process. But the following section should help you get started. (Later I show you how to save settings from the Premiere Pro Color Corrector so you can easily apply the same settings to other clips.)

Adjusting the image

Before you start changing the colors of your clips, you should set up your workspace so that it's better tailored to color correction. Premiere Pro includes a special color-correction workspace, which you can open by choosing Window➪Workspace➪Color Correction. In Figure 10-8, I am using a modified version of the color-correction workspace, which includes several elements that remain important as you work. These elements include

  ✔ **Effect Controls:** In the color-correction workspace, an Effect Controls tab appears in the Project window. This tab is important because it contains all the color-correction controls you can adjust. If you don't see the Effect Controls on-screen, you can reveal them at any time in Premiere Pro by choosing Window➪Effect Controls.

  ✔ **Reference Monitor:** This is kind of like an extra monitor that you can synchronize with the main Program Monitor. In Figure 10-8, I've adjusted it to display the YCbCr Parade scope to measure my video image as I adjust colors. Click the Gang to Program Monitor button to synchronize the Reference Monitor to the Program Monitor.

To begin correcting color, you must first apply the Color Corrector filter to a video clip. To apply the Color Corrector filter to a video clip:

  1. **Click the Effects tab in the Project window.**

     You can also open the Effects tab by choosing Window➪Effects.

  2. **Open the Video Effects bin.**

  3. **Open the Image Control bin.**

  4. **Click-and-drag the Color Corrector effect from the Image Control bin and drop it on a clip in the Timeline.**

  5. **Click the clip to which you applied the Color Corrector effect to select it, and place the Timeline CTI somewhere over the clip.**

Controls for the Color Corrector should now appear in the Effect Controls tab as shown in Figure 10-8. Click the right-pointing arrow next to Color Corrector in the Effect Controls to reveal all of the settings.

Effect controls   Reference monitor

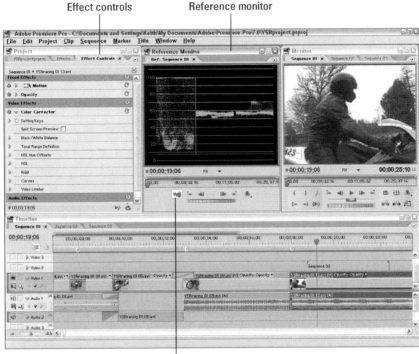

Figure 10-8:
Set up your
workspace
for color
correction.

Gang to Program monitor

 You'll find that the Color Corrector provides more predictable results and be easier to use and if you work through the settings in order. The next few sections show you how to adjust Color Corrector settings. I strongly recommend that you go through these sections in the order presented here, starting with Black/White Balance.

Black/White Balance

The Black/White Balance settings help you set a proper balance of white and black in your video image, an important first step for any color-correction work. When you expand the Black/White Balance settings, you'll see controls called Black Point, Gray Point, and White Point. Setting Black/White Balance is pretty easy:

1. **Click-and-hold the mouse button on the Black Point eyedropper.**

2. **While still holding down the mouse button, move the pointer over a spot in the Program Monitor that should represent the blackest black in the video image, and release the mouse button over that spot.**

3. Click-and-hold the mouse button on the White Point eyedropper.

4. While still holding down the mouse button, move the pointer over a spot in the Program Monitor that should represent the whitest white in the video image, and release the mouse button over that spot.

You have now set Black/White Balance for the clip. If the image seems to have an overall color cast, you can remove it using the Gray Point control. Click-and-hold on the Gray Point eyedropper, and release the mouse button over a spot in the video image that should represent neutral gray.

Tonal Range Definition

All of the colors in a video image fall into one of three categories called *tonal ranges*. These tonal ranges are shadows, midtones, and highlights. You can adjust HSL and RGB values for an overall image, or you can adjust the settings separately for each tonal range. The Tonal Range Definition control lets you specify which portions of an image are considered shadows, midtones, and highlights. Click the Preview check box under Tonal Range Definition. The video image in your monitor changes to a black, gray, and white image (as shown in Figure 10-9). Here's what those colors represent:

- Black: Shadows
- Gray: Midtones
- White: Highlights

To change the tonal range definitions, adjust the Shadows and Highlights sliders under Tonal Range Definition on the Effect Controls tab. Adjustments made here do not actually change your video image, but they affect how other color-correction adjustments are applied later on. The ability to correct colors independently for each tonal range is extremely useful because color problems are most likely to crop up in shadows and midtones. Being able to adjust colors just for shadows without affecting highlights is quite valuable; in fact, when I do color correction, I almost always just change tonal ranges rather than the whole image.

When you're done reviewing and adjusting tonal ranges, uncheck the Preview option. Only being able to see white, gray, and black could make actual color correction kind of tricky.

HSL Hue Offsets

Now it's time to actually start correcting some colors. Hooray! When you expand the HSL Hue Offsets controls, you should see four color wheels as shown in Figure 10-10. You'll find a Master color wheel, which applies changes to the entire image, as well as color wheels that correspond to the three tonal ranges described in the previous section.

Midtones

Shadows   Highlights

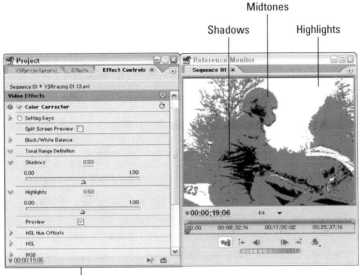

Figure 10-9:
Define tonal
ranges in
your video
image.

Click to preview tonal range definitions.

The HSL Hue Offsets wheels allow you to quickly change the color cast of
your video image. You can remove an unfavorable color cast, or add a certain
color cast to make the clip better match the rest of your project. To make
adjustments, click-and-drag the center dot on any of the color wheels. The
farther you drag the dot from the center, the more saturated the colors. This
is where that trial-and-error process I talked about earlier begins. In Figure
10-10, you can see that I've adjusted midtones and highlights but left shadows and the Master color wheel alone.

Figure 10-10:
Use the HSL
Hue Offsets
color
wheels to
change the
color cast of
your image.

If you want to make finer adjustments on the color wheel, hold down the Shift key on your keyboard as you click-and-drag on the wheels. Holding down the Shift key causes the mouse pointer to move much more slowly across the wheels.

HSL

The HSL controls allow you to adjust colors based on hue, saturation, and lightness (hence the acronym *HSL*). If you've ever used a graphics program such as Adobe Photoshop to do color correction on still images, the controls here may seem familiar. HSL settings fit into several categories:

- **Tonal Range:** If you want to adjust the whole image, choose Master in this pull-down menu. Otherwise, choose a specific tonal range to adjust.

- **Hue:** Use this control to adjust hue independently of saturation.

- **Saturation:** Adjust the saturation of colors with this slider control. (A saturation setting of zero removes all color.)

- **Brightness:** No surprises here; the Brightness slider controls brightness.

- **Contrast:** Like the name implies, this slider controls contrast in the image.

- **Contrast Center:** This slider allows you to adjust the center point upon which contrast changes are based. With the slider in the middle (50), contrast adjustments are based on the center point between white and black. The Contrast Center allows you to change the center point, which affects the way contrast adjustments are applied.

- **Gamma:** This control adjusts midtones without affecting black or white levels. The Gamma slider works well for adjusting the overall brightness of an image without affecting highlights and shadows.

- **Pedestal:** No, this does not finish your movie and place it high upon a pedestal. The Pedestal also adjusts the brightness of your image, but it has more affect on the darker pixels in the image. Use the Pedestal setting in conjunction with the RGB Gain setting.

- **RGB Gain:** This setting adjusts brightness by affecting the lighter pixels in your image.

RGB

You can adjust red, green, and blue color values in your video image using the RGB controls. RGB color is another concept you may be familiar with from working in computer graphics programs like Adobe Photoshop. As you look at RGB controls, you'll notice that you can adjust gamma, pedestal, and gain for all colors as well as red, green, and blue individually. As I mentioned in the previous section, Gamma controls midtones without affecting shadows or highlights. Pedestal affects darker colors (shadows), and Gain affects lighter colors (highlights).

The RGB Parade scope described earlier in this chapter really comes in handy when you are adjusting RGB controls. Use the RGB Parade to identify and correct chroma (color) clipping that might occur because some values are too high. As described earlier, chroma clipping can be identified by a concentration of color in a line at the top of the RGB Parade scope.

Curves

Of all the settings in the Premiere Pro Color Corrector, few encourage you to play quite as much as the Curves settings. As you can see in Figure 10-11, the Curves settings consist of four boxes, one each for Master, Red, Green, and Blue. The Master box controls brightness, and the remaining three boxes control their respective color channels.

The line in each box works like a rubber band. You can click-and-drag it to new locations, and you can use multiple control points on each line to quickly make complex adjustments. Notice the Red Curves control in Figure 10-11, which has three control points. Experiment with the Curves settings to get the best result.

Figure 10-11:
Adjusting colors with curves is quick and easy.

To remove a control point from a curve, click-and-drag the control point outside its box. The control point disappears when you release the mouse button outside the box, and the curve snaps back into its proper place.

Video Limiter

The Video Limiter controls help you prepare video for viewing on TVs and are especially useful if your project is destined for broadcast where specific limits may be in place. Basically, the Video Limiter ensures that your video conforms to the broadcast standards that you specify. If your project doesn't conform to the local broadcast-video standards, the project might get rejected by your broadcaster.

To use the Video Limiter, place a check mark next to Enable Limiter in the Video Limiter controls. The controls are organized in five categories:

- ✔ **Luma Max:** This controls the maximum luminance (light) values for the clip. The Luma Max is expressed in IRE, and the maximum IRE values allowed by broadcasters is usually 100 or 110 IRE. Check with your local broadcaster to be sure.

- ✔ **Chroma Min:** This setting controls the minimum chroma (color) values in your video. Talk to your local broadcaster about the Chroma Min setting that you should use.

- ✔ **Chroma Max:** This setting controls the maximum chroma value in the clip. Your broadcaster should provide you with a maximum allowable chroma value.

- ✔ **Video System:** Choose your video system (NTSC or PAL) here.

- ✔ **Method:** This setting lets you control the basic method by which the Video Limiter limits your luma and chroma values. You can choose to Reduce Luma, Reduce Chroma, or use Smart Limit. (The last setting is the one I recommend most of the time.)

Even if you don't color correct every single video clip, you should apply the Color Corrector to every clip destined for broadcast, if only to use the Video Limiter.

Saving your settings

Adjusting Color Corrector settings can become time consuming, and you may find that you are making the same changes to many or even all of your video clips. Fortunately the Color Corrector allows you to save and reuse settings. To save Color Corrector settings, click the right-pointing arrow next to Setting Keys and click the Save button as shown in Figure 10-12. Give your settings a descriptive name. In Figure 10-12, I give my settings a daringly original name ("My Broadcast Settings").

When the settings are saved, you can load them into the Color Corrector for any other video clip. Apply the Color Corrector to a video clip, and then click the Load Settings button. Browse to the settings file you saved earlier and open it. Your settings are then loaded.

Save Settings

Load Settings

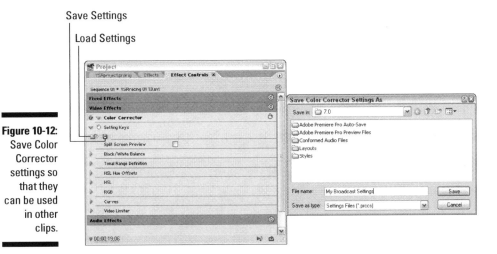

Figure 10-12:
Save Color
Corrector
settings so
that they
can be used
in other
clips.

Using the Color Match Filter

Another helpful image enhancement tool provided with Adobe Premiere Pro is the Color Match filter. This filter helps you match the colors in one video clip with the colors in another video clip. This filter is helpful when you have two scenes that were shot with different lighting conditions (or even different cameras) and you want to maintain a common look for both clips.

The Color Match filter uses two clips. The *sample clip* is the clip that has the colors or lighting that you like. The *target clip* is the clip you want to change so it looks more like the sample clip. To use the Color Match filter:

1. **Choose Window⇨Workspace⇨Color Correction if your workspace isn't already set up for color correction.**

   The Reference Monitor really comes in handy when you are color matching.

2. **Click the Effects tab in the Project window, or choose Window⇨Effects.**

3. **Open the Video Effects bin, and then open the Image Controls bin.**

4. **Drag-and-drop the Color Match filter from the Effects tab to the target clip.**

5. **Use the Jog in the Reference Monitor to display the sample clip as shown in Figure 10-13.**

If the video images in the Reference Monitor and Program Monitor move together, click the Gang to Program Monitor button to disable it. And remember, if you don't like moving the Reference Monitor's Jog with the mouse, you can also use the left- and right-arrow keys on the keyboard.

6. **Use the playback controls in the Program Monitor to display the target clip (as in Figure 10-13), and click the target clip in the Timeline to select it.**

Sample clip in Reference monitor   Target clip in Program monitor

Figure 10-13:
Use the Color Match filter to match colors in two different clips.

Gang to Program monitor

7. **Click the Effect Controls tab in the Project window, or choose Window⇨Effect Controls.**

8. **Click the right-pointing arrow next to Color Match in the Effect Controls to reveal the Color Match settings as shown in Figure 10-13.**

9. **Choose a method from the Method menu.**

    HSL (hue, saturation, lightness) is the most common method used for color matching, but you can also choose RGB (red, green, blue) or Curves if you wish.

10. **Choose what you want to match using the check boxes at the bottom of the Color Match settings.**

    If you are using the HSL matching method, you can choose whether you want to match hue, saturation, or lightness individually. For example, you may find that each clip is adequately lit, but that one has better color hue or saturation than the other. In this case, you'd disable the Match Lightness option. If you're using the RGB or Curves matching methods, you can choose whether to match red, green, or blue individually.

11. **Use an eyedropper to choose a sample color from the sample clip.**

    To use an eyedropper, click-and-hold it in the Effect Controls tab, and then move the mouse pointer over the desired color in the video image. A color is selected when you release the mouse button. The Color Match filter allows you to match colors for the master image, or you can just match one of the three tonal ranges (highlights, midtones, shadows).

12. **Use an eyedropper to choose a target color from the target clip.**

13. **Click the right-pointing arrow next to Match at the bottom of the Color match controls, and then click the Match button.**

    The image is modified. If you're not happy with the results, remember that Ctrl+Z (the Undo command) is your friend! You should click the Match button after every change you make.

As with many other color-correction tasks, the Color Match filter requires a great deal of trial and error to achieve the right look.

Chapter 11

Compositing and Animating Clips

* *

In This Chapter

▶ Using transparency to create composite scenes

▶ Animating clips and objects on-screen

* *

*H*ave you ever watched a movie where it appeared that the hero was hanging by fingertips from a ledge of a tall skyscraper, or a giant lizard creature appeared to be chasing live humans through a jungle? Of course, moviemakers don't really risk the lives of big-name stars by dangling them from skyscrapers, and they don't breed giant lizard creatures and then train them as harmless-yet-scary-looking movie extras. (Honest.) Scenes like these are created using a little bit of movie magic called *compositing*.

Guess what? You don't have to be a Hollywood movie mogul with a multimillion-dollar budget to use compositing. With some simple videographic tricks and Adobe Premiere Pro, you can create composite scenes with the best of 'em. In this chapter, I show you how. This chapter also shows you how to use Premiere Pro's animation features, which can allow you to move video scenes, titles, and other graphics across the screen.

Compositing Video

Over the years, we have come to expect sophisticated illusions in our entertainment — starships flying into a space battle, lovers standing on the bow of a long-gone ocean liner, or a weatherman standing in front of a moving weather-satellite graphic — and if you ever wanted to create some of your own, now you can: Adobe Premiere Pro is fully capable of creating such effects.

One of the great spells you can cast in the magic of moviemaking involves *compositing*. When you composite clips, you combine portions of two or more clips to make a video image that would otherwise be difficult or impossible to capture. Consider the scene I described in the introduction to this chapter, where an actor appears to be hanging by his fingertips from the fiftieth floor of a skyscraper as cars move like ants on the streets far below. Did the producers risk the actor's life and force him to hang from a tall building? Not likely — think of the insurance costs! They probably shot him hanging from a prop in a studio and then superimposed that image over a shot taken from an actual skyscraper.

Fundamental to the process of compositing is the careful layering of images. Using Premiere Pro, you can superimpose up to 99 separate video tracks upon one another. Each track contains part of the final image; by making parts of each track either opaque or transparent, you can create a convincing illusion of three-dimensional space. (See Chapter 8 for more on creating new tracks and adjusting their view.)

Adjusting the opacity of a clip

Video clips in Premiere Pro can vary between transparent and opaque. One of the most basic superimposition effects is to make a clip less opaque — that is, more transparent. The more transparent clip becomes a ghostlike image superimposed over the more opaque image behind it. You can change the opacity of an entire clip, or change it gradually throughout a clip. To adjust the opacity of a clip, follow these steps:

1. **Add a clip to the Video 1 track in a sequence.**

   Clips in the Video 1 track should not be made transparent, so you might think of Video 1 as the background layer. When you layer additional clips over it and make them transparent, the background clip on Video 1 should show through.

2. **Add a clip to a superimpose track in the sequence.**

   Video 2 and any higher-numbered tracks are all considered *superimpose tracks* because they're the ones you superimpose over a primary or background image. You can think of the video tracks in the Timeline as layers on top of each other. If you superimposed 50 tracks on top of each other, Track 50 would be the very top layer and opaque areas of that track would cover all other tracks.

   After you have added a clip to a superimpose track, the superimposed clip should appear directly above the background clip in Video 1, as shown in Figure 11-1.

3. **Click the arrow to expand the track view, as shown in Figure 11-1.**

4. **Click the Show Keyframes button in the track header for the superimpose track and then choose Show Opacity Handles from the menu that appears.**

   A yellow opacity rubberband appears on clips in the superimpose track.

5. **Click the clip for which you want to adjust opacity (doing so selects it).**

6. **Place the CTI somewhere in the selected clip.**

7. **Press Page Up on your keyboard to move the CTI to the beginning of the clip.**

8. **Click the Add/Remove Keyframe button on the track header to set a keyframe.**

9. **Move the CTI to a new place in the clip and click the Add/Remove Keyframe button again to create another keyframe.**

10. **Press Page Down on your keyboard to move the CTI to the end of the selected clip, and click the Add/Remove Keyframe button again to set another keyframe.**

11. **Click and drag on the keyframes you created to adjust the yellow opacity rubberband.**

    As you drag the rubberband down, the clip becomes more transparent. As you drag it up, it becomes more opaque.

If you find that the keyframes are kind of hard to click-and-drag with the mouse, carefully hover the mouse pointer over a keyframe. When the mouse point has a yellow dot next to it, you can click-and-drag the keyframe.

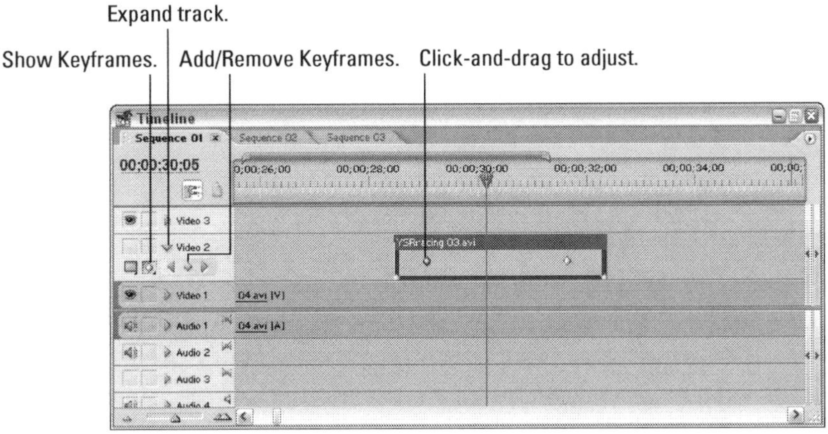

Expand track.

Show Keyframes. | Add/Remove Keyframes. | Click-and-drag to adjust.

Figure 11-1:
Use the opacity rubberband to adjust opacity throughout a clip.

Using keys

In the previous section, you adjusted the opacity of a clip to make the entire image transparent or semitransparent. But what if you only want parts of the image to become transparent while other parts of the image remain fully opaque?

You've probably heard of a video technique called *bluescreening,* often used in special-effects shots in movies, or during the evening news when a meteorologist must appear in front of a moving weather map. In actuality, the announcer is standing in front of a blue screen — usually wearing a color that clashes with the blue. Why the clash? Because you're not supposed to *see* the blue.

Here's how the blue screen becomes a weather map: Video-editing software uses a *key* — a setting that recognizes the special shade of blue and defines it as transparent. Because the wall behind the announcer is the only thing painted that shade of blue, it "disappears." In effect, the image of the meteorologist has been placed on a virtual "glass slide" and superimposed electronically over the image of the weather map. Pretty slick, eh?

Of course, if the meteorologist happens to wear a tie or blouse that *matches* the "transparent" color, you can see chunks of the weather map "right through" the person. (Oops . . .) Editors can only make *so* much movie magic; some careful videography is needed to make bluescreen-style effects work.

A blue screen key is one of many keys that work by recognizing a specific color in an image. Some keys use an alpha channel instead of a color to define transparent areas of an image. If you've worked with still graphics in a program such as Adobe Photoshop, you're probably familiar with alpha channels. An *alpha channel* is basically a layer in the image that defines transparency within the image. Generally speaking, the only time you'll use an alpha key is when you are dealing with a still graphic that was imported from a program like Photoshop or Adobe Illustrator.

The following sections show you how to use different kinds of keys to define transparent areas in your video image.

Understanding the key types

Although the example just given — a key that recognizes a blue screen behind a meteorologist — is extremely common, it isn't the only kind of key available to you in Premiere. In fact, Premiere Pro provides 14 different kinds of keys for you to use. To view a list of the keys, click the Effects tab in the Project window (or choose Window➪Effects) and then expand the Keying folder under Video Effects. Premiere Pro's keys are

✔ **Alpha Adjust:** This key works a lot like the opacity controls (described earlier in this chapter); it's for still graphics that have an alpha channel. Use this key to adjust opacity of the whole graphic, ignore the alpha channel, invert the alpha channel, or use the alpha channel as a mask.

✔ **Blue Screen Key:** Use this key when you've shot video with the subject in front of a blue screen. The blue screen must be well lit and brilliant for this key to be effective. Any shadows that the subject casts on the screen reduce the effectiveness of this key.

✔ **Chroma Key:** This key enables you to *key out* (make "disappear") a specific color or range of similar colors. With some fine-tuning, you can use this key with almost any clip. In Figure 11-2, I have applied a chroma key to the clip on the left to create the superimposition effect shown on the right. (I show how to do this in the next section.)

✔ **Difference Matte:** This matte enables you to key out the areas of two images that match each other.

✔ **Garbage Matte:** Use the Garbage Matte key to remove undesired objects that won't key out properly. When you apply a garbage matte to a superimposed clip, you can click-and-drag handles around the edge of the screen to (in effect) crop out portions of the image.

✔ **Green Screen Key:** This key works just like the Blue Screen except it uses (surprise) green instead of blue.

✔ **Image Matte Key:** This key uses a second still image to create transparency. When you use this key, you choose an image (such as a flower or a heart) to provide the basic shape for the key.

Figure 11-2:
Super-
impose
effects like
this one can
be created
with the
chroma key.

✔ **Luma Key:** Luma is short for *luminance*, which is just a fancy word for color. This key eliminates darker colors from an image.

✔ **Multiply Key:** With this key, transparency is based on bright areas on the video track underneath the superimpose track.

✔ **Non-Red Key:** This key works like the Blue Screen and Green Screen mattes, but it keys out both blue and green screens. If you encounter rough edges (called *stair-stepping*) around unkeyed objects with the Blue Screen or Green Screen keys, try using the Non-Red Key instead.

✔ **RGB Difference:** This key is similar to the chroma key, but with fewer options. This key works best when the background and subject contrast strongly.

✔ **Remove Matte:** This matte keys out the alpha channel and either the black or white background layers.

✔ **Screen Key:** With this key, the transparency is based on dark areas on the video track underneath the superimpose track.

✔ **Track Matte Key:** Use this matte with a black and white image that moves across the screen. Transparency moves with the image.

Applying a key

Applying a key to a clip is pretty easy. As explained in the previous section, a key allows portions of one image to be transparent when it is superimposed over another image. Remember, you can only apply a key to a clip in a super-impose track — that is, Video 2 or higher. To apply a key, follow these steps:

1. **Click a clip in a superimpose track to select it, and make sure that the CTI in the Timeline is somewhere over the clip.**

2. **Open the Effects tab in the Project window, or choose Window⟹Effects.**

3. **Expand the Video Effects folder, and then expand the Keying folder.**

4. **Drag and drop a key from the Effects tab to the selected clip in the superimpose track.**

5. **Click the Effect Controls tab in the left pane of the Monitor window, or choose Window⟹Effect Controls.**

   The effect controls for the selected clip should appear. The key you have applied should be listed under Video Effects.

6. **Click the right-pointing arrow next to the key to expand its controls as shown in Figure 11-3.**

   If the key uses color information — for example, the chroma key I am applying in Figure 11-3 — you may need to choose a base color for trans-parency. Click-and-hold the eyedropper in the Effect Controls, move the mouse pointer over the video image on the right side of the Monitor, and release the mouse button over the color you want to key out.

7. Adjust any other settings that may be available.

Each key is different, so experiment a bit with the settings to achieve the desired result.

Expand key controls.

Some keys have an eyedropper for choosing colors.

Figure 11-3:
Use the
Effect
Controls tab
to adjust key
settings.

Creating a matte

Some of the keys available in Premiere Pro use matte images to define transparent areas. You can create your own mattes by using a graphics program such as Adobe Photoshop, and you can create some mattes within Premiere itself. You can create mattes for a variety of purposes:

✔ A solid, brightly colored matte can help you key transparency on another clip. To create a matte of a solid color, choose File➪New➪Color Matte. Choose a color for the matte from the Color Picker. If you see a warning that the picture is out of the color gamut for your video format ("Whaddaya *mean* I can't use fluorescent puce there?"), choose another color. Then, place this matte on a track that is under the clip to which you're trying to apply a key. The brightly colored matte shows through to help you identify transparent areas and adjust as necessary. When you've made all the necessary adjustments, just delete the color matte.

✔ To mask out specific areas of an image, create a "garbage" matte and crop out the undesired object. To do this, first create a color matte (this will be your "garbage" matte) or import a background image. Next, select the image that has an object you want to crop out and add it to a superimpose track above the color matte or background image. If the image has an alpha channel, that channel automatically becomes transparent. Otherwise, you can apply the chroma key to the clip and select the color in the image that you want to make transparent. Using a still graphic as a garbage matte rather than the Garbage Matte key provided by Premiere Pro allows you to create a matte with much more complex shapes. Consider the matte in Figure 11-4, which creates the shape of a snowflake. You would never be able to create a shape like this using the Premiere Pro Garbage Matte key.

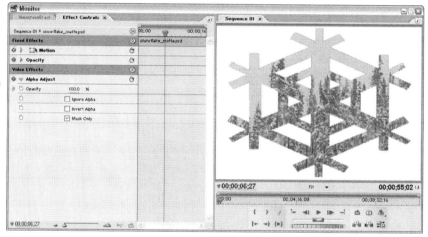

Figure 11-4:
Create a
matte in a
graphics
program if
you want
to use
complex
shapes.

When preparing a still graphic for importation into a video project, remember the importance of sizing your image to fit properly in the video image. See Chapter 6 for more on preparing still images for use in video.

Animating Clips

I know what you're thinking when you read this heading — *Why do I need to animate a video clip in which the subjects are already moving?* You may not need to animate the actual *subjects* in the video, but you can move the video image across the screen. For example, a small picture-in-picture image could sail across the screen to give a hint of action that will happen later in the movie. You can move a clip across the screen along a fixed path or a zigzag pattern, you can rotate clips, and you can distort them. To begin animating a clip, follow these steps:

1. **Click the clip in the Timeline that you want to animate to select it, and make sure that the CTI is somewhere over the clip.**

   Usually any clip that you animate should be in a superimpose track — that is, one that occupies any track above Video 1.

2. **Click the Effect Controls tab on the left side of the Monitor, or choose Window⊏⊐Effect Controls.**

3. **Under Fixed Effects, click the right-pointing arrow next to Motion to expand the Motion controls.**

Adjusting Motion controls

You can adjust the Motion controls in a variety of ways. Perhaps the easiest way to adjust a clip is to click the box next to Motion. You can then click-and-drag corners of the video image to shrink it down to a smaller size, as I have done in Figure 11-5. To move the clip, click-and-drag on the circle in the middle of the clip. If you want more precise control, use the following controls under Motion:

- ✔ **Position:** The position of the clip is expressed in pixels along an X (horizontal) and Y (vertical) axis. Zero for the X axis is the left edge of the screen, and zero for the Y axis is the top of the screen. The default position for any clip is right in the middle. For example, in NTSC-format DV video, the default position is 360 by 240. You can change the position of the clip by typing new numbers next to Position, or you can click-and-drag left or right on either Position number.

- ✔ **Scale:** The default scale for any clip is 100, which means its size is 100% of the size of the screen. Reduce the scale to shrink the clip image.

- ✔ **Scale Width:** If you remove the check mark next to Uniform Scale, you can then adjust height and width independently. With Uniform Scale unchecked, the Scale control adjusts height, and the Scale Width control adjusts width.

- ✔ **Rotation:** Use this control to rotate the clip. Expand the Rotation control and click-and-drag left or right on the clock-style rotation control to spin the image on its axis.

- ✔ **Anchor Point:** All of the other controls assume work off the clip's anchor point, which is usually in the center. If you want to rotate the clip around a corner instead of the center, for example, just move the anchor point.

If you don't like the changes you've made to the Motion controls, just click the Reset button next to Motion in the Effect Controls tab. This resets the clip back to the default settings.

Click to change size.

Reset

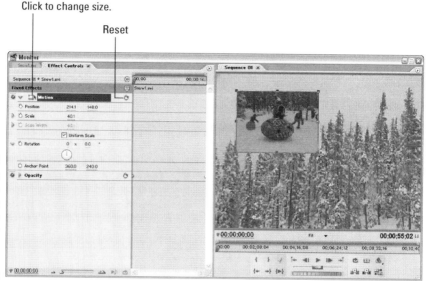

Figure 11-5:
Use the
Motion
controls to
resize or
animate a
video image.

Animating a clip

As you play with the Motion controls, you should see how easy it is to change the on-screen position, size, and orientation of a clip. But what if you want the clip to move across the screen after you've shrunk it? To do this, you must use keyframes. I explain keyframes in greater detail in Chapter 12, but to control motion with keyframes, follow these steps:

1. **Click the clip you want to animate in the Timeline to select it.**

2. **Move the CTI to the beginning of the selected clip.**

   The easiest way to do this is to first position the CTI somewhere over the clip, and then press Page Up on your keyboard.

3. **In the Motion controls for the selected clip, click the Toggle Animation button next to the control you want to animate.**

   In Figure 11-6, I am animating the Position control.

4. **Adjust the Scale, Position, and any other Motion controls you want to change.**

   These settings represent what the clip looks like and where it's positioned at the start of the animation.

5. **Click the Timeline window to make it active, and press Page Down to move the CTI to the end of the clip.**

6. **Adjust the Scale, Position, and any other Motion controls for the clip.**

    As in Step 4, these settings represent what the clip looks like and where it's positioned at the end of the animation.

When you make the adjustments described above, Premiere Pro automatically creates keyframes at the beginning and end of the clip. Premiere then automatically calculates how the clip should move and change to steadily go from one keyframe to the next. In Figure 11-6, I've started the clip off-screen to the left, and ended it off-screen to the right. As the clip plays, it appears to move across the screen.

You can add additional keyframes anywhere along the path of the clip to make more dynamic changes. Just move the CTI to a position somewhere in the middle of the clip and click the Add/Remove Keyframe button in the Motion controls, and then adjust settings as needed.

Toggle Animation   Add/Remove keyframes

Figure 11-6:
This clip moves across the screen as it plays.

Chapter 12

Affecting Effects in Your Movies

In This Chapter

▶ Having (and making) a great effect

▶ Checking over your effects arsenal

*P*ersonal computers capable of editing video have been widely available for several years now, and in the last couple of years, they've become downright cheap. This — combined with continuing price drops on DV camcorders — has led to an explosion in the number of video-editing programs available. From mild to wild, entry-level to professional, there is a video editor for every need and budget.

Not all video-editing programs are created equal, however. Many editors offer special effects you can apply to your video clips, but few offer the quality and variety available with Adobe Premiere Pro — 94 professional-grade effects. You can add even more effects from third-party vendors.

Effects can help you clean up your video or add special touches that amaze and astound your audience. What's really cool about effects is that you can add them to (or remove them from) any clip you want. Effects do not permanently change your clips, so if you aren't happy with a result, you can simply delete the offending effect. Although this book isn't the place to cover each of Premiere Pro's effects in detail, this chapter does show you the basics of using effects — including the brass-tacks specifics of using several common effects.

Understanding Effects

Adobe Premiere Pro comes with 94 effects built right in. Some of these effects may not seem immediately useful, but you may be surprised in a future project when what seems like the most obscure effect comes in handy. You can get a look at Premiere's effects by choosing Window⇨Effects, or just click the Effects tab in the Project window. Expand the Video Effects folder to reveal the following 14 categories:

✔ **Adjust:** These seven effects let you tweak levels of color and light. They can be useful for fixing color- and light-related problems in your video clips.

✔ **Blur & Sharpen:** These 11 effects run the gamut from blur to sharpen. The blur effects allow you to soften the outlines of things to simulate disorientation, or suggest speed by "unfocusing" parts of the video image. The sharpen effects perform a variety of sharpening enhancements to an image. Use these effects to sharpen images that appear too soft.

✔ **Channel:** This category includes two effects. The Invert effect inverts colors in a clip. The Blend effect enables you to blend the colors of superimposed clips.

✔ **Distort:** This folder contains 13 effects that bend, twist, or exaggerate the shape and view of your video.

✔ **Image Control:** These ten effects change the way color is viewed in your clips. They can remove a color (or range of colors) from a clip, convert a color image to black and white, or adjust the overall tint of the image (useful if, for example, you want to transform an ordinary outdoor scene into an alien landscape). Chapter 10 shows you how to use the Color Corrector and Color Match effects in greater detail.

✔ **Keying:** These effects allow you to control transparency in clips and perform compositing effects such as bluescreening. (See Chapter 11 for more on using keys in your video projects.)

✔ **Noise:** The Median effect — the only effect in the Noise category — can be used to reduce noise in the video image. If more extreme settings are applied, the image begins to look like a painting.

✔ **Perspective:** These four effects add a three-dimensional feel to your clips — for example, when you bevel the edges of the video image or create shadows.

✔ **Pixelate:** These three effects modify the pixels that make up your video image to create some unusual visual coloration and appearances. (Textures, anyone?)

✔ **Render:** The three Render effects allow you to simulate various properties of real light. One of the effects simulates lens flares — momentary bright circles that often occur in video footage when the sun reflects or glares on the lens. Although you probably work hard to avoid *real* lens flares when you shoot video, well-placed *simulated* lens flares can have a dramatic effect, especially if you are depicting a sunrise or sunset. The Lightning effect is especially cool because you can create realistic lightning on-screen.

✔ **Stylize:** These 12 effects create a variety of image modifications. With the Stylize effects you can simulate video noise (on-screen "snow"), create clip mosaics, add texturized or windswept appearances to the image, and more.

✔ **Time:** The Echo effect creates visual echoes (or double-image) of a picture. The Posterize Time effect modifies the apparent frame rate of a clip. Use this effect to make it look like you dropped frames during capture or output even if you really didn't.

✔ **Transform:** These nine effects transform the view of your clip in a variety of ways. The image can be rotated in three dimensions, you can simulate a panning effect, or you can simulate a vertical-hold problem on a TV (you can have a lot of fun with this one; just imagine your friends banging on their TVs trying to figure out why the vertical hold is messed up).

✔ **Video:** These three effects help correct video problems or prepare video for output to tape. You can apply the Broadcast Colors effect to clips when you want to filter out colors that aren't broadcast-legal, or use the Field Interpolate effect to replace missing fields knocked off the screen by interlacing. If you have a clip with many thin lines, the lines may flicker when viewed on a regular TV. Use the Reduce Interlace Flicker effect to soften the image and reduce the flickering problem.

Applying effects

To apply an effect to a clip, you simply drag the effect from the Effects tab to a clip in the Timeline. (Choose Window⇨Effects to open this tab, or click the Effects tab in the Project window.) You can adjust attributes of an effect using the Effect Controls tab. To reveal this tab, click the clip in the Timeline to select it and then choose Window⇨Effect Controls, or click the Effect Controls in the left pane of the Monitor window. The Effect Controls tab appears, as shown in Figure 12-1. Key features of the Effect Controls tab include these:

✔ Each effect applied to a clip has a separate listing under Video Effects. Click the arrow to expand the view of options for each effect.

✔ To disable an effect, click to remove the tiny circle next to the effect's title in the Effect Controls.

✔ Each effect has its own unique controls. Click the right-pointing arrow next to an effect control to view more specific controls.

✔ To enable keyframing so that the effect can be changed over time, click the Toggle Animation button, as shown in Figure 12-1. I'll show you how to use keyframes in the next section.

✔ The Effects Control tab includes a keyframe viewer, which, as you can see in Figure 12-1, looks like a miniature Timeline, complete with its own CTI (current time indicator).

✔ To add a keyframe for a control at the current location of the CTI, click the Add/Remove Keyframe button. Use the arrows on either side of any Add/Remove Keyframe button to move the CTI to the next (or previous) keyframe.

✔ Some effects have Color Pickers. In Figure 12-1, I must use the Color Picker to choose a fill color for the background after the camera view has been modified. Some Color Pickers have eyedroppers next to them. Eyedroppers are used to choose a color from the video image in the Monitor. To use an eyedropper, click-and-hold on it, move the mouse pointer over the desired color in the video image, and then release the mouse button.

✔ To quickly reset all settings back to default, click the Reset button. (I use this button a lot, especially when I'm working with keyframes.)

Using keyframes

Effects can have a variety of, er, *effects* on clips in Premiere Pro. Video clips can be blurred, recolored, distorted, and more. You can apply an effect as is to an entire clip, or you can set the effect up so it changes over time. To do the latter, however, Premiere needs a way to determine exactly how and when to make such changes. For this purpose the program uses reference points called *keyframes*. If you want an effect to change over time, you use keyframes to specify when those changes occur. Premiere Pro automatically extrapolates how the effect should progress from one keyframe to the next.

The types of keyframes I am talking about in this chapter are effect keyframes. Video codecs (the compression/decompression schemes used to make video files smaller) use another kind of keyframe called a *compression* keyframe. Although the names sound familiar, these are actually entirely different things. (See Chapter 16 for a more detailed explanation of compression keyframes.)

After you have applied an effect to a clip, you can adjust that effect using keyframes. To set keyframes, follow these steps:

1. **Locate the clip in the Timeline that has the effect you want to modify.**

2. **Select the clip, and then open the Effect Controls for the clip (Window⇨Effect Controls) if they are not already shown.**

3. **Click the Enable Animation button next to each control that you want affected by keyframes.**

   The Enable Animation button enables the use of keyframes for the effect. If the Enable Animation button is disabled, the effect will be applied evenly across the entire clip.

4. Move the CTI in the keyframes viewer (see Figure 12-1) to the exact frame where you want to set a keyframe.

You can move the CTI using the playback controls in the Monitor, or you can use the J, K, and L keys on your keyboard. Use the left- and right-arrow keys to move a single frame at a time.

5. In the Effect Controls tab, click the Add/Remove Keyframe button next to an effect control.

You need to add a keyframe for each control that you want to change. In Figure 12-1, I have applied the Camera View effect to a clip. However, I only want the camera view to change after the clip has played for a few seconds. Thus, at the first two keyframes, I set all the controls to their defaults. At the third keyframe, I adjusted the Longitude, Focal Length, Distance, and Zoom controls to the desired settings. At the last keyframe, which is at the very end of the clip, I set the exact same settings as at the third keyframe. The effect of these changes is that the clip plays normally from the beginning until it reaches the second keyframe. At that point, the camera angle starts to morph until it gets to the settings I specified at the third keyframe. At that point, the camera angle remains morphed until the end of the clip.

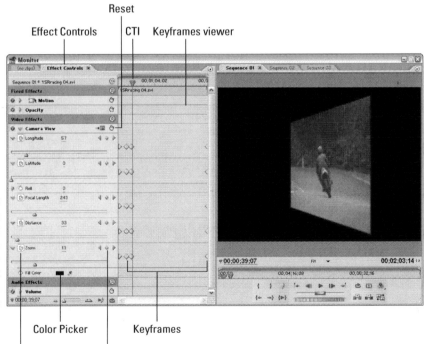

Figure 12-1:
Control your effects using the Effect Controls tab.

6. Set additional keyframes as desired.

Don't forget to use those Previous and Next Keyframe buttons. They provide an easy way to move from keyframe to keyframe. If you want to remove a keyframe, simply move to the keyframe and click the Add/Delete Keyframe button to remove the check mark. When you remove that check mark, you'll notice that the keyframe also magically disappears from the clip.

If you apply multiple effects to a clip, each effect gets its own keyframes. Thus, if you set a keyframe for one effect, don't assume that it applies to the other effects on that clip as well. To view the keyframes for an effect, click that effect in the Effect Controls tab to select it.

Removing effects

You'll probably change your mind about some of the effects you apply to your clips. Don't feel bad; this is perfectly natural. In fact, you'll find that a lot of time in video editing is spent on good ol' trial and error. You'll try an effect, you won't like it, so then you'll try something else.

To get rid of an effect, click the clip in the Timeline to select it and then choose Window⇨Effect Controls to reveal the Effect Controls tab. You have two options for removing effects from a clip:

✔ You can temporarily disable an effect by clicking the little circle next to the effect's listing in the Effect Controls tab. This can be handy because any settings that you changed for the effect are preserved. With the circle removed, the clip is disabled and is not applied to the clip when the sequence is rendered or output.

✔ You can delete an effect by clicking its title in the Effect Controls tab and pressing Delete on your keyboard. Don't worry! This will not delete the effect from Premiere Pro, it'll just remove the effect from the current clip.

Using Other Video Effects

Lots of effects are available with Premiere Pro, and I couldn't possibly describe them all here. Rather than provide a brief overview of many effects, the following sections show you a detailed approach to using a few common effects. You can adapt the techniques described here when using other effects.

Distorting video

Adobe Premiere Pro comes with a plethora of effects that you can use to distort your video. Some of the best ones can be found in the Distort and Transform folders. Distortion effects range from mild to wild. You may find that the best way to give your video a custom appearance is to apply multiple effects. Consider the clip in Figure 12-2. I have applied the Pinch effect, found in the Distort folder under Video Effects. The Pinch effect simulates a pinching or pulling of a spot in the video image.

Figure 12-2:
The Pinch effect has distorted this video clip in a most peculiar way.

When you apply the Pinch effect — just drag it from the Effects tab and drop it on a clip in the Timeline — the Pinch settings dialog box appears, as shown in Figure 12-3. The bottom of this dialog box shows a representation of the pinch that you are about to apply. You can use the grid to move the pinch point, and move the Amount slider to control the degree to which you pinch the image. (I want an extreme pinch appearance, so I've set the slider as high as it will go.)

You can open the Pinch Settings dialog box at any time by clicking the Setup next to the Pinch effect in the Effect Controls tab. Use the plus (+) and minus (–) signs in the Pinch Settings dialog box to zoom in or out on the preview window.

A minor application of the Pinch effect can give the illusion that the footage was shot using a very-wide-angle lens, also called a "fisheye" lens.

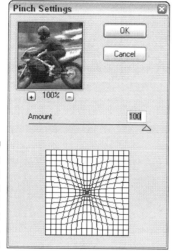

Figure 12-3:
Use this
dialog box
to control
the Pinch
effect.

Now, to really make things tricky, several seconds into the clip, I want to zoom in on the image and reduce the pinch effect. To do this, I first apply the Camera View effect (located in the Transform folder) to the clip. The Camera View effect contains, among other things, a zoom effect. Next, I add two keyframes to the clip. Between those keyframes, the zoom level goes from the default level (10) to a slightly more zoomed-in level (7). I also change the keyframes at the beginning and end of the clip to match these settings. Finally, I also create keyframes for the Pinch effect so it diminishes as the camera view zooms in. Figure 12-4 shows the keyframes that I created.

Disorienting your audience

Suppose a subject in a movie is sick or disoriented. What is the best way to communicate this to the audience? You could have someone in the movie say, "Hey, you don't look well. Are you sick?" and then the unwell person can stumble and fall down. That may be effective, but an even better way to convey a feeling of illness or confusion is to let your audience see through the subject's blurry and distorted eyes.

You can begin by shooting some footage as if from the view of the subject. Hand-hold the camera and let it move slightly as you walk. You probably don't need to exaggerate the movement, but the camera shouldn't be tripod-stable either. As you shoot, pan across the scene — but not too quickly — as if the subject were looking around the room. Occasionally you may want to dip the camera slightly left or right so the video image appears to tilt. A tilting video image has a strong disorienting effect on the viewer.

Pinch keyframes

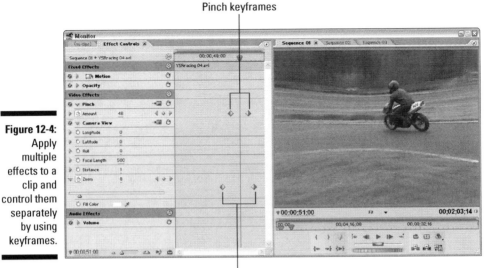

Figure 12-4:
Apply
multiple
effects to a
clip and
control them
separately
by using
keyframes.

Camera View keyframes

Now that you have some footage to work with, you can perform the real
magic in Premiere Pro. One effect that can provide a feeling of illness or disorientation is Camera Blur (found in the Blur folder). Use keyframes to adjust
camera blur throughout a clip, as if the subject's vision were moving in and
out of focus. Another good one is Ghosting (also in the Blur folder). Ghosting
produces ghost images of moving objects. Similar to ghosting is the Echo
effect, found in the Time folder, which is used in Figure 12-5. Echo gives you a
bit more control over the number and timing of echoed images.

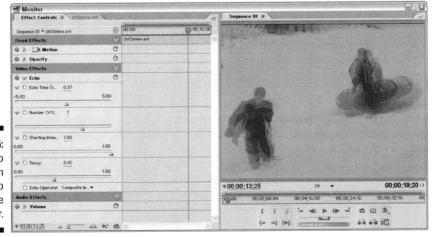

Figure 12-5:
The Echo
effect can
be used to
disorient the
viewer.

Working in the Golden Age of Cinema

Motion pictures have been around for well over a century now. You may want to use some "old" (or at least old-*looking*) footage in your movie projects, but thankfully, creating footage that looks old does not require a trip to some dank film vault deep beneath a Hollywood movie studio. You can simulate an old-fashioned look with your own video by following these steps:

- ✔ **Pay attention to your subjects and the scene.** Cowboys of the Old West didn't carry cell phones at their hips, for example, nor was the sky filled with white condensation trails left by jet airplanes. Remove objects from the scene that don't fit the period you are trying to simulate, and shoot carefully so the background doesn't depict modernity.

- ✔ **Remove color from the clip.** Perhaps the easiest way to convert a color image to grayscale is to use the Black & White filter in the Image Control folder, although I prefer to use the Color Balance (HLS) effect. Adjust the saturation level to –100, which (in effect) makes the clip grayscale. One advantage of using the Color Balance (HLS) effect is that you can use keyframes to change the effect in the middle of a clip.

  Grayscale is just a fancy way of saying "black and white." Grayscale is a more technically accurate term because "black-and-white" video images are actually made using various shades of gray.

- ✔ **"Weather" the video image.** Film tends to deteriorate over time, so if you're trying to simulate old footage, you should simulate some of that deterioration. Use the Noise effect under Stylize to add some graininess to the video image.

- ✔ **Reduce audio quality and if possible use a mono setting.** Audio recordings made 75 years ago did not use 16-bit stereo sound. To reduce quality, reduce the sampling rate of the audio when you export your movie (see Chapter 14 for more on movie export settings). Alternatively, you may want to go for the "silent movie" effect and not record any audio at all. Just use an appropriate musical soundtrack and title screens for dialog.

- ✔ **Speed up the clip.** Older film often plays back at a faster speed, so speed up the clip by selecting it, choosing Clip⇨Speed/Duration, and increasing the Speed percentage in the Clip Speed/Duration dialog box that appears.

Flipping video

Do you ever wish you could produce a mirror image of a video clip, or maybe rotate it and change its orientation on the screen? Such modifications are easy to make with Premiere Pro. Effects that you can use to flip video can be found in the Transform folder of Video Effects. These effects include two classics:

✔ **Horizontal Flip:** This effect flips the video left to right, as shown in Figure 12-6.

✔ **Vertical Flip:** This effect flips the video top to bottom.

When flipping video, watch out for letters and numbers that appear in the frame. Backward letters stick out like sore thumbs (or rude gestures) when your audience views the movie.

Figure 12-6: The Horizontal Flip effect was applied to the clip on the left.

Adding Web links to movies

The term *multimedia* is used pretty loosely these days, although few types of media are as "multi" as the movies you can create with Premiere Pro. Not only can your movies contain audio, video, and still graphics, but they can also include links to the World Wide Web. Of course, for the link to work, your audience must be watching the movie on a computer that can connect to the Internet. Also, the movie needs to be output in a format that supports Web links, such as QuickTime. Web links can be handy if you want a specific Web page to open during or after playback. To create a Web link, follow these steps:

1. **Move the CTI to the point in a sequence at which you want the link to be activated.**

2. **Choose Marker⇨Set Sequence Marker⇨Unnumbered.**

   A marker appears on the Timeline ruler. Actually, you can make it a numbered marker if you wish.

3. **Double-click the marker.**

   The Marker dialog box appears, as shown in Figure 12-7.

4. **In the URL field, type the complete URL (Uniform Resource Locator) for the link target.**

   The URL is the Web address for the site that you want to open. To be safe, it should include the `http://` part of the address. Consider the URL that you enter here carefully. Does it point to a page that will still be online several months (or even a year) from now? Consider how long users might be viewing copies of your movie.

5. **Click OK to close the dialog box.**

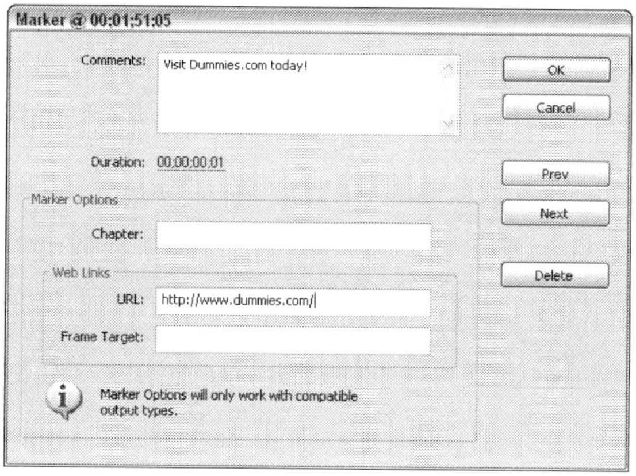

Figure 12-7:
Timeline
markers can
link to World
Wide Web
addresses.

Marker @ 00:01:51:05	
Comments: Visit Dummies.com today!	OK
	Cancel
Duration: 00:00:00:01	Prev
Marker Options	Next
Chapter:	
Web Links	Delete
URL: http://www.dummies.com/	
Frame Target:	
(i) Marker Options will only work with compatible output types.	

Test your Web link in the final output format! If it works, the desired Web page should open in a Web browser. Some formats (such as QuickTime) support Web links; others don't.

Be really, really careful when you type the address for your Web URL. Exact spelling and syntax is crucial or else your Web link is broken — and that creates a bad impression with your audience. Furthermore, because most Web servers run a UNIX-based operating system, everything after the `.com` part of the Web address is probably case-sensitive. Watch that capitalization!

Chapter 13

Working with Audio

In This Chapter

▶ Digging into audio

▶ Recording narration

▶ Tweaking audio in the Timeline (not illegal in most states)

▶ Making the best use of audio effects

*O*f all the various aspects of a video program, audio is typically the easiest to overlook. We tend to think of movies as a visual art form, but it turns out that the audible portion of a movie is nearly as important as what happens on-screen. In fact, a lot of video experts will tell you that while audiences tend to be forgiving of flaws and mistakes in a video image, they find poor-quality audio almost immediately noticeable and off-putting.

To tell the truth, I'd love to dedicate more than one chapter to audio; it's a big subject. But I think this chapter can cover the essentials — a brief look at just what audio is, followed by a hands-on delve into actually editing audio in Adobe Premiere Pro.

Understanding Audio

Consider how audio affects the feel of a video program. Honking car horns on a busy street; crashing surf and calling seagulls at a beach; a howling wolf on the moors; these are sounds that help us identify a place as quickly as our eyes can, if not quicker. If a picture is worth a thousand words, sometimes a sound in a movie is worth a thousand pictures.

What is audio? Well, if I check my notes from high school science class, I get the impression that audio is produced by sound waves moving through the air; human beings hear those waves when they make our eardrums vibrate. The speed at which a sound makes the eardrum vibrate is the *frequency*. Frequency is measured in kilohertz (kHz), and 1 kHz equals one thousand vibrations per second. A lower-frequency sound is perceived as a lower pitch or tone, and a higher-frequency sound is perceived as a high pitch or tone. The volume or intensity of audio is measured in *decibels* (dB).

Understanding sampling rates

For over a century, humans have been using analog devices (ranging from wax cylinders to magnetic tapes) to record sound waves. As with video, digital audio recordings are all the rage today. Because a digital recording can only contain specific values, it can only approximate a continuous wave of sound; a digital recording device must "sample" a sound many times per second; the more samples per second, the more closely the recording can approximate the live sound (although a digital approximation of a "wave" actually looks more like the stairs on an Aztec pyramid). The number of samples per second is called the *sampling rate*. As you might expect, a higher sampling rate provides better recording quality. CD audio typically has a sampling rate of 44.1 kHz — that's 44,100 samples per second — and most digital camcorders can record at a sampling rate of 48 kHz. The sampling rate for your project is one of the things you have to determine when you create a new project in Premiere Pro.

Delving into bit depth

Another term you'll hear bandied about in audio editing is *bit depth*. The quality of an audio recording is affected by the number of samples per second, as well as the amount of information in each of those samples. The amount of information that can be recorded per sample is the bit depth. More bits equal more information. Many digital recorders and camcorders offer a choice between 12-bit and 16-bit audio; choose 16-bit whenever possible.

Conforming audio

When you first import audio into Adobe Premiere Pro — whether you're importing music from a CD or capturing audio and video from a DV tape — Premiere *conforms* the audio to match the audio settings of your project. For example, if you created your project to use a 48-kHz sample rate (see Chapter 5 for more on starting a new project), but the audio you are importing is 44.1-kHz audio from a music CD, the imported audio is converted to 48 kHz (the sample rate of your project).

When audio is conformed, Premiere Pro doesn't actually change the audio file that is being imported or captured. Instead, Premiere creates new conformed audio files on your hard disk. By default, these conformed audio files are stored in the following subfolder of your My Documents folder:

```
Adobe\Premiere Pro\7.0\Conformed Audio Files
```

Within this folder are subfolders, one for each of your projects. When you first import or capture some audio, Premiere Pro automatically starts creating conformed audio files. Conformed audio serves two important purposes:

✔ Audio quality remains consistent throughout your project.

✔ Conformed audio files are essentially rendered audio files, meaning that audio effects and other edits can be previewed in real time.

You may notice that some audio files won't play immediately after you import or capture them. This means that Premiere Pro isn't done conforming the audio. The process happens quickly, so you shouldn't have to wait long. When a waveform appears on an audio clip, that means the audio has been conformed.

Conformed audio files use up a lot of disk space. If you're trying to clean up old files and recover some disk space, you may want to delete the conformed audio files left over from old projects that you aren't working on any more. Happily, if you decide to work on that project again later, Premiere Pro can automatically regenerate conformed audio files.

Recording Audio

When you shoot video, you probably spend extra time and effort making sure the shot is composed just right and that the lighting is favorable. You want to shoot the best quality video that is possible so that less editing work is necessary later on. You should also spend some time making sure that the audio you record is top quality. The next section offers basic tips on recording better audio. I'll also show you how to record audio using your computer and Premiere Pro.

Making sound audio recordings

Recording great-quality audio is no simple matter. Professional recording studios spend thousands, even millions, of dollars to set up acoustically superior sound rooms. Even if you don't have that kind of budgetary firepower, you can get still pro-sounding results if you follow these basic tips:

✔ **Use an external microphone whenever possible.** The built-in microphones in modern camcorders have improved greatly in recent years, but they still present problems. They often record undesired ambient sound near the camcorder (such as coughing audience members) or even mechanical sound from the camcorder's tape drive. If possible, connect an external microphone to the camcorder's mic input.

✔ **Eliminate unwanted noise sources.** If you *must* use the camcorder's built-in mic, be aware of your movements and other possible causes of loud, distracting noises on tape. Problem items can include a loose lens cap banging around, your finger rubbing against the mic, wind blowing across the mic, and the *swish-swish* of those nylon workout pants you wore this morning.

When you're recording audio in your studio (a.k.a. your office), be especially wary of ambient noise. Subtle sounds like the cooling fans inside your computer, air rushing through heating ducts, and someone playing video games in the next room all create ambient noise that *will* show up on audio recordings. If you're using Premiere Pro to record narration, you won't be able to do anything about the computer fans, but if you have other computers in the room, you definitely want to shut those down.

Do not try to disable the cooling fans in your computer, not even for just a few minutes! Modern computer processors run so hot that they can be ruined in mere seconds if they're not properly cooled.

✔ **Try to minimize sound reflection.** Audio waves reflect off any hard surface, which can cause echoing in a recording. Hanging blankets on walls and other hard surfaces is one way to significantly reduce reflection.

✔ **Obtain and use a high-quality microphone.** A good mic isn't cheap, but it can make a huge difference in recording quality.

✔ **Watch for trip hazards!** In your haste to record great sound, don't forget that your microphone cables can become a hazard on scene. Not only is this a safety hazard to anyone walking by, but if someone snags a cable, your equipment could be damaged as well. If necessary, bring along some duct tape to temporarily cover cables that run across the floor.

Recording audio in Premiere Pro

Premiere Pro allows you to record audio directly to an audio track in the Timeline. This can be especially handy for recording narration to go along with a movie project. To record audio in Premiere, your computer must have audio hardware (a sound card) that is capable of audio input (a sound card with a microphone port). And, of course, you need a microphone. To configure Premiere Pro for recording audio from your sound card:

1. **In Premiere Pro, choose Edit⇨Preferences⇨Audio Hardware.**

   The Preferences dialog box appears with the Audio Hardware group (shown in Figure 13-1).

2. **Choose the audio device you want to use for recording in the Input/Output Device menu.**

   If the hardware you want to use doesn't appear in the menu, it isn't properly installed on your computer. Choose Adobe Default Windows Sound if you just want to use your computer's sound card.

3. **Set Output Channel Mappings.**

   Audio channels available on your audio hardware are listed in this menu. On the far right side of the menu, you see icons that show how that channel is mapped for both stereo and 5.1 surround audio. To change how each channel is mapped, simply drag and drop an icon to a new channel. The channels automatically switch mappings.

4. **Click OK to close the Preferences dialog.**

Stereo ────── ┌──5.1 Surround

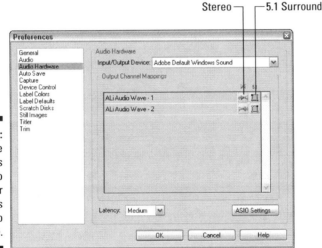

Figure 13-1:
Make sure Premiere is set up to use your computer's audio hardware.

After Premiere Pro is set up to use the correct audio hardware, you are almost ready to record your audio. I recommend that you create a new audio track for the audio you plan to record — because you'll be recording directly to an audio track in the Timeline. Next, you'll need to set the Premiere Pro Audio Mixer to record to that track. Follow these steps:

1. **Click the sequence to which you want to record to bring it to the front of the Timeline window.**

2. **Choose Sequence⇨Add Tracks.**

3. **In the Add Tracks dialog box, add one audio track and zero video or submix tracks. Click OK to close the Add Tracks dialog box.**

   You cannot record sound directly to a submix track. Submix tracks are explained later in this chapter.

4. **Click the track header of the new track you just created to make it the target track.**

5. **Click the speaker icons to remove them from all other audio tracks in the sequence.**

   Removing the speaker icons temporarily mutes the other audio tracks. This ensures that sound from those tracks won't play through your computer's speakers while you are trying to record your own audio.

6. **Place the CTI in the Timeline a little before the spot where you want to begin recording.**

7. **Open the Audio Mixer by choosing Window➪Audio Mixer.**

   Alternatively, you can open the audio workspace by choosing Window➪Workspace➪Audio. This rearranges all of the Premiere Pro windows to allow for more efficient audio mixing. (The Audio Mixer is described in greater detail in the following section.)

8. **In the Audio Mixer, click the Enable Track for Recording button as shown in Figure 13-2.**

   When you click this button, a menu appears, listing your audio hardware. Make sure the correct audio hardware is listed in the menu.

9. **Position your microphone, eliminate ambient noise, get a drink of water, and just generally make sure you're ready to go "on the air."**

10. **Click the Record button at the bottom of the Audio Mixer window.**

11. **Click Play at the bottom of the Audio Mixer window.**

    The sequence starts to play; you can watch it in the Monitor window.

12. **Speak into the microphone.**

    Try to say something interesting!

13. **Click Stop at the bottom of the Mixer window when you are done recording your audio.**

    A wave (.wav) file now appears in the target audio track, as shown in Figure 13-2. Don't be afraid to delete and re-record your narration if you're not entirely pleased with it. If you have a particularly difficult time recording good narration, consider writing out a script, and practice reciting the script a few times while the movie plays to get your timing right.

Enable Track for Recording

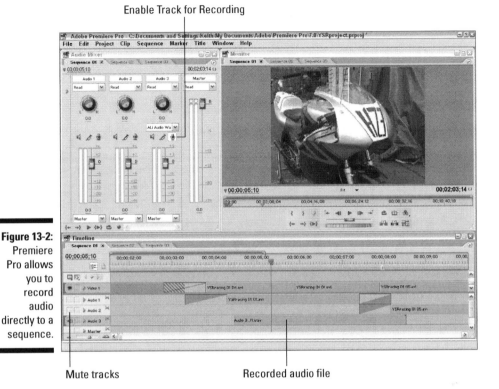

Figure 13-2:
Premiere
Pro allows
you to
record
audio
directly to a
sequence.

Mute tracks   Recorded audio file

Working with Audio in a Project

The designers of Premiere Pro thought that audio was such an important part
of a movie project that they provided a workspace specifically tailored to
audio. To open the Audio Editing workspace, choose Window⇨Workspace⇨
Audio. One of the primary features of the audio workspace is the Audio Mixer
window shown in Figure 13-3. The Mixer includes mixing controls for each
audio track, as well as master controls for the project. Audio tracks in the
current sequence are listed by number in the Audio Mixer, and the Mixer
window includes tabs for each sequence in your project's Timeline. Figure
13-3 shows an Audio Mixer that is open in a project that has three audio
tracks. Track 1 is a stereo track, Track 2 is mono, and Track 3 is 5.1 channel
surround.

Enable recording   Balance control (surround)

Balance control (stereo)   VU meter

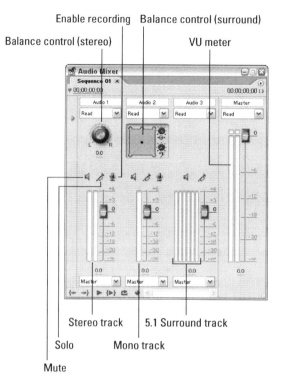

Figure 13-3:
The Audio
Mixer is
where you
control your
audio.

Stereo track   5.1 Surround track

Solo   Mono track

Mute

If you don't see all of the tracks in your current sequence listed in the Audio Mixer, you may need to click-and-drag the edge of the Mixer window to expand it.

As you play your Timeline, you'll notice that your audio registers on the VU (volume unit) meter for the corresponding track. The number of VU meters on a track depends on the format. As shown in Figure 13-3, a mono track has one VU meter, a stereo track has two, and a 5.1 surround track has six.

You can also use the Audio Mixer to control which audio tracks play and which ones don't. To mute a track, click the Mute button in the Audio Mixer for that track. The Mute indicator should turn red to indicate that it is muted.

If you only want to play one of the audio tracks, click its Solo button in the Audio Mixer. The Solo button for that track turns green, and the Mute button for every other track turns red. Click the Solo button again to turn it off.

Linking audio and video

When you insert a clip that contains both audio and video into a sequence, the audio and video tracks for that clip are usually linked together. If that's the case, then you'll notice that they both become selected when you click one of them in the Timeline. Usually this is handy, but sometimes you may want to unlink the two and edit them individually. To unlink audio and video for a clip, select that clip in the Timeline and choose Clip⇨Unlink Audio and Video. You can now select the audio and video portions of the clip individually.

Premiere Pro provides a visual clue to tell you which clips are linked and which ones are not. Linked clips have underlined names in the Timeline. The names of unlinked clips are not underlined.

Adjusting volume

I like to use a lot of different audio tracks in a project. If possible, I try to insert each new audio element on a different track. This gives greater flexibility when making adjustments to things such as volume. Different bits of audio get recorded at different levels, and you may find that one audio clip is too loud whereas another is not loud enough. You can adjust the volume for a track by using the Volume sliders in the Audio Mixer. Simply click-and-drag the slider to adjust the volume.

The volume of audio in video projects is measured in volume units (VU). Premiere's Audio Mixer includes VU meters that may appear similar to the volume meters on a tape deck or other recording device you've used before. If you've ever recorded audio on tape using an analog tape deck, you probably made sure that the audio levels got above 0 and into the red once in a while, but that average volume was below 0. But when you are working with digital audio, 0 is the maximum volume level you can have before distortion occurs. That's why if you look at the Master Audio track in the Audio Mixer, you'll notice that the VU meter scales stop at 0.

When adjusting volume — also called the *gain* — for an individual track, keep an eye on the Master VU meters in the Audio Mixer. If the meters reach 0, you'll probably get audio distortion in the final program. If 0 is reached, the red indicator at the top of the VU meter lights up red and remains lit until you click Play again.

Besides watching for audio peaks that are above 0, you should also keep an eye on the average audio levels. The VU meters dance up and down quite a bit as you play the project — adjust the volume control so the average levels are between –12 and –18 on the VU meter.

Most of the time you adjust gain for individual tracks or clips. You can adjust the overall gain for an entire clip, or you can adjust it variously throughout a clip. To adjust gain for the whole clip at once, follow these steps:

1. **Select the audio clip in the Timeline and choose Clip⬄Audio Options⬄Audio Gain.**

   The Audio Gain dialog box appears.

2. **Click-and-drag left on the dB number to reduce gain, or click-and-drag right to increase gain.**

   Alternatively, click Normalize. Doing so automatically adjusts the gain to the highest possible level without creating distortion. To reset the clip to its original gain level, restore the gain value to 0 dB.

3. **Click OK to close the dialog box.**

In addition to adjusting the overall gain of an audio clip, you can also adjust gain at individual points within the clip. Here's how:

1. **Click the arrow on the left side of the audio track to expand its view in the Timeline.**

2. **Click-and-hold the Show Keyframes button on the track header and choose Show Clip Volume from the menu that appears.**

   A yellow line representing the clip's volume appears across the clip's waveform in the Timeline. This line is called the *volume rubberband*.

3. **Move the CTI to a spot in the Timeline where you want to start adjusting gain.**

4. **Click the clip you want to adjust to select it.**

5. **Click the Add/Remove Keyframe button.**

   A round keyframe appears along the yellow volume rubberband.

6. **Move the CTI to a new location in the clip and click the Add/Remove Keyframe button again.**

   Repeat this step to create additional keyframes.

7. **Click-and-drag on keyframes to move the volume rubberband.**

   Moving the rubberband up increases gain, and moving it down decreases gain. Your volume rubberband may end up looking like the one in Figure 13-4.

If you adjust the volume rubberbands upward on any audio clips, make sure you play the clip using the Audio Mixer and keep an eye on the Master VU meter. If the master level exceeds 0, you'll need to reduce gain a bit.

Show Keyframes   Volume rubberband

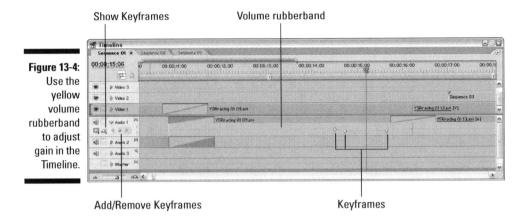

Figure 13-4:
Use the
yellow
volume
rubberband
to adjust
gain in the
Timeline.

Add/Remove Keyframes   Keyframes

Adjusting audio balance

Most audio clips have more than one channel. Stereo clips — the most common type — have left and right channels. Sounds in the left channel play out of the left speaker of a stereo system, and sounds in the right channel play out of the right speaker. (Surround sound adds even more channels, but I'll talk about that in the next section.)

You can also easily adjust the balance of mono or stereo clips using the Premiere Pro Audio Mixer. In a project with stereo audio, you see balance knobs in the Mixer as shown in Figure 13-5. Simply turn the balance knob left or right. If you turn the knob all the way to the left, audio is only sent to the left channel, coming only out of the left speaker on a system with stereo audio. Moving the audio from one channel to another is also referred to as *panning*. To adjust audio balance, follow these steps:

1. **Choose Touch from the Automation menu at the top of the track you want to pan in the Audio Mixer.**

2. **Start playing the Timeline.**

3. **Click-and-drag the balance knob in the Audio Mixer to adjust balance as the clip plays.**

   If you release the balance knob in Touch mode, the knob gradually adjusts itself back to the middle. In Figure 13-5, I have panned the audio to the left at the beginning of this clip because the motorcycle is entering the scene from the left.

Balance knob

Automation menu

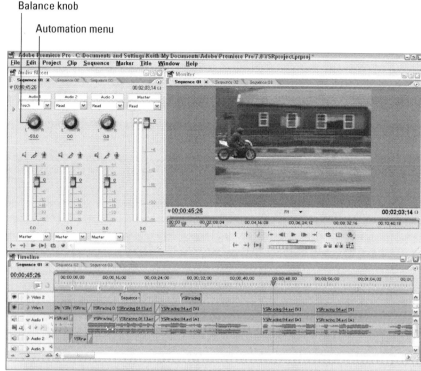

Figure 13-5:
Pan audio
using the
balance
knob in the
Audio
Mixer.

Panning 5.1 channel audio

One of the new features of Adobe Premiere Pro is the ability to use and mix
5.1 channel surround-sound audio. Surround sound is designed to immerse
the audience in the sounds of a scene by placing speakers all around the lis-
tener. Whereas stereo audio just has left and right channels, surround sound
has three front channels (left, center, right), two rear channels (left and
right), and a low-frequency channel (usually a subwoofer, the ".1" in *5.1*).

To work with 5.1 channel audio, your project must be created with 5.1 channel audio as the master audio format for the project. See Chapter 5 for more
on starting a new project. After your project is formatted for 5.1 channel
audio, you can edit audio that has been recorded in 5.1 channel format, or
you can pan mono and stereo tracks using the 5.1 channel balance control
(shown in Figure 13-6).

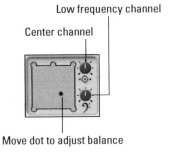

Low frequency channel

Center channel

Figure 13-6:
Surround
sound
balance can
be adjusted
dynamically
in Premiere
Pro.

Move dot to adjust balance

As you can see in Figure 13-6, the balance control is a box that represents the five main channels of surround-sound audio. To adjust balance, set the automation menu to Write and then click-and-drag the dot in the middle of the balance box toward one of the five channels. You can dynamically adjust balance by dragging the dot anywhere in the box. In Figure 13-6, you can see I've adjusted the balance slightly toward the right-rear channel.

Avoid adjusting balance too far toward the rear channels. If a viewer doesn't have rear speakers properly hooked up — a common malady in home theater systems — audio adjusted to the rear could be lost.

Using submix tracks

Another new feature of Premiere Pro is the availability of audio submix tracks. A submix track allows you to combine several different tracks in a sequence and apply edits or effects to all of those audio tracks at once. You can add a submix track to a sequence just like you would add any other video or audio track. Choose Sequence➪Add Tracks, and add one Audio Submix Track in the Add Tracks dialog box.

After you have created a submix track, sending tracks to the submix track is easy. Open the Audio Mixer and choose the submix track from the Output menu at the bottom of the Mixer. In Figure 13-7, I've sent Audio 1 and Audio 2 to the Submix 1 track. When you've sent tracks to the submix track, you can adjust volume, change balance, or apply audio effects to the submix track just as if it were any other audio track. Changes applied to the submix track then apply to all audio tracks assigned to that submix.

The audio format for a submix track should match the format for audio tracks that are sent to it. For example, send stereo tracks to a stereo submix track, and send 5.1 tracks to a 5.1 submix track. Effects and other changes might not work properly if the submix track contains mixed formats.

Figure 13-7:
Tracks
Audio 1 and
Audio 2
have been
assigned to
the Submix
1 track.

Using Audio Effects and Transitions

Adobe Premiere Pro comes with a pretty substantial collection of audio effects and transitions. Just like video effects and transitions, you can access audio effects and transitions by clicking the Effects tab in the Project window. If you don't see the Effects tab, choose Window⇨Effects. The following sections describe audio effects and transitions available in Premiere Pro.

Reviewing Premiere's audio effects

Premiere Pro comes with a wide variety of audio effects. Some of these effects can be used to make audio seem distorted or surreal; other effects simply help you repair problems in an audio track. Premiere Pro's audio effects live on the Effects tab, which you can reveal by choosing Window⇨Effects. Audio effects are divided into categories for 5.1, Stereo, and Mono format audio. Make sure you use an effect from a category that matches the format of the audio clip to which you are applying the effect. (For example, don't apply an effect from the Mono category to a 5.1 audio clip.) Audio effects offered in Premiere Pro include

- ✔ **Balance (Stereo only):** Controls balance within a stereo clip.
- ✔ **Bandpass:** Removes frequencies that fall outside a range you specify.
- ✔ **Bass:** Provides control over bass response in the clip.
- ✔ **Channel Volume (5.1 and Stereo only):** Allows you to control the volume of channels independently.

✔ **DeNoiser:** Removes unwanted background noise during quiet parts of the clip.

✔ **Delay:** Echoes the clip. Echoes the clip.

✔ **Dynamics:** Graphic controls that help you remove unwanted frequencies, balance the dynamic range of the clip, and reduce distortion.

✔ **EQ:** Adjusts audio tone much like a stereo equalizer.

✔ **Fill Left (Stereo only):** Moves the audio completely to the left channel.

✔ **Fill Right (Stereo only):** Moves the audio completely to the right channel.

✔ **Highpass:** Removes lower frequencies from the audio.

✔ **Invert:** Inverts all channels in the clip.

✔ **Lowpass:** Removes higher frequencies from the audio.

✔ **MultibandCompressor:** Compresses the dynamic range of the clip. This effect works similar to gain, but you can adjust lows without affecting highs, or vice versa.

✔ **Multitap Delay:** Provides a combination of advanced delays and rhythms. Each delay effect is called a *tap,* and you can uniquely control up to four taps with this effect.

✔ **Notch:** Removes sound at a frequency you specify. This effect can be used if the audio clip has a constant hum.

✔ **Parametric EQ:** Similar to the Equalize effect, but offering a bit more control.

✔ **PitchShifter:** Adjusts pitch in an audio clip.

✔ **Reverb:** Makes the audio sound as if it's being played in a large hall or room.

✔ **Swap Channels (Stereo only):** Swaps the left and right channels.

✔ **Treble:** Provides control over treble in the clip.

✔ **Volume:** Allows you to adjust volume with an effect rather than the Audio Mixer or the volume rubberbands.

A complete course on how to use each effect would take up nearly another whole book (each effect differs considerably from the others). Some general instructions are in order, however: To apply an audio effect to a clip, simply drag it from the Effects tab and drop it onto your audio clip in the Timeline. Depending on which filter you chose, you should be able to manipulate it using the Effect Controls tab in the Monitor window, or choose Window⇨Effect Controls. Make sure a clip is selected in the Timeline if you want to view its Effect Controls.

Using audio transitions

One of the most common reasons for adjusting gain on a clip (at least, in my experience) is to fade a clip in as it begins and fade it out as it ends. Fading sound in and out is usually barely perceptible to the viewer, but it takes a distinct "edge" off the transition as a loud noise starts or stops. And when you transition between video clips, fading the audio from the first clip out as the new clip fades in greatly improves the feel of the transition, even if the video portions of the clips do not fade in or out.

The process of fading between clips in or out has never been easier. Premiere Pro provides two audio transitions that you can apply to audio clips to quickly fade them in or out. If two clips are adjacent, the transition cross-fades the two clips. You can access the transitions under Audio Transitions on the Effects tab in the Project window (choose Window➪Effects if you don't see the Effects tab). You get two Cross Fade transitions:

- **Constant Gain:** Audio fades in or out at a constant, linear level.

- **Constant Power:** Audio fades in a manner that sounds linear to the human ear, although from a purely mathematical standpoint, it is not linear.

I use the Constant Power transition most, but you may want to experiment to get the best results for your projects. To apply a transition, simply drag-and-drop it from the Effects tab to the edge of a clip or a spot between clips. The transition appears as shown in Figure 13-8.

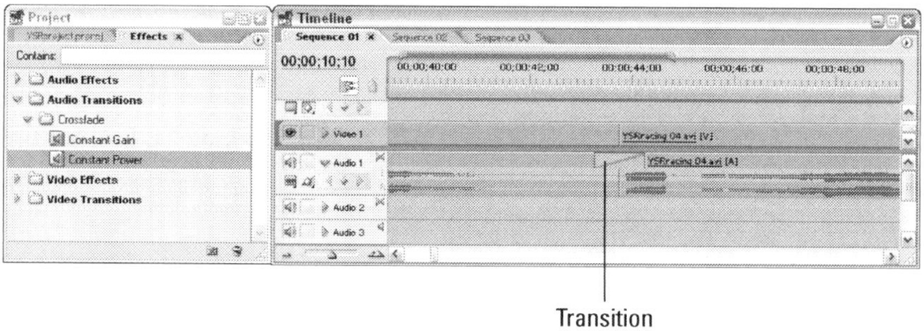

Figure 13-8:
Audio transitions make it easy to cross fade audio.

Transition

Chapter 14

Giving Credit with Titles

In This Chapter

▶ Titling your project in Premiere

▶ Creating, adding, and tweaking titles

▶ Adding graphics and animation to your titles

*I*n a rush to get to the pictures, folks who are new to video editing often overlook the importance of good audio. The same could also be said of titles — the subject of this chapter. Titles — the words that appear on-screen during a movie — are critically important in many different kinds of projects. Titles tell your audience the name of your movie, who made it, who starred in it, who paid for it, who made the titles, and who baked cookies for the cast. Titles can also clue the audience in to vital details — where the story takes place, what time it is, even what year it is — with minimum fuss. And of course, titles can reveal what the characters are saying if they're speaking a different language.

Adobe Premiere Pro includes a powerful titling tool called the Adobe Title Designer. This chapter shows you how to use this Adobe Title Designer to create on-screen words for your movie projects.

Creating Titles in Premiere

It's easy to think of titles as just words on the screen. But think of the effects, both forceful and subtle, that well-designed titles can have. Consider the *Star Wars* movies, which all begin with a black screen and the sentence, "A long time ago, in a galaxy far, far away . . . ." This simple title screen quickly and effectively sets the tone and tells the audience that the story is beginning. And then, of course, you get those scrolling words that float three-dimensionally off into space, immediately after that first title screen. A story floating through space is far more interesting than white text scrolling from the bottom to top of the screen, don't you think?

To begin creating titles for a project, open that project and choose File➪New➪Title. The Adobe Title Designer window appears, as shown in Figure 14-1. Notice also that a new menu called "Title" is added to the Premiere Pro menu bar. Before you begin actually creating text, however, I recommend that you spend some time setting up the view.

Setting up the Adobe Title Designer view

One of the first things you should do before creating titles is make sure that the Safe Title Margin is shown. To do so, choose Title➪View and make sure that Safe Title Margin has a check mark next to it. A thin green line showing the margin should appear in the title area. If you look closely you might also see a blue line slightly outside the green Safe Title Margin. The blue line is the Safe Action Margin. The Safe Action Margin is less important when designing titles because all of your titles should fall within the smaller box drawn by the Safe Title Margin.

The Safe Title and Safe Action Margins are especially important if you're producing a movie that will be viewed on TV screens. Most TVs *overscan* the image, which means that they allow some of the video image to be cut off at the edges of the screen. Some TVs overscan worse than others, but anything inside the Safe Title Margin should appear on just about any TV screen with a bit of room to spare. If you place titles outside that margin, you're taking a chance that some text may run off the screen and be unreadable. The Safe Action Margin is a bit bigger than the Safe Title Margin because readability is less important for action in the video image.

If you're creating a title to be superimposed over a video image, I recommend that you display the actual image in the Adobe Title Designer window as you work on the title. Doing so helps you decide exactly where to position the text.

To display a video image in the Adobe Title Designer, simply place a check mark next to the Show Video option, as shown in Figure 14-2. Video from your current sequence appears. You can move to a specific point in the sequence using several methods:

- ✔ Click (once) the timecode next to Show Video and then enter a specific timecode to which you want to jump.
- ✔ Click-and-drag left or right on the blue timecode next to Show Video. The video image jogs back and forth as you drag.
- ✔ Click the Sync to Timeline Timecode button (shown in Figure 14-2). This moves the video to the current location of the CTI in the Timeline.

In Figure 14-2, you can see I've moved to 00;00;06;15 in my Timeline.

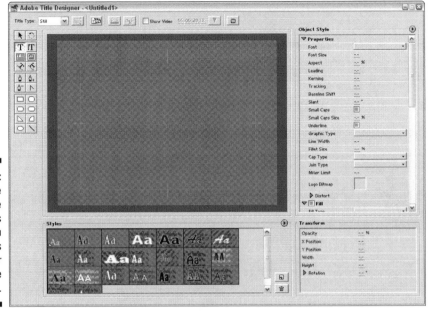

Figure 14-1:
The Adobe
Title
Designer is
where you
create titles
for your
movie
projects.

Current Timecode   Sync to Timeline Timecode

Show Video   Send Frame to External Monitor

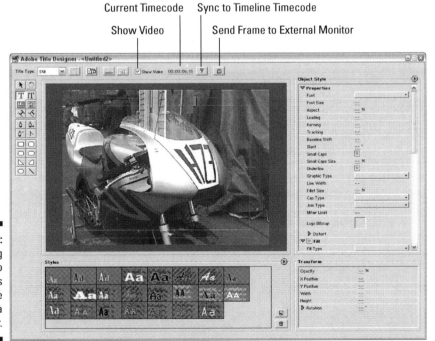

Figure 14-2:
Previewing
video
images
makes title
creation a
lot easier.

Creating text

After you have the Adobe Title Designer's view set up the way you like it, you can start adding text. From the toolbar on the left side of the Title Designer window, choose either the Horizontal or the Vertical text tool, and then click in the window and start typing. Your text appears on-screen. As you can see in Figure 14-3, the text probably doesn't look exactly the way you want it at first. To begin with, you probably want to move the text after you're done typing it. Click the Move tool and then click-and-drag the text box to a new location. Don't get too picky at this point; you'll probably move the text again later after you adjust some text attributes.

If you want long lines of text to automatically wrap to a new line when space runs out, open the Title menu from the Premiere Pro menu bar and click the Word Wrap option to place a check mark next to it.

Using title templates

Another — even simpler — way to start creating titles is to use one of Premiere's built-in title templates. Premiere Pro comes with hundreds of pre-designed templates that can save time when you're creating complete titles. To use a title template, click the Templates button in the Adobe Title Designer window. The Templates window appears, as shown in Figure 14-4.

If you want to use a template, it's best to make that decision before you start entering text for your titles. When you apply a template to a title, any text you've already entered is replaced by the stock placeholder text that comes with the template.

To preview a template, click it in the Templates list on the left, and then preview it in the upper-right corner of the Templates window. Many designs are available, so you may want to spend some time exploring them. If you scroll to the bottom of the list, you'll find folders containing elaborately designed titles that fit a variety of themes. For example, within the Professional folder, you'll find a subfolder called Medical. Here, you'll find a collection of titles that would work well in, say, an instructional video for medical topics. After you've chosen the title you want to use, click Apply in the Templates window. The Templates window closes and the template is applied to your title.

Setting text properties

Regardless of whether you use a template for your title, you'll probably want to adjust the attributes of the text in your titles to make them more to your liking. For example, you can pick a font that's consistent with the project's style (and is easy to read), pick a color that contrasts adequately with the background, adjust the size and scaling of the text, and more. To adjust text properties, click the text object once to select it, and then twirl down the arrow next to Properties in the Object Style menu.

Horizontal text

Move tool

Vertical text

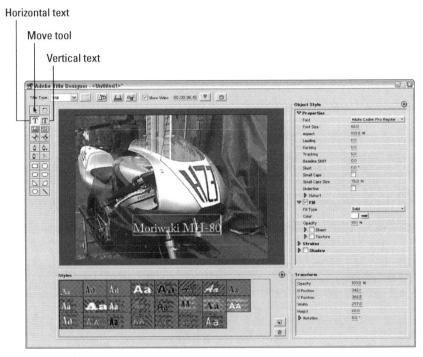

Figure 14-3:
Arrghh! Text
can be hard
to read
when you
first type it.

As you can see in Figure 14-5, many of the properties are numeric values. To change these, you can either click once and type a new value, or click-and-drag left or right to adjust the value with the mouse. Some properties — such as Font — have their own submenus. Click the box next to an item to open its submenu, and then choose an item from the submenu.

Figure 14-4:
Premiere
Pro comes
with
hundreds of
templates
for a variety
of title
styles.

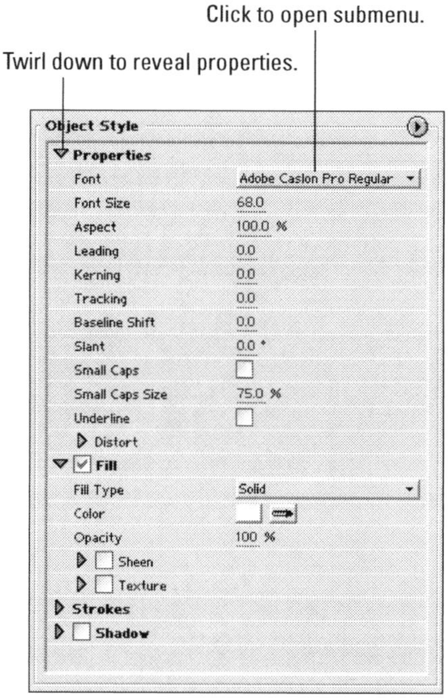

Click to open submenu.

Twirl down to reveal properties.

Figure 14-5:
Adjust text
attributes
using the
Object Style
menu on the
right side of
the Title
Designer
window.

When you've made your choices, click the arrow next to Properties to twirl the options back out of sight. Scroll down the list of items in the Object Style menu. You see a few general categories of properties to adjust, including the following:

✓ **Properties:** This is where you adjust general text properties such as font, size, and other typographic properties. For example, Leading adjusts the vertical spacing between lines of text, and Kerning fine-tunes the spacing between individual characters. The Distort subgroup of options lets you add vertical and horizontal distortions to your characters for that funhouse-mirror look.

✓ **Fill:** Here you set the color and pattern for the text. For basic text, you may want to choose "Solid" from the Fill Type menu. Gradient, bevel, and ghost patterns are also available. Choose text colors using color pickers, and adjust the opacity of the text or object. An object that is less than 100 percent opaque is slightly transparent.

✓ **Strokes:** Adjust the appearance of text on various "strokes" of the characters. Strokes in the Adobe Title Designer are basically just outlines or borders around text. This requires some experimentation to get just the right effect.

✓ **Shadow:** Use this group of options to apply a shadow to your text, as described in the next section.

Making effective titles

If you've ever worked in print or Web design, you know some of the general rules for text: Use dark text on light backgrounds; use serif typefaces for large bodies of text; don't use too many different typefaces on a page.

Video has some text rules too, although they differ considerably from print. One of the things you must take into consideration when creating text for video is the effect that interlacing has on your text. Interlacing on NTSC or PAL TV screens causes thin lines to flicker or crawl on-screen. To prevent this headache, make sure that all the lines in your text are thicker than 1 pixel. Also, avoid using serif typefaces in video, especially for smaller text. Serif typefaces — such as Times New Roman — have those extra little strokes at the ends of characters, while sans serif typefaces — like Arial — do not. Those little strokes in serif typefaces are often thin enough to cause interlacing flicker. The text you're reading right now uses a sans serif face,

while most of the text in the previous section uses a serif face. To be on the safe side, always carefully preview your titles on an external video monitor and check for flickering or other appearance problems.

Text color is another important consideration. In print and on the Web, dark text over a light background is usually best. Adequate contrast is still important, but in video, light text usually works better. The best possible combination for video is white text on a dark background. If the background is light or has mixed color, use shadows or graphics to create a dark background just for your titles.

Finally, *always* keep your titles inside the green Title Safe margin. Not only does this prevent text from running off the screen on TVs that badly overscan the image, but it also means that your text isn't running right up against the edge of the screen.

Shadowing text

If you want to apply a shadow to some text, Premiere's Title Designer provides a great deal of control. To apply a shadow to some text, first click the text in the Adobe Title Designer window to select it. In the Object Style menu, scroll the list and place a check mark next to Shadow. Then twirl down the arrow and adjust these attributes of the shadow:

- ✔ **Color:** Shadows are usually dark. Click the color swatch to open the color picker and choose a color.

- ✔ **Opacity:** Adjust this to make the shadow somewhat transparent. Some transparency makes the shadow seem more realistic.

- ✔ **Angle:** Adjust this from 0 to 360 degrees to precisely set the angle of the shadow. The default angle is 273 degrees.

- ✔ **Distance:** The distance should be greater than 0, but it shouldn't be so great that the text is blurry and difficult to read.

✔ **Size:** Adjust the size of the image, but again the shadow shouldn't over-power the text in front.

✔ **Spread:** Use this to soften or sharpen the shadow's appearance.

A shadow can help offset text from the video image somewhat, especially if the title appears over a light or mixed-color background.

Using styles

If a title template seems too fancy and manually adjusting title attributes is too time-consuming, try using one of the Adobe Title Designer's predesigned styles. More than 20 styles are available in the Styles menu at the bottom of the Title Designer window. To apply a style to some text that you have already typed, simply click the text object to select it, and then click a style from the list at the bottom of the Title Designer window. The style is automatically applied to the text.

Styles can be thought of as starting points. Even if one of the styles doesn't exactly match what you need, choosing one that is close can still save you a lot of time. After you've applied the style, you can always fine-tune attributes such as color, size, and shadows.

Orienting text

Text can be oriented in a variety of ways using the Adobe Title Designer. You've already seen horizontal text, and that's what you're likeliest to use. But you can change the orientation of your text as well. Text can appear verti-cally on the screen, or on an angle or curve that you define. On the Title Designer toolbar, you'll notice several basic text tools:

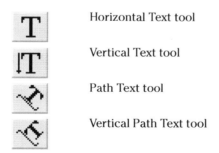

Horizontal Text tool

Vertical Text tool

Path Text tool

Vertical Path Text tool

The Horizontal and Vertical Text tools are pretty self-explanatory, so I'll assume you can figure those out for now. The Path Text tools are a bit trickier because they allow you to define the path on which your text appears. To use the Path Text tool or Vertical Path Text tool:

1. **Click the Path Text tool to select it.**

2. **Move the mouse pointer over the spot where you want the text to *begin*.**

3. **Click and drag the mouse along an angle.**

   A text baseline appears with control points at both ends, as shown in Figure 14-6. The angle described by the baseline is the angle that the characters follow at the beginning of the text.

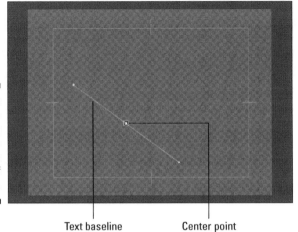

Figure 14-6:
Click-and-drag along the angle for the beginning of your text.

Text baseline   Center point

4. **Move the mouse pointer over the spot where you want the text to *end*.**

5. **Click-and-drag the mouse along another angle.**

   As before, a baseline with control points appears. The angle described by this second baseline is the angle the characters assume at the end of the text. You'll also notice that a curve will appear to connect the two baselines as shown in Figure 14-7. This curve shows the actual path that your text will follow.

6. **Begin typing some text.**

   The text should appear along the angle you defined. Adjust text properties as needed.

You may find that you need to move or resize the text. To do so, select the Move tool and drag the text object to a new location. Use the handles at the corners of the text object to resize it and change the angle. After you've fine-tuned the text position and properties, your finished result might look similar to Figure 14-8. In the figure, I've curved some text so it curves around an object in the video image.

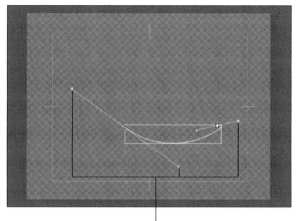

Figure 14-7:
A curving
path shows
the angle
that your
text will
follow.

Drag adjustment handles to change curve.

Animating text

Titles are often animated in video productions. Text can fly onto the screen, crawl along the bottom like a stock ticker, or scroll from bottom to top as you roll the credits at the end of your movie. You can animate text using one of two methods:

✔ Animate the title clip in the Timeline using Premiere Pro's animation tools. (For more on animating titles and other clips in the Timeline, see Chapter 11.)

✔ Use the animation tools built into the Adobe Title Designer.

Figure 14-8:
Text can be
created
along a
curve that
you define.

The second method is the less complex of the two, so it's a good general choice. To create animated titles using the Adobe Title Designer, follow these steps:

1. **In Premiere, choose File➪New➪Title.**

2. **In the Title Type menu at the top of the Title Designer window, choose Roll or Crawl.**

   Rolling titles roll from the bottom to the top of the screen, and crawling titles crawl from right to left.

3. **Create text objects for your titles.**

   If you're creating a rolling title, you can scroll down in the title area to add more titles. If you're creating a crawling title, you can scroll right.

4. **Open the Title menu on the Premiere menu bar and choose Roll/Crawl Options.**

   The Roll/Crawl Options dialog box appears.

5. **If you want the rolling or crawling title to begin off-screen, select the Start Off Screen option. If you want the title to end out of view, choose the End Off Screen option.**

6. **If you want the title to remain static for a while before it starts to roll or crawl, enter a time in frames in the Pre-Roll field.**

   If you enter 15 in the Pre-Roll field, the title appears on-screen for 15 frames before it starts to roll or crawl off the screen. This field is not available if you choose the Start Off Screen option.

7. **If you want the title to roll or crawl on-screen and then stop, enter a time in the Post-Roll field.**

   Like Pre-Roll, Post-Roll is measured in frames.

8. **If you want the title to gradually increase speed as it starts to move or gradually decrease as it stops, enter times in the Ease-In and Ease-Out fields.**

   Like Pre-Roll and Post-Roll, Ease-In and Ease-Out are expressed in frames. If you enter an Ease-In time of 15 frames, the title starts moving slowly and gradually builds up to full speed within 15 frames.

9. **Click OK when you're done.**

   Doing so closes the Roll/Crawl Options dialog box.

Although you can scroll in the work area of the Adobe Title Designer to see your entire title, you cannot preview the actual roll or crawl in the Title Designer. This is because Premiere Pro dynamically adjusts the speed of the roll or crawl based on the length of the clip in the Timeline. The entire title rolls or crawls past, whether you have the title set to play for five seconds or five minutes in the Timeline. Obviously, the more time you give the title to play, the slower it rolls by.

Adding graphics to titles

Besides text, Adobe's Title Designer also enables you to draw some basic graphics and shapes in your titles. The drawing tools can serve a variety of useful purposes including

- ✔ Draw a line under some text, thus making the text stand out a bit more on the screen. This is often done when identifying a speaker or subject on-screen (see Figure 14-9).
- ✔ A solid-colored box behind your text can help when the colors in the video image make it difficult to create adequate contrast between words and the background image.

The drawing tools can be found in the toolbar of the Title Designer window. Their functions are pretty self-explanatory; simply click a tool and then click-and-drag the shape on-screen. Use the Object Style menu to adjust colors and other attributes of the objects you draw. In Figure 14-9, for example, I've drawn a line underneath a row of text. To create the line, I actually drew a narrow rectangle and then changed the fill color to the desired color (green, though you can't see that in the monochrome image shown here).

Figure 14-9:
Subtle graphics can greatly improve the readability of text.

You may want to adjust several other attributes of your graphics as well. When you select a graphic object using the Move tool, the Title menu (located up on the main Premiere menu bar) provides access to a couple of important options:

- ✔ **Arrange:** If you want some objects in a title to overlap other objects (say, for example, text appearing over a background graphic), you'll need control over which objects are arranged on top of others. To move an item forward or back relative to other objects in the title, select that item and choose Title➪Arrange and select an option from the submenu that appears. In Figure 14-9, I created a black rounded-rectangle background graphic for the text and chose Send to Back from the Arrange menu to ensure that the graphic was behind everything else in the title.

- ✔ **Opacity:** By default, all graphics you create in a title are opaque, which means you can't see through them. You can reduce the opacity of graphic objects, thereby making them more transparent. To adjust opacity, select a graphic object and choose Title➪Transform➪Opacity. Enter a percentage less than 100 to make the object less opaque. In Figure 14-9, I placed a black oval behind the text. An opaque black oval looked like a heavy black blob — but with its opacity reduced to 50 percent, the background oval gained some subtlety. Now it still helps the text stand out, but it doesn't completely blot out the action going on behind it.

Adding Titles to Your Project

After you have created titles in the Adobe Title Designer, adding them to your project is pretty simple. When you're done creating a title, choose File➪Save to name and save the title as a file on your hard drive. The title then appears in your Project window and resides in whatever bin happened to be open when you saved the title. To help keep things organized, I recommend that you create a special bin just for titles (call it "Titles" or something similarly creative), and store all your titles there.

Adding titles to a sequence

To add a title to a project, you basically just drag it from the Project window to a video track on the Timeline. I recommend that you create a separate track in each sequence specifically for titles. To add a title to a sequence, follow these steps:

1. **Create a new video track specifically for titles.**

   To do so, choose Sequence➪Add Tracks. In the Add Tracks dialog box, add one video track. Click OK to close the Add Tracks dialog box.

2. **Right-click the name of your new track and choose Rename from the menu that appears.**

   Type a new name for the track ("Titles" should work fine).

3. **Drag the title from the Project window and drop it on the title track in your sequence, as shown in Figure 14-10.**

   As with still graphics and many other elements, the default duration for a title is five seconds.

4. **Fine-tune your title to fit the needs of your project.**

   - **To change the duration of your title:** Click-and-drag the edge of the title clip to increase or decrease its duration.

   - **To fade a title in or out:** Expand the title track and use the Opacity handles to control opacity. (See Chapter 11 for more on working with clip opacity.)

Importing titles from other programs

Adobe's Title Designer isn't your only option for creating titles for Premiere Pro projects. Many other software publishers offer programs that do nothing but generate titles. And of course, many graphics and illustration programs offer elaborate ways to create titles as well. Some designers like to create titles in Adobe Illustrator or Photoshop and then import their creations into Premiere. This is fine, but for best results, be sure to define any areas of the file that you don't want to show up on-screen (say, the background) as transparent. In Photoshop, for example, a title file would probably have two layers:

✔ **Background:** This layer is transparent.

✔ **Layer 1:** This layer has the actual title.

Save the file as a Photoshop (.PSD) document, and then import that document directly into Premiere Pro. When you're asked which layers you want to import, choose Merged Layers. You can then place the imported file in a sequence just like any other still clip. The transparent portions of the Photoshop image remain transparent in Premiere Pro.

Drag title from here.   Title overlays video clip.

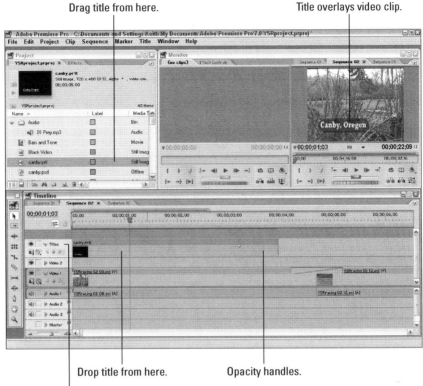

Figure 14-10:
Titles can
be added
to the
Timeline and
manipu-
lated, much
like any
other clip.

Drop title from here.   Opacity handles.

Create a title track.

Previewing titles

Previewing your titles is critical; presenting a movie with a half-obscured (or otherwise mangled) title is like slipping on a banana peel right before you want to quote Shakespeare. A word to the wise: Preview the timing of the appearance and disappearance of the titles, and review the positioning of your titles as action takes place behind the text. Make sure that the action in the video clip doesn't conflict with or obscure your titles while they are on-screen. Also double-check to make sure your titles are inside the safe margins as shown in Figure 14-11.

Titles that come from the Adobe Title Designer are generated in much the same way that black video or bars and tone are generated — automatically. Because of this, titles must be rendered before you can export the project. To render your titles in a sequence, choose Sequence⇨Render Work Area. Fortunately, titles render pretty quickly. After a few adjustments (and/or a few moments to gaze admiringly at your work), you can rest assured that your movie makes a competent entrance.

Make sure titles stay within safe margins.

Figure 14-11:
Preview
your titles
carefully.

Click to view safe margins.

Part IV
Wrapping Up Your Project

The 5th Wave   By Rich Tennant

©RICHTENNANT

THE LEVINES EDIT THEIR AFRICAN
SAFARI VIDEO

"Do you think the 'Hidden Rhino' clip should
come before or after the 'Waving Hello'
video clip?"

In this part . . .

Any chef will tell you that presentation is key to the success of any fine meal. And so it is with movie projects. When you're done editing your movie, you must prepare it for distribution, whether your audience is a few friends and family on the Internet, or a local broadcast outlet.

This part shows you how to wrap up your project and get it ready for distribution. Using what's here, you finalize your project and then distribute it on the Web, on tape, and on DVD.

Chapter 15

Finalizing the Project

I don't know about you, but I have a really hard time finishing a movie project. Some clip always lasts a few frames too long, or an effect keyframe isn't in exactly the right spot, or a title font isn't exactly what I wanted. There's always *something* — no matter how miniscule — that could be improved upon. Moviemaking is like that. But at some point, you have to give up tweaking your masterpiece and decide that it is "good enough."

Before you can actually stick a fork in your movie and call it done, you have a few tasks to do to finalize the movie and get it ready for output. You should sit back and preview the whole thing, of course, and also add elements to the beginning and end of the movie to prepare it for broadcast or delivery. Finally, you need to make sure that the project is rendered and ready for output. This chapter helps you put the finishing touches on your project.

Previewing the Timeline

I could start and end this section by simply telling you to click Play on the Program side of the Monitor to preview the current sequence. As an "oh-by-the-way," I could also mention the effects and edits may need to be *rendered* before they will play properly, although (thanks to the powerful real-time features of Adobe Premiere Pro) rendering usually isn't necessary unless your computer is below the "recommended" system specifications detailed in Chapter 2. Any portion of a sequence that has to be rendered — but isn't yet — shows a red line under the Work Area bar, as shown in Figure 15-1. A green line means the section needed to be rendered but you already rendered it. To render the unrendered portions of the Timeline, choose Sequence⇨Render Work Area (or just press the Enter key on your keyboard).

Work Area bar.   Red bars indicate you must render.

Figure 15-1:
The Work
Area bar at
the top
of each
sequence
shows you
whether
the project
must be
rendered.

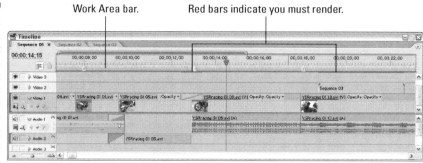

Even if your computer seems to have no trouble playing effects, transitions, and other edits in real time, those edits will still need to be rendered before the movie can actually be output to tape, DVD, or a file.

Casting a critical eye upon your project

Of course, there's more to previewing your project than simply rendering a sequence and clicking Play. Consider carefully what you are actually previewing when you play a sequence. Here are some ways to get the most out of previewing your project:

- **Watch the whole program from start to finish.** You may be tempted to periodically stop playback, reverse, and repeat sections, perhaps even make tweaks to the program as you run it. This is fine, but to get a really good "feeling" for the flow of the project, watch the whole thing from start to finish — just as your audience will. Keep a notepad handy and jot down quick notes if you must.

- **Watch the program on an external television monitor.** If you plan to export your movie to tape, previewing on an external monitor is crucial. (See the next section in this chapter for a more detailed explanation.)

- **Have trusted third parties review the project.** Moviemakers and writers are often too close to their creations to be totally objective; an "outside" point of view can help a lot. Though I worked hard to write this book (for example), my work was reviewed by various editors and their feedback was invaluable. Movie projects benefit from a similar review process. Even if you want to maintain strict creative control over your project, feedback from people who were not involved with creating it can help you see it afresh.

Previewing on an external monitor

Even if you expand Premiere Pro's Monitor window to a really big size, it still probably won't be as large as some of the displays that your audience is likely to use. A larger external monitor reveals camera movements and other flaws that might not be obvious on your computer screen. But even more important is color: Your computer monitor uses the RGB (red-green-blue) color space to generate color, but television screens generate colors differently. Properly previewing the colors of your project on a computer monitor is virtually impossible.

How you connect an external TV monitor to your computer varies depending on your hardware. If you have a video card with analog outputs, you should be able to connect your external monitor to those outputs. Some newer, high-quality video decks also have FireWire ports, which should allow you to connect a video deck directly to your computer. You can then connect a video monitor to the analog outputs on the video deck. If you're really on a tight budget, you could connect your digital camcorder to your FireWire port, set the camera to VTR mode, and connect a monitor to the analog outputs on your camcorder. Sure, you'll have a mess of cables strewn all over the place, but this method should still be effective.

If you preview your project on an external DV device, the preview playback in the Monitor window might not play back at full quality.

After you have your hardware set up, make sure Premiere Pro is configured to play out to your external monitor. Here's how to check:

1. **In your project, choose Project⇨Project Settings⇨General.**

   The General page of the Project Settings dialog box appears.

2. **Click the Playback Settings button.**

   The Playback Options dialog box opens, as shown in Figure 15-2.

3. **If your monitor is connected to a FireWire port on your computer, place a check mark next to Play Video on DV Hardware (under Video Playback).**

4. **Under Audio Playback, choose whether you want to play audio on your DV Hardware or Audio Hardware.**

   This setting only applies to video previews as you play a sequence to preview it. In Figure 15-2, I have chosen to play audio out to the Audio Hardware on my computer. I chose this because I don't have good audio speakers hooked up to my external DV hardware, but I do have good speakers on my computer.

5. **Choose whether you want real-time effects to play out to DV hardware or only on your desktop.**

   If you have some DV hardware hooked up to your computer and turned on, you'll notice that transitions and effects will play on the external monitor during previews, even though they haven't been rendered. Behold the real-time playback power of Premiere Pro! If real-time effects don't seem to play smoothly on your external monitor, choose the Desktop Only option.

6. **Choose an audio playback option under Export to Tape.**

   When I get to the point where I'm going to export my movie to tape, I've already previewed the audio enough times to know that it sounds good. Thus, in Figure 15-2, you can see that I have chosen to Play Audio on DV Hardware during export. Only choose the Audio Hardware option if you will be recording your audio separately.

7. **When you're done, click OK twice to close the two settings dialog boxes.**

Previewing video with your camcorder

If you aren't able or don't feel like connecting an external monitor to your computer, you could simply use your camcorder. (It's better than nothing!) However, your camcorder is not the ideal preview monitor for some very important reasons: First of all (and most obviously), the displays on camcorders are usually very small. Small details and problems may not show up very well on the tiny LCD screen or viewfinder of your camcorder.

Another problem with previewing video on a camcorder that people don't often consider is *interlacing*. If you'll be exporting your movie to videotape or DVD, you can assume that most of your audience will be watching the movie on standard TV screens. NTSC and PAL television displays are interlaced, meaning that each frame is drawn in two consecutive passes or *fields*. Each field contains every other horizontal resolution line. Interlacing is necessary, but it can create some anomalies in your video. Most of these anomalies involve thin lines. If a

subject on-screen is wearing a pinstriped shirt, the pinstripes will appear to crawl or waver on the screen. This is called a moiré pattern. Also, if you have titles or graphics on-screen with very thin lines, those lines may flicker annoyingly on a TV screen.

What do moiré patterns and interlacing flicker have to do with your camcorder? If you preview video on your camcorder's LCD screen, you probably won't see them. This is because the LCD screens on most camcorders are *progressively scanned* (they aren't interlaced, and all resolution lines are drawn in a single pass). Your video might have serious problems that simply won't show up on your progressive-scanning LCD monitor. The small viewfinder on your camcorder *might* be interlaced (check your camcorder's documentation), so you could try previewing the video through that — but if possible, I still recommend that you use a real TV as your external monitor.

Analog playback equipment varies greatly, so you should check the documentation for your video card and devices for specific information on video playback.

Figure 15-2:
Use the DV
Playback
Options
dialog box
to control
playback
options
for your
external
monitor.

Adding Final Video Elements

Movies and videos usually have a few elements that you may take for granted if you've never worked with professional video before. Some elements are tools that broadcast engineers normally use to adjust video equipment. These include counting leaders and color bars and tone. A third element that we'll discuss in the following sections seems like nothing at all: black video.

Creating a leader

Have you ever seen one of those spinning countdowns at the beginning of a video program? It's called a *counting leader* and is used by video engineers to ensure that the playback speed is correct and that audio and video are synchronized. The leader counts down from eight, and when it reaches two, a blip sounds. This blip helps the engineer synchronize the audio with the video. If your project is for use in broadcast or another professional environment and you will be delivering it on videotape, it should have a counting leader at the beginning of the tape.

Premiere can generate a universal counting leader. It is 11 seconds long and must be placed in the Timeline. Ideally, you should plan ahead and leave 11 seconds open at the beginning of the Timeline, although it is possible to insert that time later. To create a counting leader:

   1. **In your project, choose File⇨New⇨Universal Counting Leader.**

      Alternatively, you can click the New Item button in the Project window and choose Universal Counting Leader in the dialog box that appears.

   2. **Review the settings in the Universal Counting Leader Setup dialog box.**

      In general, I recommend that you maintain the default colors and settings unless you are just creating the leader because you think it looks cool and you'd like to use some custom colors.

      You see two audio options in the Counting Leader dialog box. The first one — Cue Blip on 2 — you should leave enabled unless you are not concerned about audio synchronization.

      Alternatively, if you're *really* concerned about synchronization, enable the Cue Blip at all Second Starts option. Doing so creates a blip at the beginning of each second during the countdown.

   3. **Click OK to close the dialog box.**

      The counting leader is generated, appearing in the Project window when it's ready.

   4. **If you have an open block of 11 seconds or more at the beginning of your sequence, simply drag the Universal Counting Leader from the Project window and drop it into the sequence.**

If you do *not* have an open 11-second block to accept the counting leader, make one. Follow these steps:

   1. **Press Ctrl+A to select all clips in the current sequence.**

      All clips in all tracks of the current sequence should now be selected.

   2. **Click the Select tool in the Premiere Pro toolbar to make sure it is the active tool.**

      The Select tool looks like an arrow and is at the top of the Premiere Pro toolbar. See Chapter 8 for more on working with the tools in the Premiere Pro toolbar.

   3. **Drag the selection to the right in the sequence so that slightly more than 11 seconds of blank space is available at the beginning of the project.**

   4. **Drag the Universal Counting Leader from the Project window and drop it on Track 1, as shown in Figure 15-3.**

   5. **If a blank space appears between the counting leader and the first clip in the Timeline (and it probably will), click the space to select it and then choose Timeline⇨Ripple Delete.**

Your project will now have an 11-second counting leader at the beginning. You'll probably have to render your entire Timeline again to create all new preview files. You should play through the whole Timeline to ensure that all of the clips still play correctly.

Drag leader from here.   Universal Counting Leader.

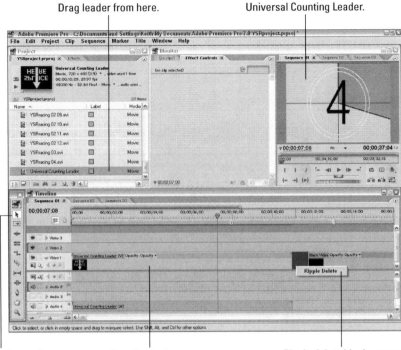

Figure 15-3:
Insert the
11-second
Universal
Counting
Leader
at the
beginning of
your project.

Select tool.   Drop leader here.   Ripple delete blank space.

Adding bars and tone to the project

Two more important movie elements — especially if you plan to export to a professional broadcast environment — are color bars and a 1 kHz tone. The pattern for color bars, shown in Figure 15-4, is standardized by the Society for Motion Picture and Television Engineers (SMPTE) and can be used to calibrate the colors on a TV monitor. The 1 kHz tone serves to calibrate audio levels.

To generate bars and tone, choose File⇨New⇨Bars and Tone. A five-second long Bars and Tone clip now appears in the Project window. As with the Universal Counting Leader described in the previous section, you can drag the Bars and Tone clip to an empty space at the beginning of a sequence.

The bars and tone don't necessarily need to appear for long, although you should consult with the video engineers at the broadcast facility or production house to find out exactly what they want. In some cases, they may only need a single frame of bars and tone, but in other cases, they may want up to 30 seconds of bars and tone at the beginning of the tape.

Color

Tint

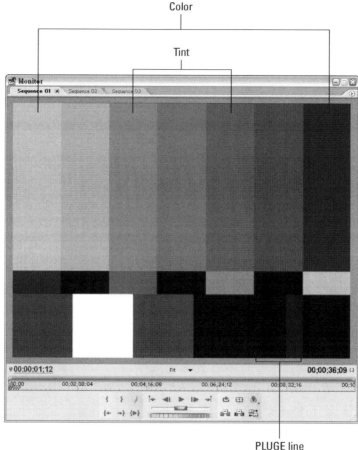

PLUGE line

Figure 15-4:
SMPTE
color bars
are used to
calibrate the
colors on
video
monitors.

Generating black video

Let's talk about nothing for a moment, shall we? By "nothing," I mean *black video* — as in "fade to black." Black video is a surprisingly important element for almost any movie project, often overlooked precisely because it seems like there's, well, nothing to overlook. Black video actually serves several important purposes:

✔ At the beginning of a movie, a stretch of black video gives the viewer a chance to get comfortable or "in the mood" after pressing Play. If the movie starts immediately once Play is pressed, the perception of the movie can be abrupt and unsettling for the viewer.

✔ At the end of the movie, black video gives the viewer some cushion space to press Stop after the credits stop rolling but before the static at the end of the tape starts. Without a bit of black video at the end of the program, that static could put someone's eye out if they're not expecting it (well, maybe it won't be *that* drastic, but you get the idea).

✔ Black video provides splicing room at the beginning of a tape. If you plan to distribute your movie on videotapes, remember that one of the most common mechanical failures on VHS tapes is the tape snapping at the beginning of the reel during rewind. This breakage can be repaired using a razor blade and some sticky tape, but some tape from the beginning of the reel is usually cut off. It would be better if a few seconds of black video were cut rather than the first few seconds of your program. If you're outputting for VHS tape, I recommend at least 60 seconds of black video at the beginning of the tape.

Like Bars and Tone or a Universal Counting Leader, black video can be generated quickly in the Project window. Choose File⇨New⇨Black Video. A five-second black video clip appears in the Project window. To change the duration of the Black Video clip, select it in the Project window and choose Clip⇨Speed/Duration. The Clip Speed/Duration dialog box appears as shown in Figure 15-5. As you can see in the figure, I have changed the duration of my Black Video clip to 45 seconds.

Calibrating color with color bars

If you have an external video monitor, you can use color bars to calibrate it. Start by playing the color bars out to the monitor, and then pause playback so that the color bars remain. Next, turn the Color knob on the monitor all the way down and take a look at the PLUGE line (see Figure 15-4). You should see three different shades of black in the PLUGE line. Adjust the brightness knob on the monitor until the middle shade and the left shade appear to be the same. Now adjust the contrast knob up, and then turn it gradually down until the right shade in the PLUGE line is barely visible.

Now you are ready to adjust the color. If your monitor has a Blue Only setting (check the monitor's control panel), turn it on. Otherwise you have to use a blue filter, which is available at many photo-supply vendors. The blue filter should be big enough to fit over the front of the monitor's screen. Adjust the Tint (or Hue) knob until the third bars from the left and right seem to match with the small bars just under them. Then adjust the Color knob so the outermost bars seem to match the small bars just under them. Turn off the Blue Only setting, and your colors are calibrated. Well done!

Figure 15-5:
Use the Clip
Speed/
Duration
dialog box
to change
the duration
of your
black video
clip.

Exporting Audio

We usually think of Adobe Premiere Pro as a video-editing program, but it can also edit and export audio. You can export audio in several different formats, including QuickTime, MP3, RealAudio, Windows waveform (WAV), and others. The simplest way to export audio from Premiere is to choose File↔Export↔ Audio. The Export Audio dialog box appears. Scroll down the Summary box to see the current export settings. The default audio-export format is Windows Waveform. If you don't like the default, click Settings and choose a different format.

Of the various formats available, I like MP3 the best because it can be played on almost any computer — as well as on countless MP3 player devices. To export an audio clip directly from Premiere as MP3, follow these steps:

1. **Select the clip in the Project window or Timeline that you want to export.**

2. **Choose File↔Export↔Audio.**

   The Export Audio dialog box appears.

3. **Click Settings.**

   The Export Audio Settings dialog box appears.

4. **Make sure that Windows Waveform is selected in the File Type menu.**

5. **Select the desired export range in the Range menu.**

   If you're exporting a clip from the Project window, you'll probably want to choose Entire Clip. Alternatively, you can export just the area between In and Out points if you have set any. If you're exporting from the Time-line, you can export the Entire Sequence or just the range covered by the Work Area Bar.

6. **Click Audio on the left side of the Export Audio Settings dialog box to reveal Audio settings.**

7. **Choose MPEG Layer-3 from the Compressor menu.**

8. **Choose additional quality settings in the Sample Rate, Sample Type, Channels, and Interleave menus.**

   Remember, higher-quality audio will produce larger file sizes.

9. **Click OK to close the Export Audio Settings dialog box.**

10. **Choose a name and location for the file and click Save.**

    The MP3 file is exported by Premiere Pro.

As I mentioned above, you can export audio in various other formats as well, including RealAudio and Windows Media Audio. (See Chapter 16 for more on exporting in the RealAudio and Windows Media formats.)

Exporting Still Images

Premiere Pro enables you to export still graphics from your movies, which can be handy for a variety of reasons. For example, you may want to display some stills from the movie on a promotional Web page. Just keep in mind that stills extracted from video are of much lower quality than stills shot with a conventional still camera (film or digital).

If you want poster-quality promotional shots of your movie, bring a high-quality still camera along with you during a video shoot — and use it to take some pictures of the scenes or subjects in the movie.

To export a still image from Premiere Pro, follow these steps:

1. **Move the CTI in the Timeline to the exact frame that you want to export.**

2. **Choose File➪Export➪Frame.**

   The Export Frame dialog box appears.

3. **Click Settings to open the Export Frame Settings dialog box.**

4. **Choose an export format from the File Type menu.**

   The available export formats for still frames are Windows Bitmap, Compuserve GIF, Targa, and TIFF. Bitmap or TIFF will provide the highest quality, but GIF is more Web-friendly. Export to Bitmap or TIFF if you plan to edit the still graphic further in a graphics program such as Adobe Photoshop.

5. **Click OK.**

6. **Choose a location and name the file, and then click Save.**

   The still image is saved.

You should edit any still images exported from video, especially if the image comes from interlaced video. Fast-moving objects in the image may have interlacing jaggies, which are horizontal distortions of the image caused by interlacing, and if the video came from a rectangular-pixel video image, it appears distorted on computer screens. (Check out Chapter 20, where I show you how to correct these problems using Adobe Photoshop.)

Chapter 16

Sending Your Project to the World Wide Web

In This Chapter

▶ Using the Web as your screening room

▶ Choosing a player program

▶ Exporting movies for online consumption

1 don't know about you, but I have so much fun working on movie projects in Adobe Premiere Pro that I almost forget that other people might want to see my work. After all, sharing your movies is one of the main reasons for editing them in the first place, right?

You can share your completed movies with the world in many different ways. This chapter shows you how to share your movie projects in the online world of the Internet. I help you identify some of the special problems involved with putting movies online, I help you choose a player program for your movies, and I show you how to export your movies in a variety of Web-friendly formats using the Adobe Media Encoder.

Introducing the World's Largest Screening Room

It's hard to believe, but the World Wide Web has been with us for over ten years now. As for the Internet (of which the World Wide Web is a part), in a few years, it will reach middle age. The good folks who built the foundations of the online world envisioned it as an efficient global information exchange, though I doubt they envisioned folks like you and me exchanging full-motion video online. Video, and especially streaming video, is at odds with the fundamental design of the Internet for two key reasons:

✔ **Bandwidth:** Most Internet users still have slow dial-up connections. In the United States (for example), over two-thirds of all Internet users were still using dial-up connections in mid-2003. That's potentially a problem because video files tend to be large — so large that even broadband users still can't watch full broadcast-quality video over the Internet. For most of us, many video files — even those with drastically reduced quality — are simply too big to download in a reasonable amount of time.

✔ **Packet delivery:** Data is transmitted over the Internet in packets rather than in steady streams. This makes data transfer over the Internet reliable, but not fast.

Data is broken down into packets before being transmitted over the Internet. These packets can travel over many different pathways to the destination, where they are reassembled in the correct order to form a Web page, e-mail message, or any other file that is shared online. Compare this to, say, a radio or television broadcast where data is transmitted in a continuous wave. Packet delivery is very reliable because it does not require a single unbroken connection between the sender and the receiver. Confused? Imagine you want to give your phone number to someone across a crowded room. You could try yelling across the room (a broadcast) but because of all the other noise, the other person might miss a number or two. A more reliable method would be to write your phone number on a piece of paper and send it via messenger to the other person. The paper method would be slower, but at least you know the recipient will get the correct phone number.

So what's the point of all this technical discussion about bandwidth and packets? I bring it up because you must be aware of the potential problems before you start sharing video over the Web. Video for the Web must be highly compressed, the frame size must be reduced, and you must accept some sacrifices in quality.

Video can be distributed over the Internet in one of two ways:

✔ **Download:** Users download the entire movie file before it can be viewed.

✔ **Stream:** The movie plays as it downloads to the user's machine. Some of the video is *buffered* (portions of the file are temporarily stored on the user's hard drive) to provide uninterrupted playback. The three predominant formats for streaming video are QuickTime Streaming, RealMedia, and Windows Media Streaming Video. In each case, special server software is required to host streaming media.

Regardless of which distribution method you choose, the export process for the movie from Adobe Premiere Pro is still the same. You export the movie as a file that resides on your hard drive. Whether that file is later streamed is determined by whether you use streaming server software on your Web server.

If possible, I recommend that you produce several different versions of your movie for the Web. Produce a lower-quality movie for people on slow dial-up connections, and a higher-quality movie for folks with broadband access. You may also want to offer versions for several different players. For example, you could offer a RealMedia version and a Windows Media version. Let's face it, some people are very touchy about using software from certain companies. In practical terms, offering your movie in only one format is sure to limit the size of your audience.

Selecting a Player

Distributing your movie digitally actually means distributing it as a file — so you have to make sure your intended audience can open that file. If you're distributing on a DVD, this usually isn't a problem; DVD players have their own built-in software for playing movies. But if you're distributing a movie file over the Internet, your audience has to have the right program to play your movie. As the moviemaker, you have two basic choices:

✔ Assume that your audience already has the necessary software installed.

✔ Direct your audience to download the necessary software from a Web site.

The following sections describe some common software players for your movies.

QuickTime

Apple QuickTime (depicted in Figure 16-1) is an almost-ubiquitous media player in the personal computer world — which makes it a good overall choice for your audience. QuickTime is available for Macintosh and Windows systems. QuickTime can play MPEG and QuickTime media. The QuickTime Player also supports progressive download, where files begin playing as soon as enough has been downloaded to allow continuous playback. The free QuickTime Player is available for download at

```
www.apple.com/quicktime/download/
```

Apple also offers a version of QuickTime called QuickTime Pro. Key features of QuickTime Pro include

✔ Full-screen playback

✔ Additional media-management features

✔ Simple authoring tools

✔ Advanced import/export options

Figure 16-1:
Apple's
QuickTime
is one
of the most
common
and best
media
players
available.

As an owner of Adobe Premiere Pro, you don't need the extra features of QuickTime Pro; it doesn't do anything that Premiere can't do already. Your audience really doesn't need QuickTime Pro either (unless of course they want to watch movies in full screen.) The standard QuickTime Player should suffice in most cases. QuickTime-format files can be exported directly from Premiere Pro using the Adobe Media Encoder.

RealPlayer

Another very popular media player is RealPlayer from RealNetworks. RealPlayer is available for Macintosh, Windows, and even Unix-based systems. The free RealPlayer software is most often used for RealMedia streaming media over the Internet, although it can also play MPEG-format media as well. The Adobe Media Encoder includes a *codec* (compressor/decompressor software program, as discussed in Chapter 4) for exporting movies in the RealMedia format. To download the RealPlayer in its various incarnations, visit

```
www.real.com/
```

Although RealNetworks does offer a free version of the RealPlayer (pictured in Figure 16-2), you have to look carefully for the Free RealPlayer or Free RealOne Player links to download it. RealNetworks offers other programs that aren't free of charge but do have additional features. RealNetworks has specialized in the delivery of streaming content, and it offers a variety of delivery options. You can use its software to run your own RealMedia streaming server, or you can outsource "broadcast" duties to RealNetworks.

A complaint often heard about RealPlayer is that the software tends to be intrusive and resource-hungry once installed — and that the program itself collects information about your media-usage habits and sends that information to RealNetworks. Although RealPlayer is extremely popular, consider that some folks out there simply refuse to install RealNetworks software on their computers. Although RealMedia is an excellent format, I recommend that you offer your audience a choice if you plan to use it; include another format such as QuickTime or Windows Media.

Figure 16-2:
RealPlayer
is a very
popular
media
player, often
used for
streaming
media on
the Internet.

Windows Media Player

Microsoft's Windows Media Player (version 7 or newer) can play many common media formats. I like to abbreviate the program's name as *WinMP* because, well, it's easier to type. WinMP comes preinstalled on computers that run Windows Me or Windows XP. Although the name says "Windows," versions of WinMP are also available for Macintosh computers that run OS 8 or higher. In fact, Figure 16-3 shows WinMP being used in Mac OS X. WinMP is even available for Pocket PCs and countless other devices. WinMP is available for free download at

```
www.microsoft.com/windows/windowsmedia/download/
```

WinMP can play video in MPEG and AVI formats. Premiere Pro can output both of these formats, but they're not terribly useful for online applications because they're big and have an appetite for resources. Windows Media Player can also play Windows Media Video (WMV) format, and Premiere Pro can output that as well by using the Adobe Media Encoder. I like the WMV format because it provides decent quality (for Web movies) with incredibly small file sizes.

Figure 16-3:
Windows Media Player is required for viewing Windows Media–format movies.

What are the compelling reasons for choosing WinMP (shown in Figure 16-3) over other players? Choose Windows Media Player as your format if

✔ **Most or all of your audience members use Windows.** Most Windows users already have WinMP installed on their systems, so they won't have to download or install new software before viewing your Windows Media-format movie.

✔ **You want the look, but not the expense and complexity, of streaming media.** If you don't want to deal with the hassle of setting up and maintaining a streaming-media server, Windows Media-format files can provide a workable compromise. WinMP does a decent simulation of streaming media with *progressive downloadable video*: When downloading files, WinMP begins playing the movie as soon as enough of it is downloaded to ensure uninterrupted playback.

✔ **You're distributing your movie online and extremely small file size is more important than quality.** The Windows Media format can offer some remarkably small file sizes, which is good if your audience downloads your movie over slow dial-up Internet connections. I recently placed a 3:23-long movie online in Windows Media format, and the file size was only 5.5MB (megabytes). Of course, the movie wasn't broadcast quality. It had 32 kHz stereo audio, a frame size of 320 x 240 pixels, and a frame rate of 15 frames per second (fps). Although the quality was relatively low (compared to, say, DVD), it was superior to the quality offered by other formats, given the file size and length of the movie.

Exporting Your Movie

You are reading the second edition of this book. When I wrote the first edition, called simply *Adobe Premiere For Dummies*, I covered version 6.5 of Adobe Premiere. When I got to the section on exporting a movie for the Web, I had to write three wildly different sections for each of the three Web-friendly formats: QuickTime, RealMedia, and Windows Media Video. This is because each format used its own special little export tool, each with its own special set of complex instructions.

Thankfully, Adobe has simplified things greatly in Adobe Premiere Pro. When you want to export a movie in a Web-friendly format, you use the new Adobe Media Encoder and follow the same basic steps no matter which format you plan to use. To begin exporting your movie in a Web-friendly format, follow these steps:

1. **Click somewhere in the Timeline window to make it active, and make sure that the sequence you want to export is in front.**

   Remember, each sequence is like its own separate Timeline. The only way to export more than one sequence at a time is to nest sequences. (See Chapter 8 for more on nesting sequences.)

2. **Press the Enter key.**

   Doing so ensures that everything in the sequence has been rendered. When rendering is complete, the sequence starts to play in the Monitor. Go ahead and stop playback if you have already previewed your movie and you know you're ready to export.

3. **Choose File⇨Export⇨Adobe Media Encoder.**

   The Transcode Settings dialog box appears as shown in Figure 16-4.

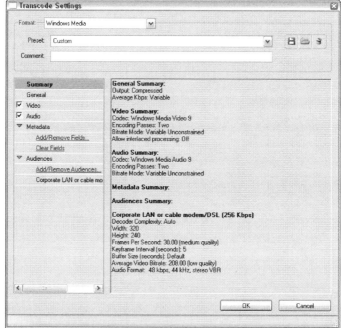

Figure 16-4:
Choose an
export
format and
settings
here.

4. **Choose an export format from the Format menu.**

   Remember, if you're exporting for the Web you want to choose QuickTime, RealMedia, or Windows Media. I'll describe the nuances of each format in the following sections.

5. **Choose a preset from the Preset menu.**

   The exact choices here vary depending on which format you are exporting. Again, I describe specific presets in the following sections.

6. **In the pane on the left side of the Transcode Settings window, make sure that check marks appear next to Audio and Video.**

   Of course, if you only want to export audio, remove the check mark next to Video, and vice versa.

7. **Click General in the pane on the left side of the Transcode Settings window and review general options on the right.**

   General options vary greatly depending on the format. I describe those options in the following sections.

8. **Click Video on the left and review video settings on the right.**

   See the following sections for information on video settings.

9. **Click Audio on the left and review audio settings on the right.**

   Guess what? Audio settings also vary greatly depending on the format. See the following sections for more.

10. **Click Metadata on the left.**

11. **Click Add/Remove Fields under Metadata.**

   The Select Metadata dialog box appears as shown in Figure 16-5. The exact fields listed in this dialog box vary depending on your export format. If you've ever watched movies online, you've probably noticed that most movie players can show the name of the movie, the author, a copyright notice, and other information in a text box as the movie plays. You can add that information to your own movie using these metadata fields.

12. **Place a check mark next to the metadata fields that you want to use and click OK to close the Select Metadata dialog box.**

   In Figure 16-5, you can see that I have chosen the Title, Author, and Copyright fields.

Figure 16-5:
Choose metadata fields for your movie.

13. **Enter data for your metadata, as shown in Figure 16-6.**

14. **Click a listing under Audiences and review settings for that audience preset.**

15. **Click Summary again at the top of the left-hand pane and review all of the movie settings.**

   The settings should reflect any changes you made in Steps 6–14. If everything looks acceptable, click OK. If you see a Choose Name dialog box appear, enter a name for your customized preset and click OK.

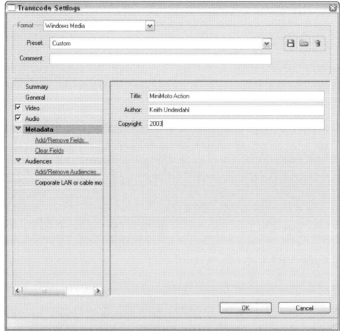

Figure 16-6:
Enter
information
in your
metadata
fields.

16. In the Save File dialog box, choose an option from the Export Range menu.

In most cases, you'll want to export the Entire Sequence, but you can also choose to export just the Work Area if you have specified a work area that only encompasses part of your sequence.

17. Choose a location in which to save the movie, enter a name in the File name field, and click Save.

When you click Save, the movie is exported. You'll see a Rendering dialog box that tells you the progress of the export. A "remaining time" estimate is given; it might be a while, especially if this is a long project. In the next few sections, I help you sort out some of the specific settings for each export format.

Exporting for QuickTime

QuickTime is a very popular format for sharing movies online because it provides a good balance of file size and quality. Before you can export to QuickTime format, you must have QuickTime Player 6 or later installed on your computer. See the section on Apple QuickTime earlier in this chapter for information on downloading this software.

General settings

When you export a movie in QuickTime format, the first settings you'll need to check in the Transcode Settings dialog box (see the previous section on exporting movies) are the General settings. Review the following General settings:

- **✓ Loop:** Check this option if you want the movie to loop back to the beginning and start playing again when the movie is finished.

- **✓ Compress Movie Header:** Check this option if the movie will be served on a streaming media server.

- **✓ Autoplay:** This option causes the movie to start playing as soon as it is opened.

- **✓ Hinted Movie:** This option enables streaming as well as progressive download, which means the movie starts to play before the entire file has been downloaded. The player program calculates the amount of download time remaining and starts playback when it figures that the whole thing will be downloaded before the movie reaches the end.

- **✓ Make Movie Self-Contained:** This ensures that the whole movie occupies a single file. You'll want to keep this option checked for any movie you share online.

- **✓ Optimize Hints:** If the movie will be on a streaming server with a lot of bandwidth, check this option so that more people can access the file simultaneously. Otherwise, leave this option unchecked because it greatly increases the file size.

- **✓ Video Hinter Track:** If the file will be streamed, this option must be checked.

- **✓ RTP Payload Encoding:** The Realtime Transport Protocol (RTP) is part of a streaming movie file that tells the player what kind of data is being sent. In general, you should choose the Use Native Encoding if Possible option, but if you audience seems to have a lot of problems opening and playing your movie, you may want to try choosing the Always Use QuickTime Encoding option.

- **✓ Packet Size Limit/Packet Duration Limit/Interval:** If your audience seems to have a hard time downloading a streaming movie with acceptable quality, smaller or shorter packets should provide more reliable streaming.

- **✓ Audio Hinter Track:** As with the Video Hinter Track, this option should be checked for streaming movies. Note that you can also set packet size, duration, and interval limits for audio.

Keyframes: Not just for effects anymore

Although they share a name with effect keyframes, compression keyframes are entirely different. Basically, a compression keyframe is a picture of the entire video image. When video is compressed, a keyframe might only occur once every one, five, or even ten seconds. All of the frames between those keyframes — the in-between frames are called *delta* frames — contain information about only the things in the video image that have changed.

Cartoon animation provides a good analogy for compression keyframes. Suppose an animator wants to draw a rabbit hopping around near a tree. The animator will probably draw one picture that includes the tree, grass, and other background objects. Next, the animator draws individual frames that show the rabbit hopping this way and that, as rabbits are wont to do. These frames are drawn on clear sheets of plastic called *cells*. Each cell can then be overlaid and photographed in front of the drawing of the tree and background. This method saves the artist a lot of work, because the tree and the background only have to be drawn once.

When you compress video, keyframes are kind of like the background drawing of the tree and the grass. The frames in between — the delta frames — are like the cells showing the rabbit. Just as artists save effort, keyframes help codecs reduce file size because less information has to be stored.

Most codecs allow you to specify how often you want keyframes to be created. A longer interval between keyframes usually reduces file size, but the longer the movie plays, the more stuff on screen is likely to change between keyframes. This means that each keyframe contains less information, and the delta frames contain more. As a result, your files bloat rather than shrink. Long keyframe intervals work well for video without a lot of action. For example, if the video consists primarily of an interview where the person doesn't move much and the background remains almost totally static, long keyframe intervals are probably safe. But if your movie has a lot of action and movement, you'll need to use keyframe intervals of just one or two seconds.

Video settings

I know what you're thinking: Some of those General settings didn't seem too general. Fortunately, the QuickTime video settings are easier to sort through. Click Video in the left pane of the Transcode Settings dialog box and review these settings:

- ✔ **Codec:** As described in Chapter 4, the codec is the compressor/decompressor scheme used to compress the movie to a smaller file size. There are many, many choices in the Code menu, but for online use, one of the Sorensen codecs is probably best.

- ✔ **Width/Height:** These boxes control the size of your video image. Remember to maintain the same aspect ratio (usually 4:3) of your source footage so as not to distort the video image. See Chapter 4 for more on aspect ratios. Keep in mind that larger video sizes mean larger files.

- **Frame Rate:** Broadcast-quality video usually has a frame rate of 25 or 30 frames per second (fps). Online movies often use a frame rate of 15fps to help reduce file size.

- **Keyframe Distance:** Compression keyframes help video compress more efficiently. A longer interval between keyframes reduces file size and quality.

- **Datarate:** A higher datarate means higher video quality, and of course higher file sizes.

- **Spatial Quality:** This setting controls how the video image is compressed. Higher quality results in larger files. (I'll bet you didn't see that one coming!)

Audio settings

QuickTime's audio settings are actually pretty simple. You can choose an audio codec from the Codec menu (the QDesign Music 2 codec works well), select mono or stereo output, and specify a frequency. A frequency of 44 kHz provides CD-quality audio, but keep in mind that high-quality audio can inflate the size of your files in a big hurry. If your exported files are too big, you may want to start here and reduce the audio frequency, as well as switch from Stereo to Mono.

Exporting Advanced RealMedia

I don't think I'm going out on a limb to suggest that Apple and Microsoft can be a little competitive sometimes. Apple's QuickTime and Microsoft's Windows Media Player are clearly aimed at the same online multimedia market, but they're not the only major players in that market. RealPlayer from RealNetworks is very popular and has been in widespread use for many years. Premiere Pro can export movies in RealMedia format, which is the format used by RealPlayer.

One of the nice things about using RealMedia is that the files can dynamically adjust to various bandwidths. You only have to create one RealMedia file, but the quality that users receive depends on the speed of their Internet connections.

Another nice thing about exporting in RealMedia format is that the settings are pretty easy to review and understand. When you click General on the left side of the Transcode Settings dialog box, the only two options you see are Allow Recording and 2 Pass Encoding. Uncheck Allow Recording if you want to prevent audience members from recording a copy of your movie. The 2 Pass Encoding option increases the time it takes to export the movie, but the reduced file size and increased quality is worth the wait. With two pass encoding, the encoder first analyzes the movie on one pass, and then actually encodes it on a second pass based on the analysis it made during the first pass.

Video and audio settings for RealMedia export are pretty simple as well. You can choose a codec (choose the newest one unless compatibility with old RealPlayer software is important), a Video Content option (choose the option that best matches your movie), the Height, the Width, and the Resize Quality. I usually just leave the Resize Quality on High Quality Resize. In the Audio options, choose whether most of your audio is music or voice.

The only truly complex settings in RealMedia export are under Audience. The audiences you see listed in the left pane of the Transcode Settings dialog box vary depending on which preset you chose. In Figure 16-7, I have chosen the RM9 NTSC Streaming Modem preset because the majority of my audience for this movie uses a modem connection. Click one of the audience listings on the left to review and adjust settings on the right. Settings include

- **Bitrate Encoding:** For streaming movies, choose Constant Bitrate. If your movie won't be streamed, choose a Variable Bitrate (VBR) option. Note that if you choose a VBR option, you can only adjust settings for a single audience group.

- **Constant Bitrate:** Slide this option right to increase quality and file size.

- **Maximum Video Frame Rate:** If the user's Internet connection can't keep up, RealPlayer dynamically drops frames (if the word "dynamic" can be used when speaking of such a tragedy). Still, you can set a maximum frame rate here if you wish.

- **Codecs:** Four codec menus allow you to set basic compression levels for various types of content. I usually just accept the defaults in all four menus.

- **Maximum Startup Latency Time:** Before a streaming movie can start to play, some of the movie must be buffered on the user's computer. This slider allows you to adjust the maximum amount of time that the user must wait while video is buffered.

- **Maximum Keyframe Interval:** RealMedia intelligently decides when to set compression keyframes, particularly if you use two pass encoding. You can set a maximum interval for keyframes using this slider, if you wish.

- **Enable Loss Protection:** Sorry, this setting doesn't make sure you never lose your keys. Enable this option if your movie will be on a streaming server. This option helps prevent data packets from being lost during streaming.

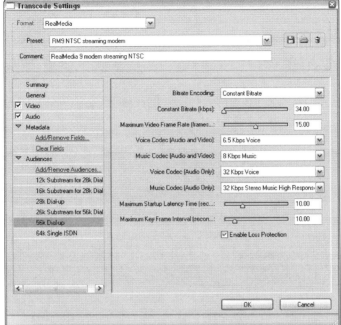

Figure 16-7:
RealMedia
export lets
you
customize
settings for
each
audience.

Exporting Windows Media

Another Web-friendly export option available in Adobe Premiere Pro is
Windows Media. This export option produces Windows Media Video (WMV),
an efficient export format for online media. WMV-format video supports progressive download (also called *hinted download*), which means it starts to
play as soon as a sufficient amount of data has been received to ensure continuous playback from start to finish. Versions of Windows Media Player —
the only program that can play Windows Media Video — are available for
both Windows and Macintosh systems.

Premiere Pro can export using Windows Media 8 or Windows Media 9 codecs.
When you look through the Windows Media presets available in the Transcode
Settings dialog box, you'll see presets labeled WM8 and WM9. Like RealMedia,
reviewing the actual settings for Windows Media export is pretty simple.
Beginning with the General settings, you can choose to output either
Compressed or Uncompressed video. That's it for General settings. I can't
think of too many reasons to export uncompressed Windows Media Video,
except perhaps to edit it in an application specific to Windows Media.

Windows Media export also provides few Video and Audio settings. In each settings group, you see a codec menu, an Encoding Passes option, and a Bitrate Mode menu. In general, I recommend sticking with a Windows Media 9 codec for audio and video, and (as with RealMedia), two encoding passes because that greatly improves the file size and quality of your exported Windows Media Video. Choose a variable bitrate unless the movie will be streamed. In Video options, you also see a check box for the Allow Interlaced Processing option. Don't check this option unless your exported movie will be viewed on regular TVs (in which case, you really shouldn't be exporting in Windows Media format anyway).

Like RealMedia, the Windows Media 9 codec supports multiple audience levels for a movie, as shown in Figure 16-8. To add an audience for your movie, click Add/Remove Audiences in the left pane of the Transcode Settings dialog box and place a check mark next to each audience you want to use. Audience settings include

- **Maximum Bitrate:** This option appears only if you chose the Constant bitrate mode under Video options. Adjust the bitrate down to reduce file size, or up to increase quality. This setting is not shown in Figure 16-8 because I chose a variable bitrate mode under Video settings.

- **Width/Height:** As you'd expect, these boxes control the height and width of your video image.

- **Frames Per Second:** Reducing the frame rate to 15 can greatly reduce your file sizes.

- **Keyframe Interval:** As explained earlier in this chapter, a longer interval between compression keyframes can greatly reduce file size, except in very high-action video.

- **Buffer Size:** Whether streaming or progressive download, some of the movie must be buffered on the user's computer before playback can begin. This setting controls how long the user must wait. Most of the time you'll probably want to leave this on Default, but you can specify a different time if you wish.

- **Average Video Bitrate:** A smaller average bitrate reduces the file size. This option isn't available if you have chosen a Constant bitrate.

- **Peak Video Bitrate:** This option appears only if you chose the Variable Constrained bitrate mode under Video options. This peak bitrate is the bitrate that the video will have under ideal download conditions.

- **Peak Video Buffer Size:** This option appears only if you chose the Variable Constrained bitrate mode under Video options. This setting controls the maximum buffer size for poor Internet connections.

✔ **Image Quality:** This option appears only if you chose the Constant bitrate mode under Video options. Reduce the image quality to reduce the file size.

✔ **Audio Format:** Remember, audio quality has a huge affect on file sizes. If you export your movie and the file is too big, try dropping the audio format to the next lower quality.

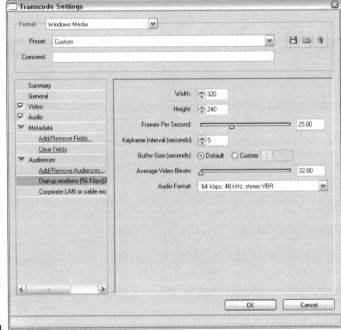

Figure 16-8:
Adjust settings for each audience when exporting to Windows Media Video.

Chapter 17

Exporting Your Movie to Tape

*A*lthough analog video may seem old-fashioned, it is still a very common method for sharing video. It's also pretty reliable. When you share movies on CD-ROM or the Internet, you have to worry about your possible users' mishmash of bandwidth capabilities — and whether they have the right playback software. And even with DVDs, some players simply refuse to play some discs. But in the case of VHS videotapes, you know that your tapes play reliably in almost any VHS tape deck. You also know that virtually every human being in your target audience already owns at least one VHS tape deck and a TV.

This chapter helps you prepare your movies for playback on videotape. After your movie is ready, I show you how to export your movie from Adobe Premiere Pro to videotape.

Preparing for Analog Playback

Exporting video to an analog source is also a far less complicated process than exporting for a digital source. The main difference is that you don't have to worry about codecs and player software. Your only real concern is that you have the right hardware for export, and that your computer runs well enough to export without dropping frames or causing other problems. Generally speaking, if your computer meets the system requirements for running Adobe Premiere Pro (see Chapter 2) and you are able to capture video successfully, you shouldn't have any trouble exporting to tape.

Getting your movie ready for tape

Before you export your movie to tape, you should make sure that your movie is actually ready. Naturally, you should review the project and all of your edits. Because any movie you export to tape will be viewed primarily on broadcast-style TVs, you should also check the following:

- **Does the movie need any broadcast-style elements?** If your movie is going to a broadcast outlet — even a local public-access cable channel — you may need to provide color bars and tone at the beginning or end of the tape. There is also a (remote) possibility that the broadcaster wants a counting leader at the beginning of the tape. Contact the broadcaster and ask them to provide any specific requirements. I show you how to generate and use counting leaders and bars and tone in Chapter 15.

- **Are the project settings properly adjusted?** In your project, choose Project⇨Project Settings⇨General. In the Project Settings dialog box that appears, click the Playback Settings button. The DV Playback Settings dialog box appears, as shown in Figure 17-1. Make sure that the Play Audio on DV Hardware option is set under Export to Tape. Click OK once to close the DV Playback Settings dialog box.

- **Is the movie compatible with the appropriate broadcast standard?** Review settings in the General Project Settings (Project⇨Project Settings⇨ General). If your movie is standard sized (not widescreen) and is viewed on NTSC TVs, the Frame Size should be 720 by 480, the Display Format should be 29.97 fps Drop-Frame Timecode, and the Pixel Aspect Ratio should be NTSC (0.9). For standard size PAL video, the frame size should be 720 by 576, the Display Format should be 25 fps, and the Pixel Aspect Ratio should be PAL (1.067). See Chapter 4 for more on video standards.

- **Does the movie contain broadcast-illegal colors?** If the footage in your movie was originally shot with a DV camcorder, there's a good chance that it contains color or light values that exceed local broadcast rules and standards. This probably isn't an issue if your project is not destined for broadcast, but if your project *will* be broadcast, you should use the Video Limiter feature of the Premiere Pro Color Corrector to remove illegal colors. (See Chapter 10 for more on using the Color Corrector.)

- **Have you previewed your project on a TV monitor yet?** Previewing your movie on a real TV monitor can help you identify problems such as weird colors or titles that get cut off at the edge of the screen. (See Chapter 15 for more on previewing your movie on an external monitor.)

Setting up your recording hardware

Though DVDs are quickly becoming the standard for video exchange, VHS videotapes are still a common video medium. If your ultimate plan is to put your video on a VHS tape, you can use one of three methods:

✔ **Export directly to a VHS deck connected to your computer.** This generally requires special hardware such as a high-quality video card. If you were able to capture video from a VHS deck, you should be able to export to it as well. Device control is only available on higher-quality, professional-grade tape decks. A few newer, professional-style S-VHS decks now have FireWire ports, making the process of connecting the VCR to your computer much, much easier.

✔ **Export video through the analog outputs on your digital camcorder.** With your camcorder connected to your FireWire port, the camcorder can serve as a digital-to-analog converter to the VHS deck. Some camcorders do not allow analog output and FireWire input at the same time, so you'll have to experiment with your own camcorder to see if it works. Also, when using this method, Premiere Pro's device control can only control the camcorder, not the analog deck.

✔ **Export video to your digital camcorder, and then dub it to the analog deck later.** This approach should work even with the cheapest consumer-grade hardware. If your camcorder doesn't allow simultaneous digital input and analog output, simply export the video to a DV tape in the camcorder and then later dub it to a VHS tape using the camcorder's analog outputs.

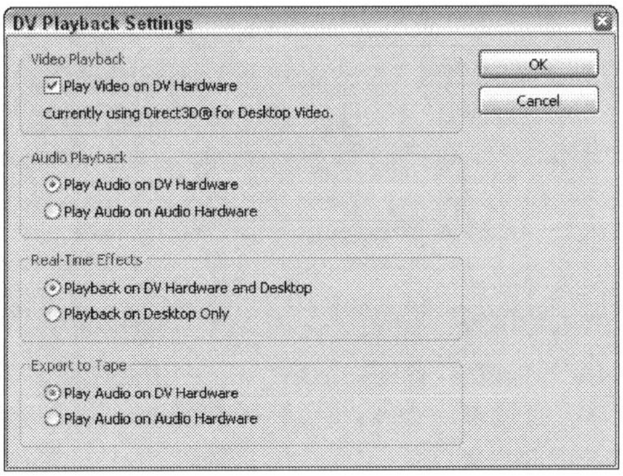

Figure 17-1:
Make sure
that your
audio will
play out
to DV
hardware
during
Export
to Tape
operations.

DV Playback Settings

Video Playback
☑ Play Video on DV Hardware
Currently using Direct3D® for Desktop Video.

Audio Playback
⦿ Play Audio on DV Hardware
◯ Play Audio on Audio Hardware

Real-Time Effects
⦿ Playback on DV Hardware and Desktop
◯ Playback on Desktop Only

Export to Tape
⦿ Play Audio on DV Hardware
◯ Play Audio on Audio Hardware

OK
Cancel

Blacking and coding a tape

If you plan to export your movie to a tape in a DV device (such as a digital camcorder), Premiere Pro assumes that there is already timecode on the videotape to which you are about to export. But if you are using a brand-new tape that you just peeled out of its plastic shrink-wrap, the tape has no timecode yet. You can rectify this situation by doing what video pros call *blacking and coding* the tape — recording black video and timecode onto the tape before you record anything else.

The easiest way to black and code a tape is to simply put your DV camcorder in a dark, quiet room and press Record with the lens cap on. Come back in an hour when the tape is full. Voila! Your tape now has black video and timecode recorded on its entire length. Another way to black and code a tape is to create a project in Premiere Pro that contains nothing but black video (with *no* audio), and then export that project to the tape. You might be tempted to just black and code the first minute or two of a tape, but I have found that with some devices, this can cause a recording glitch when the end of the original timecode is reached during export.

Preparing your computer to export video

Remember back when you were getting ready to capture video into your computer? You probably spent some time preparing your system to ensure that you didn't drop any frames during capture. As with capturing, exporting video is also resource-intensive, and you must carefully prep your computer to ensure there aren't any dropped frames as you lay the movie down on tape. Before you export a movie to tape, double-check the following:

- Make sure all unnecessary programs are closed, including your e-mail program, MP3 jukebox, and Web browser. Every open program uses up memory and processor resources that should be devoted to video export.

- Disable memory-resident programs — for example, antivirus programs and any programs that have icons in the Windows system tray (the area in the lower-right corner of the screen, next to the clock).

- Disable screen savers and power-management settings to ensure they don't kick on in the middle of a long export operation.

- Defragment your hard drive. A recently defragmented disk is important to ensure efficient operation during video capture and export.

Exporting Your Movie

After you have prepared your movie, computer, and recording deck for export to tape, you're ready to begin the actual export process. The steps you follow vary a little bit depending on whether you are exporting with or without device control. How do you know? If you are exporting to a DV device (a digital camcorder or a DV deck), Premiere Pro can probably control that device using the same FireWire connection that actually transfers the video. Some high-end analog tape decks also facilitate device control via your computer's serial port. If you have one of these setups, your deck should have come with software and instructions for setting up device control in Premiere Pro.

If you don't have device control, you'll have to juggle your hands as you manually press Record on your tape deck while beginning export in Premiere. The following sections show you how to export video with and without device control.

Exporting to tape with device control

Years ago, when computer manufacturers introduced Plug and Play hardware, many old-timers scoffed. "Plug-and-*pray*," it was often called, especially when it didn't work. Thankfully, years of development have made Plug and Play — combined with device control — a crucial asset of IEEE-1394 (FireWire) technology. Connect a digital camcorder to your FireWire port, turn it on, and within seconds, you should be controlling camcorder functions using your computer. I've been using digital video equipment for a few years now, and it still amazes me every time I click Play in Premiere and the tape in my *camcorder* starts to roll. In fact, thanks to device control, I have *more* control over the camcorder in Premiere Pro than I do when trying to manipulate the buttons on the camcorder itself.

Generally speaking, a DV tape will only have timecode on it if somebody (probably you) blacked and coded it beforehand (as described earlier in this chapter). I suggest getting that out of the way well *before* you get to this point.

Device control makes exporting video to tape really easy. If you are exporting to a device that has device control (such as a digital camcorder), follow these steps:

1. **Connect your recording device (your camcorder or tape deck) to your computer and turn it on.**

   Make sure the camcorder is turned on to VTR (player) mode, and not to Camera mode.

2. **After you make sure that the sequence you want to export is active and currently in front in the Timeline window, press Enter to make sure everything in the sequence is rendered.**

3. **Choose File⇨Export⇨Export to Tape.**

   The Export to Tape Settings dialog box appears, as shown in Figure 17-2.

4. **Make sure a check mark is placed next to the Activate Recording Device option.**

   The only time you would disable this option is if you're exporting video through a video converter connected to your computer's FireWire port. (I describe video converters in Chapter 21.)

5. **If the tape already has timecode on it, select the Assemble at Timecode option and specify a timecode where you want recording to begin.**

   As you can see in Figure 17-2, I'm starting my movie at about the one-minute mark on my tape.

   If you are exporting NTSC video, you might notice that you can't choose the timecode 00;01;00;00. If you want to start recording the movie about one minute into the tape, you'll need to choose the timecode 00;01;00;02 as I have in Figure 17-2. The reason for this is that NTSC video uses drop-frame timecode — which skips frames 00 and 01 at the beginning of every minute, except at every tenth minute. (See Chapter 4 for more on how drop-frame timecode works.)

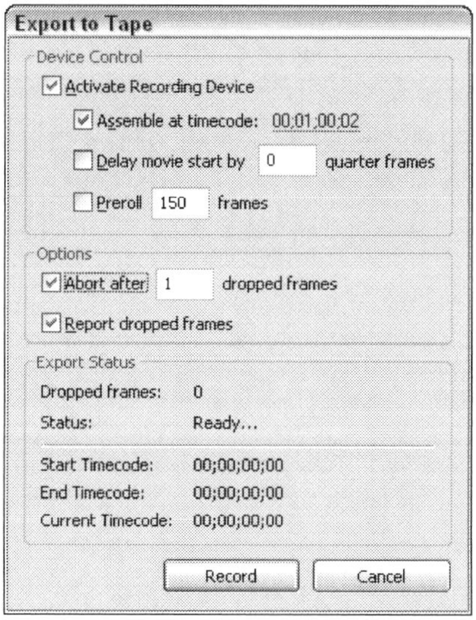

Export to Tape

Device Control
- ☑ Activate Recording Device
  - ☑ Assemble at timecode: 00;01;00;02
  - ☐ Delay movie start by [0] quarter frames
  - ☐ Preroll [150] frames

Options
- ☑ Abort after [1] dropped frames
- ☑ Report dropped frames

Export Status
- Dropped frames: 0
- Status: Ready...

- Start Timecode: 00;00;00;00
- End Timecode: 00;00;00;00
- Current Timecode: 00;00;00;00

[Record] [Cancel]

Figure 17-2:
Make sure that the Activate Recording Device option is selected.

6. **Enter the number of quarter frames, if any, that you want to delay before the movie starts playing.**

   Some devices need a delay between receiving the *record* command and the actual movie.

7. **Enter the number of frames that you want to preroll the tape in the Preroll field.**

   Preroll allows the reels in the tape deck to spin up to the correct speed before recording begins. I recommend at least five seconds (150 frames for NTSC video, 125 frames for PAL video) of preroll.

8. **Place a check mark next to Abort after.**

   Of course, you can tell Premiere Pro to only abort export after 2 or 3 or 50 frames have been dropped, but even 1 dropped frame is an unacceptable quality problem. If you have trouble with dropped frames during capture, review the earlier sections of this chapter and Chapter 2 to make sure your computer is ready and that it meets the specs for running Premiere Pro.

9. **Click Record.**

   Your movie is recorded on the tape.

Steps 5 through 7 above require that there is already timecode on the tape to which you are exporting. Although you can often get away with skipping those three options — especially if you already placed a section of black video at the beginning of your sequence — I recommend that you black and code your tapes before exporting to them.

Exporting to tape without device control

Exporting to tape without device control is a tad clumsy, but it is possible. You basically just use your own magic flying fingers to press Record on the tape deck *as you click Play* in Premiere Pro. Here's how:

1. **Connect your hardware and cue the tape to the point at which you want to start recording.**

2. **Click the sequence you want to export to bring it to the front of the Timeline window.**

3. **Press Enter to ensure that everything in the sequence has been rendered.**

   When the sequence is done rendering, the CTI automatically moves to the beginning of the sequence and starts to play. Make sure that the movie plays on your external monitor or camcorder display. When you are sure that your movie is playing on your external monitor, stop playback.

4. **Place the CTI at the beginning of the sequence.**

5. **Press Record on the tape deck or camcorder you are using to record.**

6. **Click Play in the Program side of the Monitor to play the sequence.**

Step 3 not only ensures that the sequence is rendered, but also serves as a test to make sure your hardware setup is going to work. This test is crucial because if you don't see the video from the Timeline playing out on the external hardware, you can bet that nothing is getting recorded onto your tape either.

Chapter 18

Recording DVDs

* *

* *

*I*n June 2003, right around the time I started to write this edition of *Adobe Premiere Pro For Dummies*, the video-rental industry announced that for the first time since DVD movies became available in 1997, DVD rentals surpassed VHS tape rentals. In just six short years, DVD has gone from a high-tech gadget used by only the most hardcore videophiles to the industry standard for movie distribution.

DVDs aren't just changing the way we watch movies; DVDs are also changing the way we *make* movies. Recordable DVD drives are now cheap and widely available, and software companies are rushing to add advanced DVD authoring tools to their video-editing programs. Adobe first offered DVD authoring tools in Premiere 6.5, and they now offer an advanced DVD authoring program called Adobe Encore DVD that integrates well with Adobe Premiere Pro.

This chapter shows you how to put your movie projects on DVD using Adobe Premiere Pro. I also show you how to use Encore DVD because I believe it is an invaluable addition to your Premiere editing system.

Understanding DVD Basics

You've probably noticed that DVD (Digital Versatile Disc) has become *the* hot method for distributing movies today. However, until recently, the process of mastering a DVD movie was complex, and the hardware for recording (a.k.a. *burning*) DVDs was prohibitively expensive. Thankfully, all that is changing. DVD burners are now available for less than $200, and blank recordable DVD discs are around $1 each, or maybe even less if you shop around. In fact, blank recordable DVDs are now cheaper than VHS tapes, and they're certainly lighter and easier to mail, meaning that distributing your movies has never been more simple or affordable.

Comprehending DVD standards

One of the things I love about VHS tapes is that once I record a movie onto a tape, I know it'll play in just about any VCR. Likewise, I can usually look at the tape and immediately know how much video it holds. For example, a tape labeled T-120 is going to hold about 120 minutes of NTSC video. Alas, DVDs are a little more complicated. Although many DVD players can play the DVDs that you record yourself, some players have trouble with them. And of course, the amount of space on a blank DVD is usually listed computer-style (gigabytes) rather than human-style (minutes). If a blank DVD says it can hold 4.7GB, how many minutes of video is that, exactly? The next few sections answer the most common questions you'll have about recording DVDs.

How much video can I cram onto a DVD?

A standard recordable DVD of the type you are likely to record yourself has a capacity of 4.7GB, which works out to a little over two hours of high-quality MPEG-2 video (MPEG-2 is the codec used by DVD video). Two hours is an approximation; as I show later in this chapter, quality settings greatly affect how much video you can actually squeeze onto a disc. Some professionally manufactured DVDs can hold more because they are double-sided or have more than one layer of data on a single side. Table 18-1 lists the most common DVD capacities.

Table 18-1	DVD Capacities	
Type	*Capacity*	*Approximate Video Time*
Single-sided, single-layer	4.7GB	More than 2 hours
Single-sided, double-layer	8.5GB	4 hours
Double-sided, single-layer	9.4GB	4.5 hours
Double-sided, double-layer	16GB	More than 8 hours

You've probably seen double-sided DVDs before. They're often used to put the widescreen version of a movie on one side of the disc, and the full-screen version on the other. Unfortunately, there is currently no easy way for you to make double-sided or double-layer DVDs in your home or office. These types of discs require special manufacturing processes, so (for now) you're limited to about two hours of video for each DVD you record.

When double-layer discs are manufactured, the layers are actually recorded separately and then glued together (yes, really) using a special transparent glue. This is a very complex process, so don't try to make your own double-layer DVDs with super glue; it won't work.

What is the deal with the DVD-R/RW+R/RW alphabet soup?

When it comes to buying a drive to record DVDs, you're going to see a lot of similar yet slightly different acronyms thrown around to describe the various formats that are available. The basic terms you'll encounter are

- **DVD-R (DVD-Recordable):** Like a CD-R, you can only record onto this type of disc once.

- **DVD-RW (DVD-ReWritable):** You can record onto a DVD-RW disc, erase it later, and record something else onto it.

- **DVD-RAM (DVD-Random Access Memory):** These discs can also be recorded on and erased repeatedly. DVD-RAM discs are only compatible with DVD-RAM drives, which pretty much makes this format useless for movies because most DVD players cannot play DVD-RAM discs.

The difference between DVD-R and DVD-RW is simple enough. But as you peruse advertisements for various DVD burners, you'll notice that some drives say they record DVD-R/RW, whereas others record DVD+R/RW. The dash (-) and the plus (+) aren't simply a case of catalog editors using different grammar. The -R and +R formats are unique standards. If you have a DVD-R drive, you must make sure that you buy DVD-R blank discs. DVD-R drives are typically made by Apple, Hitachi, Panasonic, Pioneer, NEC, Toshiba, Samsung, or Sharp.

Likewise, if you have a DVD+R drive, you must buy DVD+R blank discs. Manufacturers that offer DVD+R drives include Dell, Hewlett-Packard, Philips, Sony, and Yamaha.

The differences between the -R and +R formats are not major. Either type of disc can be played in most DVD-ROM drives and DVD players. And as of this writing, both formats are widely available. I do not recommend one over the other, although I have noticed that blank +R discs tend to be a little more expensive.

One more thing: When you buy DVD-R discs (that's *-R*, not +R), make sure you buy discs that are labeled for General use, and not for Authoring. Not only are DVD-R for Authoring discs more expensive, but they are not compatible with most consumer DVD-R drives. This shouldn't be a huge problem because most retailers only sell DVD-R for General discs, but it's something to double-check when you buy blank media.

What are VCDs and SVCDs?

You can still make DVD movies even if you don't have a DVD burner.

Yes, you read that correctly. Okay, technically you can't make *real* DVDs without a DVD burner, but you can make discs that have menus just like DVDs and play in most DVD players. All you need is a regular old CD burner and some blank CD-Rs to make one of two types of discs:

✔ **VCD (Video CD):** These can hold 60 minutes of video, but the quality is about half that of a DVD.

✔ **SVCD (Super VCD):** These hold only 20 minutes of video, but the quality is closer to (though still a little less than) DVD quality.

The advantage of VCDs and SVCDs is that you can make them right now if you already have a CD burner but not a DVD burner. Adobe Premiere Pro can export movies in VCD or SVCD format, and I'll show you how later in this chapter. Just keep in mind that VCDs and SVCDs are not compatible with all DVD players.

A great resource for compatibility information is a Web site called VCDHelp. com (`www.vcdhelp.com`). Check out the Compatibility Lists section for compatibility information on specific brands and models of DVD players.

Preparing your movie for DVD playback

Perhaps the best thing about DVDs is their ability to play back movies at optimum quality, regardless of whether the movie has been played once or a hundred times. The digital nature of DVDs means they don't suffer from the generational loss problems of analog videotapes (see Chapter 4 for a detailed explanation of generational loss).

Viewers expect very high quality from DVD movies. They're more likely to buy high-quality TVs so that they can watch their DVDs on crisp, bright displays. This means you're going to have to work especially hard to make sure that your movies are properly prepared for DVD. For best results, capture and edit your program at full DV quality. This means

✔ **NTSC:** 720x480 frame size, 0.9 pixel aspect ratio, 29.97 frames per second, drop-frame timecode, 48 kHz (16-bit) audio

✔ **PAL:** 720x576 frame size, 1.067 pixel aspect ratio, 25 frames per second, 48 kHz (16-bit) audio

Consider these specifications to be the *minimums*. If you're working with widescreen footage, the pixel aspect ratio for NTSC footage should be 1.2, and for PAL footage it's 1.422. (For more on pixel aspect ratios, timecode, frame rates, and video standards, see Chapter 4.)

Another thing you may want to do to prepare your movies for DVD is to create some chapter references, which enable viewers to jump quickly from scene to scene. In Chapter 8, I show you how to create sequence markers that can later be used as chapter references in DVD movies.

Recording DVDs with Premiere Pro

Not so long ago — in fact, in the last version of Adobe Premiere — recording a movie onto DVD was a complex and time-consuming process. Thankfully, Premiere Pro greatly simplifies the process with an Export to DVD feature that is easy to understand and use. When you're done editing a project in Premiere, you can record it directly to a blank recordable DVD in your computer's DVD burner.

If you export a movie from Premiere Pro directly onto a DVD, keep in mind that the movie simply plays start-to-finish, as if it were a videotape. If you want the DVD to have menus and all the other fancy controls that DVDs usually have, you'll need to use a more advanced DVD authoring program such as Adobe Encore DVD. I'll show you how to use Encore DVD later in this chapter. I'll also show you how to make VCDs and SVCDs in Premiere Pro. If you want to make a VCD or SVCD, you must follow a different procedure than the one described for DVDs in the following section.

Before you export a movie to DVD, make sure that your DVD burner is installed. If it's an external burner, make sure the power is turned on and that all cables are properly connected. If you start the export process without making sure your burner is ready, you'll waste a lot of time doing the same steps twice.

Exporting to DVD

As with so many things in life, starting the process of exporting to DVD is easy. After you get into it, however, you find there are actually a lot of steps to follow. Also, the process will take a long time; if you're recording two hours of video on a DVD it could take Premiere Pro several hours to prepare the movie and burn the disc.

I recommend that you start the export process when you know your computer won't be needed for anything else for at least several hours. I typically start a burn at night before going to bed. Also, disable screen savers or power saving settings on your computer so that the export process isn't interrupted.

When you, your movie, and your computer are ready for DVD export, follow these steps:

1. **Click the sequence you want to export to bring it to the front of the Timeline window.**

   If you only want to export a portion of the Timeline, slide the ends of the yellow Work Area bar at the top of the Timeline so that only the desired portion of the sequence is covered by the bar. You may want to do this if your Timeline includes elements for tape export such as a long stretch of black video or a counting leader.

2. **Choose File⟳Export⟳Export to DVD.**

   The Export to DVD dialog box appears.

3. **In the General options, enter a name for your disc.**

   The default name is a cryptic number that doesn't mean much to any-body. Actually, if you squint real hard at the numbers, you'll see that they actually represent the current date and time. I recommend you choose Custom from the Disc Name menu and enter a custom, descrip-tive name for the movie.

4. **If you created sequence markers to use as chapter references, place a check mark next to the Chapter Points At option.**

5. **Enable the Loop Playback option if you want the movie to play over and over and over and over . . . .**

   I recently produced a product demonstration video intended for play-back on a TV set up at a trade show booth or store kiosk display. The movie was only a couple of minutes long, and looping playback meant that the movie would play continuously without requiring constant human intervention of the DVD player's Play button.

6. **Click Encoding on the left side of the Export to DVD dialog box.**

   Encoding options appear to the right.

7. **Choose a preset from the Preset menu.**

   Which preset you choose depends on several important factors. The name of each preset provides important clues:

   • **NTSC** or **PAL:** Choose a preset that matches the video standard used by your footage.

   • **DV** or **Progressive:** Only choose a Progressive preset if you know the movie will be used on progressive-scan equipment. This means that both the DVD player and the display unit (such as a progres-sive scan HDTV unit or a projector) must both have a progressive scan mode. If your movie will be viewed on conventional TVs, choose a DV preset.

   • **4Mb** or **7Mb:** This number tells you the target bit rate in megabits (Mb) for the movie. If the movie is short, choose a 7Mb preset for best quality. If the movie is more than an hour, choose a 4Mb preset to ensure that the whole program fits on a single disc.

   • **VBR 2 Pass** or **CBR 1 Pass:** Choose a variable bit rate (VBR) or con-stant bit rate (CBR) preset. A VBR preset takes twice as long to encode because the movie is first analyzed before it is actually encoded. This analysis allows the encoder to compress the movie more efficiently, using a high bit rate when necessary and a low bit rate when it is less likely to affect playback quality. Most VBR presets use a target bitrate of 4Mb, except for the 7Mb VBR 2 Pass SurCode for Dolby Digital presets, which should only be used if your project contains 5.1 channel audio.

Although you can usually find a preset that matches your needs, you can also adjust encoder settings individually if you wish. To do so, click Edit. I'll show you how to adjust the various encoder settings in the next section.

8. **If you only want to export the sequence between the In and Out points you set in Step 1, choose Work Area from the Export Range menu. If you want to export the whole sequence, choose Entire Sequence from the Export Range menu.**

9. **Leave the Fields menu alone.**

   The setting in this menu is determined by the preset you chose in Step 5.

10. **Enable the Maximize Bitrate option.**

    This option forces Premiere Pro to use the highest bitrate that allows the movie to fit on the disc. Unless you chose a CBR preset and you're in a hurry to get the disc recorded, there is really no reason not to choose this option. If you enable Maximize Bitrate, you can also enable the Force Variable Bitrate option. This option is only applicable to CBR presets, but if you're choosing this option, you probably should have chosen a VBR preset to begin with.

11. **Click DVD Burner on the left side of the Export to DVD dialog box.**

12. **Make sure that your DVD burner is selected in the DVD Burner menu, as shown in Figure 18-1.**

    If your burner isn't available in the list, make sure that its power is turned on and that all cables are properly connected. If the burner's power wasn't on (for example), you'll need to click Cancel in the Export to DVD dialog box and go back to Step 1.

13. **Choose the number of copies you want to record.**

14. **Make sure that the Burner Status says Ready.**

    If the Burner Status says Media Not Present, you need to insert a blank recordable DVD disc of the correct format and then click Rescan. If the status says Incompatible Disc, you probably have a CD-R disc in the drive, or a recordable DVD that is not the correct format for your burner. When a proper disc is inserted and the status says Ready, the bottom of the dialog box provides an estimate of the disc space required for your movie, as well as the space that is still available on the blank disc.

15. **Choose a Record Option.**

    Most of the time you'll probably just want to choose Record, which records the disc. If you choose Test Only, a disc image is written to your hard drive to test for errors, but no disc is burned. If you choose Test and Record, a test image is created, and if no errors occur, the disc is burned.

16. **Click Summary on the left side of the Export to DVD dialog box and review the settings that appear on the right.**

17. **When you're ready to burn the disc, click Record at the bottom of the Export to DVD dialog box.**

    The disc is recorded.

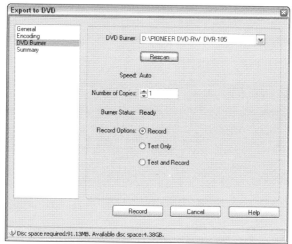

Figure 18-1:
Make sure
that your
DVD burner
is selected
and ready
for
recording.

Customizing DVD settings

Most of the time, using one of Premiere Pro's presets to format your DVD is a good idea. However, if you are a tinkerer and want to tweak the individual audio and video settings, you can do so by clicking Edit in the Encoding options of the Export to DVD dialog box. When you click Edit, the Transcode Settings dialog box appears as shown in Figure 18-2. The following sections show you how to review and adjust the available video and audio settings. Click OK at the bottom of the Transcode Settings dialog box when you are done reviewing settings.

Video settings

To begin reviewing video settings, click Video on the left side of the Transcode Settings dialog box. Video settings will appear to the right, as shown in Figure 18-2.

Many of the video settings are self-explanatory and should match the settings used in your project. In particular, the TV Standard, Aspect Ratio, Frame Rate, Program Sequence, and Field Order settings should match your project. You can choose CBR or VBR Bitrate Encoding, and you can choose one or two encoding passes (Bitrate Encoding and Encoding Passes are explained in Chapter 16).

You can also fine-tune the Target, Maximum, and Minimum Bitrate settings if you wish. For example, if you have a very short movie, it's probably safe to boost up the Target and Maximum bitrate settings a bit if you're using VBR encoding. If you're using CBR encoding, you'll have just a single Bitrate slider control.

At the bottom of the Video settings, you see menus called M Frames and N Frames. You can usually ignore these menus and use the default settings. But if you really must know, these menus control how compression works. MPEG video has three different kinds of frames: I, P, and B frames. Basically, an I frame is a complete image, and a P frame is a "predicted" image based on information in the previous I or P frames. A B frame is a "bidirectional" predicted frame that looks forward or back. The M Frames menu lets you specify the number of B frames between I and P frames. Why this menu is called "M Frames" rather than "B Frames," I have no idea. The N Frames menu specifies the number of frames between I frames, and it must be a multiple of the M Frames setting. Increasing the M and N Frames settings allows the video to compress more efficiently, but it also causes some cheaper DVD players to skip during playback.

Audio settings

To review audio settings, begin by clicking Audio on the left side of the Transcode Settings dialog box. The settings here depend on which codec you choose in the Codec menu. The available codecs are

- ✔ **MainConcept MPEG Audio:** This is a good codec to choose if your project contains stereo audio. This codec allows you to specify a bitrate for the audio.
- ✔ **PCM Audio:** This is another codec that works well with stereo audio.

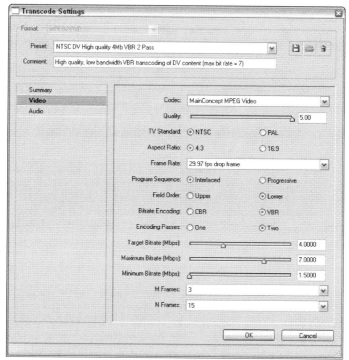

Figure 18-2:
Choose
video
settings for
your DVD
movie here.

✔ **SurCode for Dolby Digital:** Use this codec if your program uses 5.1 channel Dolby Digital audio. Although this codec is included with Premiere Pro, you can only use it for free three times before you must purchase it. The Premiere Pro plug-in encoder costs $149. Visit www. surcode.com for purchasing information.

Recording VCDs and SVCDs

In the previous section, I mentioned two other possible destinations for your MPEG-2 movies — VCD (Video Compact Disc) and SVCD (Super VCD). Both use regular CD-R (Compact Disc-Recordable) media for recording. Believe it or not, you can record up to 74 minutes of full-motion MPEG-2 video and audio onto a VCD. A SVCD can only hold about half as much video, but the quality is slightly higher and you can include more audio and subtitle tracks. The video quality of VCD and SVCD video is generally lower than that of DVD video, but it's as good as — or better than — VHS video.

The appeal of VCDs and SVCDs is obvious. Although DVD burners and blank DVD media are getting cheaper, they are still not as common or affordable as common CD burners and blank CD-Rs. VCDs and SVCDs provide an economical way to share high-quality video, although you should keep in mind that some DVD players cannot play VCDs and SVCDs. For player-compatibility information, I recommend that you check out a Web site such as that maintained by VCDHelp.com (www.vcdhelp.com), featured in Chapter 15 of this book.

You cannot burn VCDs or SVCDs using Premiere Pro's Export to DVD feature, but you can export movies in VCD or SVCD format. After the movie is exported in the proper format, you have to use a third-party CD mastering program to actually *record the disc*. To export a movie in VCD or SVCD format, follow these steps:

1. **Click the sequence you want to export to bring it to the front of the Timeline window.**

   If you only want to export a portion of the Timeline, slide the ends of the yellow Work Area bar at the top of the Timeline so that only the desired portion of the sequence is covered by the bar. You may want to do this if your Timeline includes elements for tape export such as a long stretch of black video or a counting leader.

2. **Choose File⇨Export⇨Adobe Media Encoder.**

   The Transcode Settings dialog box appears.

3. **Choose either MPEG1-VCD or MPEG2-SVCD in the Format menu.**

   VCDs can hold about one hour of video, but the video quality is much lower than DVD quality. SVCDs approach DVD quality, but they can only hold about 20 minutes of video.

4. **Click a preset from the Preset menu.**

   If you are making a VCD, you can choose only between a PAL or NTSC single-pass preset. If you chose SVCD in the Format menu, you have more preset choices:

   • **NTSC** or **PAL:** Choose the TV standard that matches your footage and target audience.

   • **High CBR** or **Standard VBR:** The High presets have a constant bitrate of 2.42 Mbps. The Standard presets have a target bitrate of 2.376 Mbps and a maximum bitrate of 2.42 Mbps. Choose one of the Standard presets if your movie is more than ten minutes long.

   • **1 Pass** or **2 Pass:** As explained earlier in this chapter, two encoding passes increase encoding time, but the video is also compressed more efficiently. Choose a 2 Pass preset if your movie approaches the 20-minute capacity of the SVCD.

5. Click Video on the left side of the Transcode Settings dialog box.

Video settings appear on the right, as shown in Figure 18-3. Review the video settings and adjust as necessary. For explanations of the various video settings, see the previous section on customizing DVD settings.

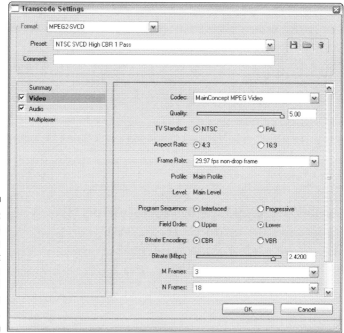

Figure 18-3: Premiere Pro can export movies in SVCD format as well.

6. Click Audio on the left side of the Transcode Settings dialog box and review the audio settings that appear to the right.

7. Click Multiplexer on the left side of the Transcode Settings dialog box and make sure that VCD or SVCD (as appropriate) is chosen on the right.

8. Click OK to close the Transcode Settings dialog box.

9. In the Save File dialog box that appears, choose either Entire Sequence or Work Area in the Export Range menu.

If you choose Work Area, only the section you identified in Step 1 is exported.

10. Name your movie and choose a location in which to save it.

11. Click Save.

The Save File dialog box closes and the Rendering dialog box appears. The process of rendering your movie in the correct format may take a few minutes. When rendering is complete, you're left with a file on your hard drive. To actually put this file on a disc, you need to use a CD-mastering program that can create VCDs and SVCDs. In Figure 18-4 (for example), I am using a program from Roxio called DVD Builder, a tool that comes with the popular Easy CD Creator program.

Figure 18-4: You must use a third-party program to burn a VCD or SVCD.

Using Adobe Encore DVD

If you've ever watched a movie on DVD, you probably used a menu to access certain features of the DVD. Adobe Premiere Pro can record your movies to DVD, but it cannot make menus.

Wait! Don't get all bummed out just yet. Sure, Premiere Pro can't make fancy, interactive DVD with all kinds of menus and special features, but plenty of other programs can. One of those programs is Adobe Encore DVD. By itself this program retails for about $550, but you can get it along with Premiere Pro in the Adobe Video Collection for about $1000. Premiere Pro and Encore DVD play well together, and Encore DVD offers some advanced features that are usually only found in much more expensive DVD authoring programs. Advanced features of Encore DVD include

- ✔ **Create dynamic disc menus.** Create menus that the audience can use to navigate the features of the DVD. Tight integration between Encore DVD and Adobe Photoshop makes the creation of menus and graphics much easier if you are already a Photoshop fan.

- ✔ **Author double-sided and double-layer DVDs.** As described earlier in this chapter, double-layer and double-sided DVDs can only be recorded at a professional DVD manufacturing facility. However, Encore DVD can author projects intended for these larger-capacity formats. Rather than exporting directly to a DVD disc, Encore exports your finished project to digital tape for transport to the DVD manufacturer. Contact your DVD manufacturer for specific guidelines on authoring double-sided, double-layer discs.

- ✔ **Transcode many different kinds of media into DVD format.** Encore DVD can take many different kinds of media and convert it to the MPEG-2 format used on DVDs. This conversion process is called *transcoding*.

- ✔ **Add subtitles, alternate audio tracks, and other features to the DVD.** Encore DVD uses timelines similar to Premiere Pro's Timeline to help you assemble and organize content. Like Premiere Pro, an Encore DVD project can have multiple timelines.

Encore DVD is a pretty sophisticated program. I don't have room in this book to fully explain all of the features and capabilities in Encore, but I can show you how to assemble a basic project. The next couple of sections show you how to export a project from Premiere Pro for use in Encore DVD.

Exporting a DVD movie from Premiere Pro

Encore DVD has some basic video editing features, but you and I know that you're much better off getting all your editing done in Premiere Pro. First of all, keep in mind that your movie must conform to specs that are DVD-compatible:

- ✔ **NTSC:** Frame size must be 720x480, 720x486, or 704x480. The frame rate must be 30, 29.97, 24, or 23.976 fps (frames per second).

- ✔ **PAL:** Frame size must be 720x576, or 704x576. The frame rate must be 25 fps.

For more on video standards and project settings, see Chapters 4 and 5, respectively. If your project meets the above standards, export the movie from Premiere Pro by following these steps:

1. **Click the Sequence you want to export to bring it to the front of the Timeline window.**

   If you only want to adjust a portion of the sequence, adjust the yellow work area bar at the top of the sequence so that it only covers the portion of video that you want to export.

2. **Choose File⇨Export⇨Adobe Media Encoder.**

3. **In the Transcode Settings dialog box, choose MPEG2-DVD in the Format menu.**

4. **Choose a Preset and review audio and video settings as described earlier in this chapter.**

5. **Click OK when you are done reviewing Transcode Settings.**

6. **In the Save File dialog box that appears, choose a location for the movie file and enter a file name.**

7. **Choose an option in the Export Range menu.**

   If you want to export the entire sequence, choose Entire Sequence. Otherwise, choose Work Area to export only the area selected under the work area bar in Step 1.

8. **Click Save.**

The Rendering dialog box appears and your movie is rendered. When rendering is complete, you actually have two files on your hard drive. One file contains the video and has the file name extension .m2v. The other file contains the audio for the project, in wave (.wav) format.

Assembling a project in Encore DVD

When you first launch Adobe Encore DVD, the program window seems kind of empty. To get started on a new movie project, first choose File⇨New Project. In the New Project Settings dialog box that appears, choose your video standard (NTSC or PAL) and click OK. A new empty project window appears. To assemble the project, work the following sections in order.

Importing assets

After you have a new project created, you need to import the movie you edited in Premiere. All of the media you use in a DVD project — video, audio, and still images — are called assets. To import audio or video, choose File⇨Import as Asset. The Import as Asset window appears as shown in Figure 18-5. If you exported a movie from Premiere Pro using the steps I described in the previous section, you'll have separate files for the audio and video for each sequence. In Figure 18-5, I am preparing to import four files, which consist of the audio and video for two different sequences that I exported.

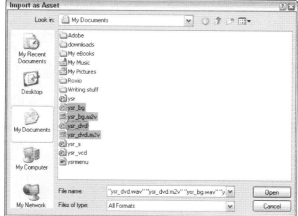

Figure 18-5:
Make sure
you import
both the
audio and
video for
each
sequence.

Creating menus

Menus allow viewers to control your movie and access various features. To create a new menu, choose Menu➪New Menu. A new menu is created using the default menu template, which is usually a boring black screen.

Encore DVD provides several nice-looking menu backgrounds and buttons. To access these items, click the Library palette or choose Window➪Library. The library includes a list of .psd and .png files. The .psd files are menu backgrounds, and the .png files are predesigned buttons and screen elements. To add a background or button to the menu, simply drag–and drop it from the Library palette to the menu.

I usually prefer to use my own graphics for menu backgrounds. To use your own image, first prepare the still image for use in video as described in Chapter 6. Import the image into Encore as an asset, and then drag–and drop it from the Project window to the menu. In Figure 18-6, I have used a still graphic that started out as an exported frame from a movie in Premiere Pro.

Notice in Figure 18-6 that I used some Photoshop magic to stylize the image to remove some detail and make it a little darker. Images with less detail — and dark areas over which to place text and buttons — make your menus a lot easier to use.

Of course, it isn't much of a menu if there aren't some buttons to press. To add buttons:

1. **Drag and drop a button image (.png) from the Library palette to the menu.**

2. **Click the Text tool (see Figure 18-6) to activate it.**

Text tool   Library palette

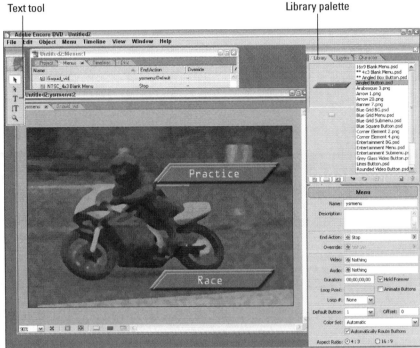

Figure 18-6:
You can use
your own
background
images for
menus.

3. **Click-and-drag over the text of your new button (which probably says something like "Text") to select the text. Begin typing to replace the placeholder text with your own helpful words.**

   Button text should be short and sweet. Ideally I try to keep button text to one word or less. (Less?) When the button text is entered, it's time to specify a link for the button. The link is what happens when the button is pressed.

4. **Open the Project window (choose Window⟿Project if you don't see it) and position it so that your menu button is visible.**

5. **Drag–and drop a video file from the Project window to the menu button.**

   The menu button is now linked to that video file.

Working with timelines and adding audio

When you link a video file to a menu button, Encore DVD automatically creates a timeline for that video file. You should see the timeline appear in your list of assets in the Project palette. Double-click the timeline to open it. A Timeline window opens, as well as a Monitor window. As you can see in Figure 18-7, it all looks suspiciously similar to Premiere Pro!

Audio file.

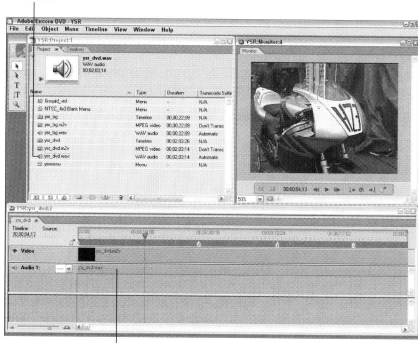

Figure 18-7:
Encore's
Timeline
interface
looks a
lot like
Premiere!

Drop audio file here.

The main thing you need to do in the Timeline is add the audio file to the project. Remember, the audio and video were imported as separate files. To add the audio, simply drag and drop the correct audio file from the Project palette to the Audio track in the Timeline, as shown in Figure 18-7.

Wrapping up the project

After you've created menus, linked assets to menu buttons, and made sure your audio and video are where it all should be, you are ready to preview the project. To do so, choose File⇨Preview. A viewer window opens with a preview of your DVD.

If everything previews okay and all of your buttons and whatnot seem to work properly, you're ready to build the DVD. Follow these steps:

1. **Click the Disc palette to bring it to the front (or choose Window⇨ Disc).**

2. **Give the disc a name and choose a size in the capacity menu.**

   An indicator tells you how much space is used by your movie.

3. **When you're ready, click Build Project.**

   Save the project if you are prompted to do so.

4. **In the Make DVD Disc window, make sure your DVD burner is selected in the Recorder menu, and choose a Write Speed and the Number of Copies.**

   Even though your DVD burner might be capable of very fast Write Speeds, the recording process is less likely to produce errors if you use a slower speed.

5. **Click Next.**

   A Summary screen appears. Make sure the Media size and Compatibility information settings look correct — and then click Build to begin recording the disc. A progress bar tells you the progress of the burn.

That's it! You're ready to share your DVD movie with the world.

Part V
The Part of Tens

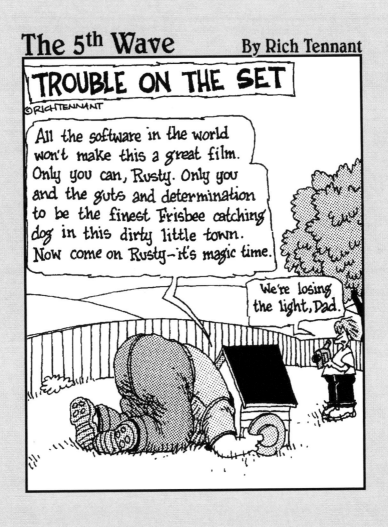

In this part . . .

If you've ever used a *For Dummies* book before, you know what this part is all about. The chapters in this part provide top-ten lists to help you find useful stuff by tens — ten great tips and tricks for moviemaking, ten software add-ons for Adobe Premiere Pro, and ten cool tools (well, okay, some are enough fun that you *could* call 'em toys) for your movie production studio.

Chapter 19

Ten Movie-Making Tips and Tricks

In This Chapter
▶ Shooting special effects
▶ Shooting better video
▶ Dealing with environmental conditions

*W*ith a name like "Adobe Premiere Pro," it's easy to believe that this software is only meant for "pros" that work at TV stations and video-production companies. But the reality is that the power of this software can be appreciated by virtually anyone who is enthusiastic about making movies. If you're relatively new to video production, or you're a dedicated video hobbyist, this chapter is for you — it provides ten tips and tricks to help you make better movies. See how many of these ideas you can incorporate into your own projects!

Transporters, Twins, and Timelines

Think of all the special effects you've ever seen in movies and TV shows. I'll bet the most common effect you've seen is where a person or thing seems to magically appear or disappear from a scene. Sometimes a magician snaps his finger and blinks out of the picture. Other times people gradually fade in or out, as when crews on *Star Trek* use the transporter.

Making people appear and disappear from a scene is surprisingly easy. All you need is a camcorder, a tripod, and Adobe Premiere Pro. Basically you just position the camcorder on the tripod and shoot *before* and *after* scenes. The subject should only appear in one of the scenes.

Once you've recorded your "before" and "after" clips and captured them into Premiere (see Chapter 6 for details), edit them into the Timeline, one after the other. If you don't use a transition between the clips, the subject will appear to "pop" into or out of the scene. If you want the subject to fade into the scene, apply a Cross Dissolve transition between the two clips (see Chapter 9 for more on using transitions). In Figure 19-1, my subject (Soren) is fading into the scene.

Figure 19-1:
Make your subject magically appear (or disappear)!

An extension of this effect is to have two occurrences of the same subject in a single picture. Consider the image shown in Figure 19-2. It appears that there are two Sorens fighting each other. This trick was achieved by first shooting one half of the image, and then shooting the other half. As you can see in Figure 19-3, one clip was placed in track Video 1, and the other clip — we'll call it the *overlay clip* — was placed in track Video 2. I then applied the Crop effect to the overlay clip so it only covered half the screen. Notice in Figure 19-4 that I have cropped 50% off the right side of the clip.

Figure 19-2:
Are you really seeing double?

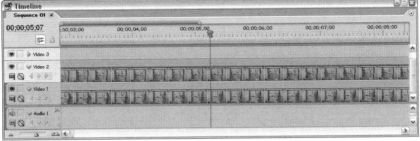

Figure 19-3:
Creative use of over-lays in the Timeline provide the illusion.

Figure 19-4:
I used the Crop effect to remove half of the overlay clip.

To make a subject magically appear or disappear effectively, follow these basic rules:

✔ **Use a tripod.** A tripod is absolutely mandatory to make this effect work. You won't be able to hold the camera steady enough by hand, and a jiggling camera ruins the results.

✔ **Don't move the camera between shots.** The camera must remain absolutely still between the before and after shots. If you have to reposition the camera, or if someone bumps it, reshoot both scenes. If your camcorder has a remote control, use that to start and stop recording so your finger doesn't move the camera at all.

✔ **Shoot the "before" and "after" scenes quickly.** If you're shooting outdoors, shadows and lighting can change quickly. Even subtle light changes will be apparent when you edit the two scenes together later.

✔ **Don't disturb the rest of the scene.** If your subject moves a chair or picks up an object between the "before" and "after" shots, the scenes will appear inconsistent when edited together.

Seeing Stars

So you want to shoot your own science-fiction epic? All you need is a script, some willing actors, a few props from the local toy store, and you're ready to make your futuristic movie.

Well, you're *almost* ready. No sci-fi movie would be complete without a scene of spaceships flying through space, and that means you'll have to create a field of stars to serve as a backdrop. You can put stars behind your spaceships using one of two methods:

- ✔ **Edit the backdrop in later.** Most professional moviemakers shoot their spaceship models in front of a blue or green screen. The video image of the spaceship is then composited over a picture of a star-filled sky during the editing process. Professionals use this method because they can use more realistic looking star fields, and, well, just because they can. See Chapter 11 for more on compositing.

- ✔ **Create a star-field backdrop.** If you don't have the time or patience to build a bluescreen studio and composite your video, just shoot the spaceships in front of a star-field backdrop that you create. The best way to create a star field is to sew sequins onto black velvet. The velvet will absorb virtually all light that falls on it, while the sequins reflect brightly.

Sequins sewn to a velvet backdrop will also tend to twinkle slightly. Of course, any sci-fi geek will tell you that twinkling stars are technically inaccurate, for the same reason that spaceships and explosions don't actually make noise in the vacuum of space. The twinkling of stars that we Earth-bound humans witness is an effect caused by our atmosphere. I doubt that the Galactic Overlord will come and vaporize you over this minor technicality, but be prepared for scoffs from a few space-opera fanatics.

Forcing a Perspective

We humans perceive the world as a three-dimensional space. When you look out upon the world you see color and light, and you can tell which things are close to you and which things are farther away. This is called *depth perception.* Bats use a sort of natural radar for depth perception, which is fine for winged creatures that flap in the night, but we humans perceive depth using two eyes. Our eyes focus on objects, and our brains interpret the difference between what each eye sees to provide depth perception. Without two eyes, the world would look like a flat, two-dimensional place, and activities that require depth perception (say, a game of catch) would be very difficult, if not impossible.

A video camera only has one eye — which means it has no depth perception — which is why video images appear as two-dimensional pictures. You can use this to your advantage because you can make objects look like they're right next to each other when they're actually very far apart. Video professionals use this trick often, and call it *forced perspective*.

Consider the video image in Figure 19-5. It looks like a locomotive and train cars parked in a train yard, but looks are deceiving in this case. As you can see in Figure 19-6, the locomotive in the foreground is a scale model, and the train cars are real and about 50 yards away.

Figure 19-5:
A typical industrial scene?

To make forced perspective work, you must

✔ **Compose the shot carefully.** The illusion of forced perspective works only if the scale looks realistic for the various items in the shot. You'll probably have to fine-tune the position of your subjects and the camera to get just the right visual effect.

✔ **Focus.** If objects are very far apart, getting both of them in focus may be difficult. To control focus, follow these steps:

    1. Set the zoom lens at the widest setting by pressing the zoom control toward "W" on the camcorder so the lens zooms all the way out.

Figure 19-6:
Not quite.
The
camera's
eye is easily
deceived.

2. **Turn off auto-focus (as described in your camcorder's owner's manual).**

3. **Set the focus to infinity.**

   Some manual focus controls have an Infinity setting. If your camcorder does not, manually adjust the focus so objects that are 20 or more feet away are in focus.

4. **Position the camera five to ten feet from the closer subject in your forced-perspective shot.**

   Check carefully to make sure everything is in focus before you shoot; move the camera if necessary. With most camcorders, everything beyond a distance of about five feet will probably be in focus when you zoom out and set focus to infinity.

In Figures 19-5 and 19-6, I show you how a small object in the foreground blends well with a large object in the background. But it can also work the other way around. In fact, model-railroad enthusiasts often use forced perspective to make their train layouts seem bigger than they really are. Mountains, trees, and buildings in the background are made smaller to provide the illusion that they are farther away.

Making Your Own Sound Effects

Believe it or not, some professional videographers will tell you that sound is actually more important than video. The reasoning goes like this: A typical viewing audience is surprisingly forgiving of minor flaws and glitches in the video picture. The viewer is able to easily "tune out" imperfections, which partially explains why cartoons are so effective. However, poor sound has an immediate and significant effect on the viewer. Poor sound gives the impression of an unprofessional, poorly produced movie.

Great sound doesn't just mean recording good quality audio. Another key aspect of your movie's audio is the sound *effects*. I don't just mean laser blasts or crude bathroom noises, but subtle, everyday sounds that make your movie sound much more realistic. These effects are often called *Foley sounds*, named for sound-effects pioneer Jack Foley. Here are some easy sound effects you can make:

- **Breaking bones:** Snap carrots or celery in half. Fruit and vegetables can be used to produce many disgusting sounds.

- **Buzzing insect:** Wrap wax paper tightly around a comb, place your lips so that they are just barely touching the paper, and hum so that the wax paper makes a buzzing sound.

- **Fire:** Crumple cellophane or wax paper to simulate the sound of a crackling fire.

- **Footsteps:** Hold two shoes and tap the heels together, followed by the toes. Experiment with different shoe types for different sounds. This may take some practice to get the timing of each footstep just right.

- **Gravel or snow:** Use cat litter to simulate the sound of walking through snow or gravel.

- **Horse hooves:** This is one of *the* classic sound effects. The clop–clop-clopping of horse hooves is often made by clapping two halves of a coconut shell together.

- **Kiss:** Pucker up and give your forearm a nice big smooch to make the sound of a kiss.

- **Punch:** Punch a raw piece of steak or a raw chicken. Of course, make sure you practice safe food-handling hygiene rules when handling raw foods: Wash your hands and all other surfaces after you are done.

- **Thunder:** Shake a large piece of sheet metal to simulate a thunderstorm.

- **Town bell:** To replicate the sound of a large bell ringing, hold the handle of a metal stew pot lid, and tap the edge with a spoon or other metal object. Experiment with various strikers, lids, or other pots and pans for just the right effect.

Filtering Your Video

Say you're making a movie showing the fun people can have when they're stuck indoors on a rainy day. Such a movie wouldn't be complete without an establishing shot to show one of the subjects looking out a window at the dismal weather. Alas, when you try to shoot this scene, all you see is a big, nasty, glaring reflection on the window.

Reflections are among the many video problems you can resolve with a lens filter on your camcorder. Filters usually attach to the front of your camera lens, and change the nature of the light passing though it. Different kinds of filters have different effects. Common filter types include

- ✔ **Polarizing filter:** This type of filter often features an adjustable ring, and can be used to reduce or control reflections on windows, water, and other surfaces.

- ✔ **UV filter:** This filter reduces UV light, and is often used to protect the lens from scratches, dust, or other damage. I never use my camcorder without at least a UV filter in place.

- ✔ **Neutral-density (ND) filter:** This filter works kind of like sunglasses for your camcorder. It prevents overexposure in very bright light conditions, reducing the amount of light that passes through the lens without changing the color. If you experience washed-out color when you shoot on a sunny day, try using a ND filter.

- ✔ **Color-correction filters:** Many different kinds of color-correction filters exist. These help correct for various kinds of color imbalances in your video. Some filters can enhance colors when you're shooting outdoors on an overcast day; others reduce the color cast by certain kinds of light (such as a greenish cast that comes from many fluorescent lights).

- ✔ **Soft filter:** These filters soften details slightly in your image. This filter is often used to hide skin blemishes or wrinkles on actors who are more advanced in age.

- ✔ **Star filter:** Creates star-like patterns on extreme light sources to add a sense of magic to the video.

Many more kinds of filters are available. Check with the manufacturer of your camcorder to see whether they offer filters specially designed for your camera, and also check the documentation to see what kind of filters can work with your camcorder. Many camcorders accept standard 37mm or 58mm threaded filters. Tiffen is an excellent source for filters, and their Web site (www.tiffen.com) has photographic samples that show the effects of various filters on your images. To see these samples, visit www.tiffen.com and click the link for information on Tiffen Filters. Then locate a link for the Tiffen Filter Brochure. This online brochure provides detailed information on the filters offered by Tiffen.

Working with Assistants

Professional moviemakers are very picky about the way they work. You can learn a lot from the pros, but the reality is that a majority of your video "shoots" will be pretty informal. Whether you're shooting a wedding, sporting event, birthday party, or some other special event, you can encounter a variety of problems:

✔ You'll have little or no control over lighting and noise.

✔ Your subjects won't want to rehearse, much less perform multiple takes.

✔ You won't always have a crew of professional videographers and sound engineers.

✔ Worst of all, your shoot won't be catered. (The horror!)

Whenever I plan to shoot video, I always try to enlist at least one assistant. Usually it's my 10-year-old son (as in Figure 19-2), and although he isn't the most experienced or highly trained video professional (yet), he is a willing trouper. His help is invaluable, but before the shoot, I always brief him on the basics — be quiet, avoid bumping the equipment, and be aware of where the lens is pointed.

Rehearse!

Everybody knows what rehearsal is, but in most cases, you probably don't have a script to memorize. So what is there to rehearse? You should carefully consider and plan every aspect of your video shoot. For example, if you plan to move the camera while you shoot, practice walking the path of travel to make sure there aren't any obstacles that might block you. If you're using a tripod, practice panning to make sure you can do it effectively. Other things to check and rehearse beforehand include

✔ If your camcorder has an audio meter, check the sound levels before you start recording. Have your subjects speak; check the levels of their speech.

✔ Have subjects go through the motions of the shoot, and then coach them on how to stand or move so they show up better in the video.

✔ Check your camera's focus. If objects in the foreground cause your camcorder's auto-focus feature to "hunt" for the correct focus, turn off auto-focus and adjust your focus manually.

✔ Check to see whether the shot is overexposed. On some higher-end camcorders, any overexposed shot shows up as a zebra-stripe pattern in the viewfinder or LCD display. Otherwise you'll have to make a careful judgment and adjust exposure as necessary. Read your camcorder's documentation to see whether it lists any special exposure settings that may help you out.

To Zoom or Not to Zoom?

If every camcorder owner makes a single mistake, it's zoom-lens abuse. On most camcorders, the zoom feature is easy and fun to use, encouraging us to use it more than is prudent. The effect of constantly zooming in and out is a disorienting video image that just looks, well, amateurish. Here are some general zoom lens guidelines to follow on any video shoot:

✔ If possible, avoid zooming in or out *while* you're recording. It's usually best to adjust zoom *before* you start recording.

✔ If you must zoom while recording, try to zoom *only once* during the shot. This will make the zoom look planned rather than chaotic.

✔ Consider actually moving the camera rather than zooming in or out.

✔ Prevent *focus hunting* (where the auto-focus feature randomly goes in and out of focus) by using manual focus. Auto-focus often hunts while you zoom, but you can easily prevent this. Before you start recording, zoom in on your subject. Get the subject in focus, *and then turn off auto-focus.* This should lock focus on the subject. Now, zoom out and begin recording. With focus set to manual, your subject remains in focus as you zoom in. On most camcorders, anything farther than about ten feet away will probably be in focus if you set the camera's focal control to infinity.

✔ Practice using the zoom control gently. Zooming slowly and smoothly is usually preferable, but it takes a practiced hand on the control.

 If you have a difficult time using the zoom control smoothly, try taping or gluing a piece of foam to the zoom-slider button on your camcorder. The foam can help dampen your inputs on the control.

Dealing with the Elements

You may at times deal with extremes of temperature or other weather conditions while shooting video. No, this section isn't about making sure the people in your movies wear jackets when it's cold (although it's always wise to bundle up). I'm more concerned about the health of your camcorder right now, and several environmental factors can affect it:

✔ **Condensation:** If you quickly move your camera from a very cold environment to a very warm environment (or vice versa), condensation can form on or even inside the lens. Avoid subjecting your camcorder to rapid, extreme temperature changes.

✔ **Heat:** Digital tapes are still subject to the same environmental hazards as old analog tapes. Don't leave your camcorder or tapes in a roasting car when it's 105 degrees out. Consider storing tapes in a cooler. (But not the one holding your lunch!) Your videotape cooler shouldn't contain any food or liquids. Simply placing the tapes in an empty cooler helps insulate them from temperature extremes.

✔ **Water:** A few drops of rain can quickly destroy the sensitive electronic circuits inside your camcorder. If you believe that water may be a problem, cover your camcorder with a plastic bag, or shoot your video at another time if possible.

✔ **Wind:** Even a gentle breeze blowing across the screen on your camcorder's microphone can cause a loud roaring on the audio recording. Try to shield your microphone from wind unless you know you'll be replacing the audio later during the editing process.

Another environmental hazard in many video shoots is the sun — that big, bright ball of nuclear fusion that crosses the sky every day. The sun helps plants grow, provides solar energy, and helps humans generate Vitamin D. But like all good things, the sun is best enjoyed in moderation. Too much sunlight causes skin cancer, fades the paint on your car, and overexposes the subjects in your video. Natural skin tones turn into washed-out blobs, and sunlight reflecting directly on your camcorder's lens causes light flares or hazing in your video image. Follow these tips when shooting outdoors in bright sunlight:

✔ **Use filters.** Earlier in this chapter, I describe how lens filters can improve the video you shoot. Neutral-density and color-correction filters can reduce overexposure and improve color quality.

✔ **Shade your lens.** If sunlight reflects directly on your lens, it can cause streaks or bright spots called *lens flares.* Higher-end camcorders usually have black hoods that extend out in front of the lens to prevent this. If your camcorder doesn't have a hood, you can make one, using black paper or photographic tape from a photographic-supply store. (Check the video image to make sure your homemade hood doesn't show up in the picture!)

✔ **If possible, position your subject in a shaded area.** This will allow you to take advantage of the abundant natural light without overexposure.

✔ **Avoid backlit situations.** If your subject is in shade and you shoot video at such an angle that the background is very bright, you'll wind up with a severely backlit situation where your subject is just a black shadow against a brightly glowing background. Shoot subjects against a more neutral or dark background whenever possible.

✔ **Wear sunscreen.** Your video image isn't the only thing you should protect from the sun!

Picture-in-Picture

If you have a somewhat fancy TV, it might have a feature called "picture-in-picture." This feature allows you to watch your favorite show in a small window on the screen while your significant other watches another show on the main screen.

Picture-in-picture — or *PIP* for short — is also a common video effect. For example, during a sporting event, a small picture might show an interview with one of the players while the action of the game fills the rest of the screen. You can make your own PIP effects in Adobe Premiere, an act made even easier now that Premiere Pro allows multiple sequences. You can create and edit a separate sequence just for the small included picture, and then later nest that sequence in the main sequence for your project. Chapter 8 shows you how to nest sequences, but the steps for creating a picture-in-picture effect in Premiere Pro are as follows:

1. **In your movie project, create a new sequence by choosing File↪New↪Sequence.**

2. **Edit clips into the new sequence.**

   The content of this new sequence should make up a little mini-movie, which will play the PIP window.

3. **When you're done assembling the PIP sequence, switch the Timeline over to the main sequence for the project.**

4. **Drag the sequence from the Project window to a superimpose track (Video 2 or higher) in the Timeline.**

   Your PIP sequence is now nested in the main sequence.

5. **Position the CTI in the Timeline so that it is somewhere over the nested sequence, as shown in Figure 19-7.**

6. **Click the nested sequence to select it, and then click the Effect Controls tab in the Monitor window.**

   If you don't see the Effect Controls tab, choose Window↪Effect Controls.

7. **In the Effect Controls, click the arrow next to Motion to reveal the Motion controls.**

8. **Reduce the Scale setting so that it is less than 100.**

   The Scale setting controls the size of the picture-in-picture window. Most picture-in-picture effects should use a Scale setting of less than 40, but you'll have to experiment a bit to get a size that looks right to you.

9. **Click on Motion in the Effect Controls to highlight it.**

   Control handles should appear around the PIP window in the right pane of the Monitor.

10. **Position the mouse pointer over the center of the PIP window in the right pane of the Monitor, and then click-and-drag the window to a new position in the screen.**

In Figure 19-7, I have moved the PIP window to the upper-right corner of the screen.

Obviously, this is something you will want to play around with to arrive at the exact settings that work best for you. But as you can see, picture-in-picture effects are actually pretty easy in Adobe Premiere Pro!

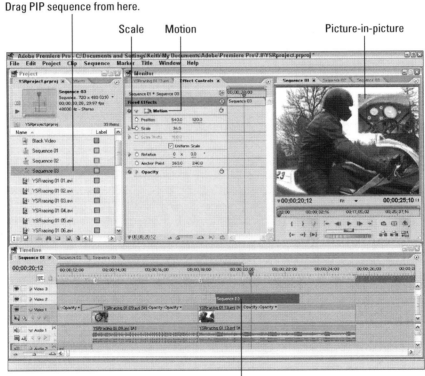

Drag PIP sequence from here.

Scale   Motion

Picture-in-picture

Figure 19-7: Use nested sequences to create picture-in-picture effects.

Nested sequence

Chapter 20

Ten Essential Software Add-Ons for Adobe Premiere

Many years ago, software companies worked hard to make single software programs that could serve a variety of needs. If you used office-productivity software ten or more years ago, you may remember massive software packages like Enable or Symphony. You may also remember that although those packages did many things, they didn't do any of those things *well*.

In recent years, the trend in software development has been to create individual programs that do a few things *very* well. Not only does this provide us users with more powerful applications, it's also more profitable for the software companies because they can sell many smaller (but still expensive) programs rather than one big, discounted software suite that not everybody uses in the same way. This approach does seem to ensure that the well-crafted special tools will find their way to the users who can appreciate them best.

Adobe Premiere Pro is a good example of this modern style of software development. It does video editing extraordinarily well, but other tasks — such as illustration, image editing, word processing, e-mail, card games — are left out. To really make effective use of Premiere Pro, you're probably going to need some additional programs to use alongside it. This chapter identifies some programs that I think you may find useful as you edit video projects with Premiere.

Adobe Video Collection

If you haven't yet purchased Adobe Premiere Pro, you should seriously consider buying the Adobe Video Collection. It costs a little more — the suggested retail price of the Adobe Video Collection Standard Edition is $999, a $200 premium over Premiere Pro — but includes a collection of extremely valuable tools:

- ✔ After Effects
- ✔ Audition
- ✔ Encore DVD
- ✔ Premiere Pro

A Professional Edition of the Adobe Video Collection retails for $1,499 and includes the aforementioned items plus After Effects Professional and Adobe Photoshop. Either edition represents significant savings over purchasing each program separately.

Adobe Photoshop

When it comes to still-image editing, Adobe's Photoshop is widely recognized as the industry standard. Photoshop comes with the Adobe Video Collection Professional Edition, or you can buy it separately for $609. If that price gives you sticker shock, you may want to consider Photoshop Elements, which retails for only $99.

You'll probably find Photoshop an invaluable tool as you work. Photoshop includes a variety of filters that allow you to apply special effects to images or fix various problems. Of special interest are the Video filters. Consider the image shown in Figure 20-1 — a frame I exported from a DV-format project in Premiere Pro (File➪Export➪Frame). Look carefully at the image and you'll notice that it has two main problems:

✔ If you look closely at the image in Figure 20-1 (or any still-image that you export from a DV-based movie project), it appears elongated, and the subjects seem slightly distorted. This is because the DV footage from which the frame was exported has rectangular pixels, but Photoshop works with square pixels.

✔ The image has what I call "interlacing jaggies." Because the original footage was interlaced, fast-moving portions of the image have an ugly pattern of horizontal distortions.

Figure 20-1:
Still graphics exported from inter-laced DV footage will appear distorted in Photoshop and other graphics programs.

Both these problems are easily fixed in Photoshop. First, we can fix the elongation problem by simply adjusting the size of the picture:

1. **In Photoshop, choose Image⇨Image Size.**

   The Image Size dialog box appears.

2. **In the Image Size dialog box, remove the check mark next to Constrain Proportions.**

   If the frame was exported from DV footage with a 4:3 aspect ratio, the image size will be 720 x 480 pixels. All you need do is change the image size so it conforms to a 4:3 aspect ratio.

3. **Change the Width value from 720 pixels to 640 pixels. Make sure that the Height is still 480 pixels.**

4. **Click OK.**

   The image shape should now be more natural, but there are still those interlacing jaggies to get rid of.

5. **Choose Filter➪Video➪De-Interlace.**

A small dialog box appears. Here you can choose to eliminate odd or even fields, and whether to generate the replacement fields by duplication or interpolation. I generally recommend that you choose Interpolation, but the Odd or Even choices may need some experimentation on your part.

When Photoshop de-interlaces an image, it actually deletes every other horizontal line of the image and replaces each deleted line with a new line. It can generate these replacement lines in one of two ways: *duplication* or *interpolation*. If the lines are generated through duplication, the line above (if you deleted the even lines) or below (if you deleted the odd lines) is copied to create the new replacement line. If the lines are generated through interpolation, Photoshop compares the lines above and below the missing line and generates a new line that is halfway between in terms of appearance. Interpolation usually gives a smoother appearance to the image.

6. **Click OK and view the results.**

If you're not satisfied, choose Edit➪Undo, and then open the De-Interlace filter again and choose different options. My finished result looks like Figure 20-2.

Figure 20-2:
The picture looks much better after Photoshop is used to adjust the size and de-interlace the image.

BorisFX

Premiere Pro comes with a lot of built-in effects, but even so, you may find that none of them are exactly what you were hoping for. Fear not; plenty of third-party software developers such as Boris (www.borisfx.com/) produce plug-ins for Premiere that give you bigger and better special effects to use in your projects.

Boris produces a variety of visual effects plug-ins for programs such as After Effects, Final Cut Pro, and Premiere. BorisFX helps you create animations, image distortions, unlimited layers of composition, rain and other weather effects, and more. If you want, you can even wrap a video image around a 3-D sphere and then shatter the image into a hundred pieces.

Another software tool available from Boris is Graffiti — an advanced titling tool that provides a huge array of options for animation and text creation. You can import the results into your Premiere project.

CineForm Aspect HD

An emerging technology in digital video is *high-definition (HD) video*. As the name implies, HD video offers much higher image quality. HD formats typically record 720, 1080, or even more horizontal lines of resolution. This is much higher than typical DV-format video, which (as described in Chapter 4) is usually closer to 500 lines. HD video also offers a variety of frames rates up to 60 frames per second (fps). As HDTVs become more and more common, HD video is sure to become the predominant video standard in a few years.

Until recently, HD cameras were very expensive. We're talking small-house-in-the-suburbs expensive. JVC, however, has recently released an affordable HD camcorder called the JY-HD10U that sells for around $3500. HD video is now within the realm of affordability, and HD cameras are sure to keep getting even cheaper and becoming more widely available.

Premiere Pro can edit HD video, but you'll find that real-time editing capabilities are lacking. If you plan to edit a lot of HD video, you may want to check out Aspect HD from CineForm (www.cineform.com). CineForm has announced that Premiere Pro will be fully supported by Aspect HD, which allows real-time editing of effects, transitions, and motion in HD video in Premiere Pro. This plug-in retails for $1200, which is a lot, but if you plan to edit HD video, you may find this tool indispensable.

Media Players

Rather than list a specific program here, I'm going to talk about a category of programs. If you'll be producing movies for computer playback, either over the Internet or on CD-ROM, you must carefully consider what format you'll use to export the movie as well as what player the audience will use. To ensure that you can accurately test the viewing experience that your audience will have, you must have the latest versions of any media-player programs they're likely to use. (I describe the three most common media players in detail in Chapter 16.)

Even if you have a specific format and/or player that you favor, you owe it to yourself to keep current on the latest technologies. You may find that as you experiment with various formats and players, some formats offer a more favorable quality-versus-file-size balance than what you've been using. Whether you are using a Macintosh or Windows, I strongly recommend that you download and install the following four players:

✔ **Apple QuickTime:** www.apple.com/quicktime/

✔ **DivX Player:** www.divx.com/

✔ **RealNetworks RealPlayer:** www.real.com/

✔ **Microsoft Windows Media Player:** www.microsoft.com/windows/
windowsmedia/

PanHandler

Starting in the 1970s, there was a long period during which not much changed in the realm of home-audio technology. Home stereos sprouted remote controls, and CD players replaced LP turntables, but the state of the art for speakers and amplifiers remained largely unchanged. Beginning in the 1990s, however, home-theater systems became common, where a system of at least five speakers provided a true surround-sound experience in suburban living rooms.

Today it seems almost everyone has a home theater system, and you can produce movies that take advantage of surround sound. Premiere Pro adds the ability to work with surround sound — a.k.a. 5.1 channel audio — but if you work with surround sound a lot, you may want look at a third-party program such as PanHandler from Kelly Industries (www.kellyindustries.com/). PanHandler enables you to encode your sound for surround-sound systems and control audio panning throughout the audio track. It provides a very easy-to-use interface for controlling the audio channels and retails for $99.

Panopticum Effects

Panopticum (www.panopticum.com/) is another developer of numerous plug-ins for Adobe programs, including After Effects, Illustrator, Photoshop, and of course, Premiere. Interesting Premiere plug-ins available from Panopticum include

✔ **Engraver:** Adds the appearance of an engraving to images. The plug-in does this by adding thin engraving lines like those you might see on paper currency.

✔ **Fire:** Fire and explosions are always fun in movies, but they aren't always safe or cost-effective to shoot. Panopticum's Fire effect helps you create realistic burning effects without worrying that you might singe your eyebrows off.

✔ **Lens Pro:** Create lens and glass distortion effects with this plug-in.

Panopticum effects act as plug-ins in Premiere; once they're installed, you can access them directly from the Premiere Effects tab.

Pixelan Effects

One of the things I love about Adobe software is that third parties can expand the original program's capabilities by developing plug-ins. I've featured a number of third-party plug-in developers for Premiere throughout this chapter, and another developer to consider is Pixelan (www.pixelan.com/). Pixelan produces truly advanced transition and effects plug-ins for Premiere and various other editing applications.

Pixelan's SpiceMASTER is an effects plug-in that provides hundreds of custom effects and wipes. SpiceMASTER effects can be controlled with fine precision, allowing you to get just the right look, be it mild or wild.

SmartSound Music Tools

I probably don't have to tell you how important good music is for your movie projects. And if you've spent time trying to locate and get permission for good music, I probably also don't have to tell you how expensive good music can be. Thankfully, a company called SmartSound has come to your rescue with affordable programs that help you generate a wide variety of soundtrack music. The music can be of almost any length, comes in a wide variety of styles, and best of all you can use it royalty-free!

Music programs are available for as little as $50, with professional-oriented programs starting at around $300. Additional royalty-free music is always being added to the SmartSound online libraries. Find out more at www.smartsound.com.

Ultimatte Compositing Plug-ins

Many of the most advanced special effects involve compositing multiple images, layering them upon one another. Premiere Pro does have some pretty good compositing tools built in, but if you want even more control and superior performance, you may want to use a plug-in from Ultimatte (www.ultimatte. com/), a maker of professional video-compositing hardware and software. Ultimatte (it's a pun, not a typo) offers plug-ins for Premiere that include

- **Ultimatte software:** Exercise precise control over bluescreen and green-screen removal with the Ultimatte software.

- **Screen Correction:** Use this plug-in to correct for unevenly lit blue- or greenscreens. Unevenly lit screens usually cause problems for Premiere's own bluescreen and greenscreen transparency keys.

- **Grain Killer:** Use this plug-in to filter out blue- or greenscreen noise in an image.

Chapter 21

Ten Tools (and Toys) for Your Production Studio

*T*he bare essentials of what you need to make great movies are a digital camcorder, a good computer equipped with a FireWire port, and Adobe Premiere Pro. Those three basics can get you started. But so many other tools (some would say "toys") can make your editing life easier and your movies that much better. This chapter features ten items you may find invaluable as you work with Premiere. (Well, okay, maybe some items aren't indispensable, but at least they're a whole lot of fun!)

Before you buy any video gear, make sure it matches the video-broadcast standard (NTSC, PAL, or SECAM) that you are using before placing your order. This is especially important when purchasing camcorders, monitors, and video decks. (For more on broadcast standards, see Chapter 4.)

Audio Recorders

I know, I know, your camcorder records audio along with video, and it's already perfectly synchronized. So what's the point of a dedicated audio recorder? Well, you may need the capabilities of an audio recorder in many situations. Take, for example, these three:

- You may want to record a subject who is across the room — in which case, have the subject hold a recorder (or conceal it so it's off-camera), and attach an inconspicuous lavalier microphone.

- You may want to record only a special sound, on location, and add it to the soundtrack later. For example, you might show crashing waves in the distant background, but use the close-up sound of those waves for dramatic effect.

- You can record narration for a video project, tweak it till it suits you, and then add it to the soundtrack of your movie.

Recording decent audio used to mean spending hundreds or even thousands of dollars for a DAT (digital audio tape) recorder. However, these days I think the best compromise for any moviemaker on a budget is to use a MiniDisc recorder. MiniDisc player/recorders can record CD-quality audio onto MiniDiscs as computer files in .WAV format — which can be easily imported into a Premiere Pro project. Countless MiniDisc recorders are available for less than $200 from companies that include Aiwa, Sharp, and Sony.

Don't forget a slate!

If you use a secondary audio recorder, one of the biggest challenges you may face is synchronizing the audio it records with video. Professionals ensure synchronization of audio and video by using a *slate* — that black-and-white board that you often see production people snapping shut on camera just before the director yells "Action!"

The slate is not just a kitschy movie prop. The snapping of the slate makes a noise that can be picked up by all audio recorders on scene. When you are editing audio tracks later, this noise will show up as a visible spike on the audio waveform. Because the slate is snapped in front of the camera, you can later match the waveform spike on the audio track with the visual picture of the slate snapping closed on the video track. If you're recording audio with external recorders, consider making your own slate to ease audio-video synchronization.

Dream Camcorders

If you recently purchased your first digital camcorder, you're probably impressed by the image quality it produces, especially compared to older consumer technologies like 8mm, Hi8, and S-VHS. Most digital camcorders are also packed with features that were considered wildly advanced just a few years ago.

But you know how the old saying goes: The grass is always greener, and all that. As impressive and wonderful as your camcorder may seem, you'll soon find even better products out there. As you get more serious about moviemaking, one of the first things you should do is upgrade to a really serious camera. High-end (yet somewhat affordable) DV camcorders are becoming so advanced now that even the pros are using them.

When you're ready to step up to the next level of DV camcorder, look for the following features that make some digital camcorders better than others:

✔ **CCD:** The *charged coupled device* is the unit in a camcorder that captures a video image from light. Most consumer-grade camcorders have one CCD, but higher-quality units have three, one for each of the standard video colors (red, green, and blue). Three-CCD cameras — also called *three-chip* cameras — capture much sharper, more saturated images.

✔ **Progressive scan:** Many cheaper camcorders capture only interlaced video. This can create a variety of problems — such as the interlacing "jaggies" that I've shown in Chapter 20 and elsewhere in this book — especially if you're editing a project for distribution on DVD, HDTV, or the Web. Higher-quality camcorders usually offer a progressive-scan mode.

✔ **24P shooting mode:** A few high-end camcorders (such as the Panasonic AG-DVX100) now offer a shooting mode called 24P, which means the unit can shoot at 24 frames per second in progressive-scan mode, emulating a 16mm or 35mm film camera. Footage shot in 24P mode can be easily edited in Adobe Premiere Pro and then distributed on film without the need for any format changes and associated editing difficulties. This feature isn't for everybody, but if you have been a film producer or enthusiast for a while, you'll appreciate the 24P format.

✔ **Resolution:** Okay, this one can get confusing; resolution is defined and listed in many different ways. Some spec sheets tell you how many thousands of pixels, but this isn't always a good indication of ultimate video quality. Instead, I recommend that you look at horizontal resolution lines. A high-quality digital camcorder should capture at least 500 lines of resolution.

✔ **Audio:** Many high-end DV camcorders have big, condenser-style microphones built onto them — a definite improvement in audio quality compared to the built-in mics on cheaper camcorders, but also look for
external audio connectors so you can use a remote microphone if you
need to. For external audio, I recommend XLR-style (also called *balanced
audio*) microphone connectors.

✔ **Lens:** Any digital camcorder still needs a good old-fashioned "analog"
glass lens to collect and focus light. A bigger, higher-quality lens produces
better video images. Make sure that any camcorder you get accepts filters
on the lens. Many more-expensive cameras offer interchangeable lenses.

✔ **Zebra pattern:** Most professional-grade camcorders display a zebra-stripe
pattern in the viewfinder on overexposed areas of a shot. This can be
extremely helpful, especially when you're adjusting exposure manually.

✔ **Manual control rings:** A lot of cheaper digital camcorders have manual
focus, exposure, and zoom controls on small dials or slider switches —
often difficult to use (provided you can *find* the things). Try to get a
camera with large, easy-to-use control rings around the lens for focus,
zoom, and exposure.

If you're willing to spend at least $1,500 for a camcorder, there are lots of good
units to choose from. The camcorder market is always changing, but Table 21-1
lists some longtime-favorite, high-quality "prosumer" digital camcorders. Just
imagine the great movies you'll make with one of these cameras!

Somebody must have worked overtime to coin the term *prosumer* to mean
high-end consumer products that give you pro-level output. (Will the word
itself catch on? I wouldn't "prosume" to say.)

Table 21-1	Dream Camcorders	
Manufacturer	*Model*	*Street Price (U.S. Dollars)*
Canon	GL2	$1,900–$2,700
Canon	XL1S	$3,200–$4,500
JVC	GY-DV500U	$3,500–$4,200
Panasonic	PV-DV952	$1,300–$1,500
Panasonic	AG-DVX100	$2,900–$4,000
Sony	DCR-VX2000	$2,200–$3,000
Sony	DCR-VX9000	$4,000–$5,000

The "street prices" listed in Table 21-1 are estimates I made by surveying various Web sites and retail outlets. The actual price you pay may be quite different, but the table gives you a ballpark figure so you can make a general price comparison for these various cameras.

DVD Burners

When Apple first released its G4 Macintosh with SuperDrive in 2001, it seemed remarkable that a complete DVD (Digital Versatile Disc) authoring system could be had for *just* $5,000. But prices dropped fast, and in less than a year, Apple was already selling iMacs capable of recording DVDs for less than $2,000. Nowadays you can buy recordable DVD drives that work with virtually any computer for less than $200, and I don't even want to speculate what they'll cost next week (or a few months from now, when you read this).

DVD burners — *burner* is the not-so-technical term used interchangeably with *recorder* — are useful for a variety of reasons. With a DVD burner, you can record up to 4.7GB (gigabytes) of data onto a single disc. Adobe Premiere Pro can record your project directly to DVD, which can then be watched in virtually any DVD player. With an advanced DVD authoring program like Adobe Encore DVD, you can design fancy navigation menus for your discs.

Some new computers now come with DVD burners built in. You can also add a DVD burner to your computer, as an internal or external drive. Internal drives usually require an available EIDE interface, the same kind of interface used by your CD-ROM, CD-RW, or DVD-ROM drive. External drives usually use a FireWire (IEEE-1394) or USB 2.0 connector. Check the documentation for your computer to see whether it supports USB 2.0. If not — and computers sold before summer 2002 usually don't —your computer's USB port probably isn't fast enough to support a DVD burner. See Chapter 18 for more on DVD formats and standards.

As I mention in Chapter 2, computer hardware is delicate and expensive. If you don't have experience upgrading or repairing PCs, you may want to have a DVD burner professionally installed in your computer rather than tackle the job yourself.

Filters

Adobe Premiere Pro contains many effects and tools that you can use to improve the quality — or change the appearance — of your video images. But sometimes it's quicker to tweak the light coming into the camera than to fuss with the digital image later — and some image issues are better dealt with using lens filters. Filters usually attach to the front of your camcorder's lens using a threaded fitting. Check your camcorder housing to determine whether it has a threaded filter fitting. Also check the documentation that came with your camcorder to find out what size and type of filter(s) can be used with your camcorder.

Many consumer-grade camcorders accept 37mm filters; prosumer camcorders usually accept 58mm or larger filters.

Filters can serve many important purposes, including

- **Protecting the lens:** A UV filter is often used primarily to protect the camcorder's lens from foreign objects and the elements. If the filter gets scratched or damaged, it will be a lot cheaper to replace than the camcorder's lens.

- **Improving lighting:** Countless filters are available to help you improve lighting problems on your shots. A neutral-density filter, for example, improves color in bright sunlight; color-conversion and color-compensation filters can increase or decrease the saturation of a specific color in a shot.

- **Reducing glare and reflections:** If a window or other shiny surface appears in your shot, an undesired glare or reflection may appear. Use a polarizing filter to eliminate or control the glare.

- **Creating special effects:** Certain filters can be used to create star patterns around light points, soften the video image, simulate fog, and more.

Filters can usually be purchased at photographic supply stores, although some consumer electronics stores may have them in their camcorder accessories sections. If nothing else, I recommend that you use a UV filter at all times to prevent damage to your camcorder's lens. But filters can also greatly improve or enhance your video images, so you may find it worthwhile to look seriously at a wide range of them. For more on video filters, check out the Tiffen Web site (www.tiffen.com).

Microphones

Virtually all camcorders have built-in microphones. Most digital camcorders boast 48-bit stereo sound-recording capabilities, but you'll soon find that the quality of the audio you record is still limited primarily by the quality of the microphone you use. Therefore, if you care even a little about making great movies, you *need* better microphones than the one built into your camcorder.

Your camcorder should have connectors for external microphones, and your camcorder's manufacturer may offer accessory microphones for your specific camera.

One type of special microphone you may want to use is a *lavalier* microphone — a tiny unit that usually clips to a subject's clothing to pick up his or her voice. You often see lavalier mics clipped to the lapels of TV newscasters. Some lavalier units are designed to fit inside clothing or costumes, though some practice and special shielding may be required to eliminate rubbing noises.

You might also use a condenser microphone to record audio. Some prosumer camcorders come with large, boom-style condenser mics built in. Although these are nice, if you want to record the voice of a subject speaking on camera they may still be inferior to a hand-held or lavalier mic.

Microphones are generally defined by the directional pattern in which they pick up sound. The three basic categories are cardioid (which has a heart-shaped pattern), omnidirectional (which picks up sound from all directions), and bidirectional (which picks up sound from the sides). Figure 21-1 illustrates these patterns.

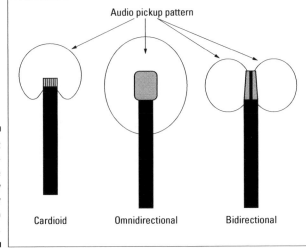

Figure 21-1: Microphones are defined by how they pick up sound.

A good place to look for high-quality microphones is a musicians' supply store. Just make sure that the connectors and frequency range are compatible with your camcorder or other recording device (check the documentation). You may also want to check with your camcorder's manufacturer; it may offer accessory microphones specially designed to work with your camcorder. Finally, the Internet is always a good resource as well. One especially good resource is www.shure.com, the Web site of Shure Incorporated. Shure sells microphones and other audio products, and the Web site is an excellent resource for general information about choosing and using microphones.

Monitors

Although the computer on which you use Adobe Premiere Pro already has a monitor (at least, I *hope* it does), computer monitors are not the ideal place to preview video as you edit. This is especially true if you ultimately plan to output your movie back to tape or DVD where it will be played on regular TVs. If you want to ensure the highest quality for your video image, you need to use an external video monitor.

An external monitor must be a broadcast-style monitor. This is because the way broadcast TV monitors display colors is different from the method computer monitors use. Colors that look fine on the computer screen may be distorted or washed out on an NTSC or PAL monitor.

Okay, from a strictly technical standpoint, your monitor can be any old TV, although (if your budget allows) I recommend buying a high-quality monitor intended for video-production use. With an external monitor connected, you can configure Premiere Pro to play video out to the monitor as you edit. If you have a high-quality video capture card, it probably already has analog video outputs, or it has a breakout box that includes analog video outputs. Connect the monitor to the correct output as instructed in your card's documentation. Alternatively, you might be able to connect your DV camcorder to your FireWire port, and *then* connect the monitor to the camcorder's analog output. This may not work on some camcorders, so some experimentation may be in order.

Is your desk too crowded for a video monitor? Build upward! You can purchase or build a rack that stacks your external video monitor above your computer monitor. Just make sure that all your monitors are properly ventilated, use monitors that don't exceed the rated weight limit of your rack, and make sure you secure everything for earthquake safety (which can also help your equipment withstand vibration from severe weather outside, rampaging small children indoors, and other miscellaneous chaos).

Multimedia Controllers

I don't know about you, but manipulating some of Premiere Pro's playback and editing controls with the mouse isn't always easy. Sure, there are keyboard shortcuts for most actions, and you may find yourself using those keyboard shortcuts quite a bit. In particular, I find that controlling playback with the J, K, and L keys is a lot easier than using the mouse, and using the arrow keys to frame forward or back is vastly superior to dragging the Jog control back and forth in the Monitor window.

Useful though the keyboard may be, there is an even better way. You can also control Premiere with an external multimedia controller, such as the ShuttlePro from Contour A/V Solutions or ShuttlePRO v. 2 from Contour Design. The ShuttlePro, shown in Figure 21-2, features 13 buttons and a two-part dial control in an ergonomically designed housing. The overall design of the ShuttlePro is based on professional video-editing controllers. The dials can operate Premiere Pro's shuttle and jog controls, and the various buttons control various other program features. The unit plugs into a USB port, which can be found on virtually any modern computer. You can find out more about multimedia controllers online at

```
www.contouravs.com
www.contourdesign.com
```

Figure 21-2:
Multimedia controllers make editing in Premiere Pro fun and easy!

Tripods and Other Stabilization Devices

The need for image stabilization will probably become apparent the first time you watch your footage on a large TV screen. No matter how carefully you try to hold the camera still, some movement is going to show up on the image. Of course, there are plenty of times when hand-held is the way to shoot, but there are plenty of other times when a totally stable image is best. To get that stability, you need a tripod.

Tripods are generally available for as low as $20 at your local department store. Alas, as with so many other things in life, when you buy a tripod you get what you pay for. High-quality video tripods incorporate several important features:

- **Dual-stanchion legs and bracing:** This gives the tripod greater stability, especially during panning shots. Braces at the base or middle of the tripod's legs also aid stability.

- **High-tech materials:** You'll soon get tired of lugging a 15- to 20-pound tripod around with your camera gear. Higher-quality tripods usually use high-tech materials (including titanium, aircraft-quality aluminum, and carbon fiber) both strong and lightweight, making the gear less cumbersome to transport and use.

- **Bubble levels:** This helps you ensure that your camera is level, even if the ground underneath the tripod isn't.

- **Fluid heads:** This ensures that pans will be smooth and jerk-free.

- **Counterweights:** The best tripods have adjustable counterweights so the head can be balanced for your camera and lens (telephoto lenses, for example, can make the camera a bit front-heavy). Counterweights allow smooth use of the fluid head while still giving you the option of letting go of the camera without having it tilt out of position.

For a tripod with all these features, you can expect to spend at least $300 (if not much, much more). If that kind of money isn't in your tripod budget right now, try to get a tripod that incorporates as many of these features as possible.

Tripods aren't the only stabilization devices available. You may also want to keep a monopod handy for certain occasions. As the name suggests, a monopod has only one leg (just as tripods have three legs, octopods have eight, and . . . never mind). Although this means that some camera movement is inevitable — you have to keep the camera balanced on the monopod — resting the monopod on the ground can give you more stability than you'd have if you simply hand-held the camera. For moving shots, you may want to try a mobile stabilizer such as a Steadicam (www.steadicam.com). Devices like the Steadicam use a system of weights and harnesses to keep the camera remarkably stable even as the operator moves around a scene.

Video Converters

You have a computer with a FireWire port, and you want to capture some analog video. What are you going to do? You have many, many solutions, of course. You could install a video capture card, but a good one is expensive and installing it means tearing apart your computer. If you're lucky, you might be able to connect an analog video source to the analog inputs on your digital camcorder and then connect the camcorder to the FireWire port. This method is clumsy, however, and it simply won't work with some camcorders.

A simpler solution may be to use an external *video converter* — usually a box that connects to your computer's FireWire port. The box includes analog inputs, so you can connect an analog VCR or camcorder to the box. The unit itself converts signals from analog media into DV-format video, which is then captured into your computer — where you can easily edit it using Premiere Pro.

 If you have worked with analog video a lot, you're probably aware that each time you make a copy of the video some quality is lost. This is called *generational loss* (see Chapter 4 for more on this subject). Video converters like the ones described here don't present any more of a generational-loss problem than a standard video capture card: After the signal is converted to digital, generational loss is no longer a problem until you output the video back to an analog tape again.

Most converter boxes can also be useful for exporting video to an analog source. You simply export the DV-format video from Premiere Pro, and the converter box converts it into an analog signal that you can record on your analog tape deck. Among other advantages, this method of export saves a lot of wear and tear on the tape-drive mechanisms in your expensive digital camcorder. Features to look for in a video converter include

✔ Analog output

✔ Broadcast standard support (NTSC or PAL)

✔ Color-bar output

✔ Multiple FireWire and analog inputs/outputs

Video converters typically range in price from $250 to $700 or more. Table 21-2 lists a few popular units.

Table 21-2	Video Converters		
Manufacturer	*Model*	*Street Price*	*Web Site*
Canopus	ADVC-100	$250–$300	www.canopuscorp.com/
Data Video	DAC-2	$600–$750	www.datavideo-tek.com/
Dazzle	Hollywood DV Bridge	$225–$250	www.dazzle.com/

Video Decks

Because it's so easy to simply connect a FireWire cable to your camcorder and capture video right into your computer, you may be tempted to use your digital camcorder as your sole MiniDV tape deck. If you're on a really tight budget, you may not have much of a choice, but otherwise I strongly recommend a high-quality video deck. A video deck not only saves wear and tear on the tape drive mechanisms in your expensive camcorder, but it can also give you greater control over video capture and export back to tape. Professional video decks are expensive, but if you do a lot of video editing, they quickly pay for themselves — both in terms of the greater satisfaction and quality you're likely to get from your finished movie and in less money spent on camcorder maintenance. Table 21-3 lists some decks to consider.

Table 21-3		DV Video Decks	
Manufacturer	*Model*	*Formats*	*Street Price*
JVC	DVS2U	MiniDV, S-VHS	$1,000
Panasonic	AG-DV1000	MiniDV	$950
Sony	GVD-1000 VCR Walkman with 4-inch LCD screen	MiniDV	$1,200

When shopping for a professional-grade MiniDV deck, you can also look for decks that support the DVCAM or DVCPRO tape formats. In general, decks that support these more robust, professional-grade DV-tape formats also support MiniDV.

Part VI
Appendix

The 5th Wave   By Rich Tennant

"Why don't you try blurring the brimstone and then putting a nice glow effect around the hellfire."

In this part . . .

The appendixes of many books are where authors stick information that seems somehow important, yet doesn't seem to fit anywhere else. *Adobe Premiere Pro For Dummies* is no exception. This book includes just one appendix, a glossary of terms relating to video editing and Adobe Premiere Pro. I throw the odd technical term into the discussion in this book now and then — so if you see something you don't understand, check the glossary.

Appendix

Glossary

● ●

AAF (Advanced Authoring Format): A new industry-standard video format for exchanging media-project files across a variety of platforms. AAF files are like edit-decision lists (EDLs), but the AAF format is not unique to any particular manufacturer or type of equipment. Adobe Premiere Pro can output AAF files. *See also* EDL.

alpha channel: Channel used to define any transparent areas in a digital image.

analog: Technology that records data as a wave with infinitely varying values. Analog recordings are usually electromechanical, so they often suffer from generational loss. *See also* digital, generational loss.

aspect ratio: The shape of a video image as determined by its proportions (width compared to height). Traditional television screens have an aspect ratio of 4:3, meaning the screen is four units wide and three units high. Some newer HDTVs use a "widescreen" aspect ratio of 16:9. Image pixels can also have various aspect ratios. *See also* HDTV, pixel.

bars and tone: A video image that serves the function of the "test pattern" used in TV broadcasting: Standardized color bars and a 1-kHz tone are usually placed at the beginning of video programs. This helps broadcast engineers calibrate video equipment to the color and audio levels of a video program. The format for color bars is standardized by the SMPTE. Adobe Premiere Pro includes a bars and tone generator. *See also* SMPTE.

bit depth: The amount of data that a single piece of information can hold depends upon how many bits are available. Bit depth usually measures color or sound quality. A larger bit-depth number means a greater range of color or sound.

black and code: The process of recording black video and timecode onto a new camcorder tape. This helps prevent timecode breaks. *See also* timecode, timecode break.

capture: The process of recording digital video or other media from a camcorder or VCR tape onto a computer's hard drive.

CCD (charged coupled device): This is the unit in camcorders that interprets light photons and converts the information into an electronic video signal. This signal can then be recorded on tape. CCDs are also used by digital still cameras.

chrominance: A fancy word for color. *See also* luminance.

clip: One of various segments making up the scenes of a video program. Individual clips are edited into your video-editing program's timeline to form complete scenes and a complete story line. *See also* Timeline.

coaxial: Most wires that carry a cable TV signal use coaxial connectors. Coaxial connectors are round and have a single thin pin in the middle of the connector. Coaxial cables carry both sound and video. Most TVs and VCRs have coaxial connectors; digital camcorders usually do not. Coaxial cables usually provide inferior video quality when compared to component, composite, and S-Video cables. *See also* component video, composite video, S-Video.

codec: A scheme used to compress, and later decompress, video and audio information so it can pass more efficiently over computer cables and Internet connections to hard drives and other components.

color gamut: The total range of colors a given system can create (by combining several basic colors) to display a video image. The total number of individual colors that are available is finite. If a color cannot be displayed correctly, it is considered *out of gamut.*

color space: The method used to generate color in a video display. *See also* color gamut, RGB, YUV.

component video: A high-quality connection type for analog video. Component video splits the video signal and sends it over three separate cables, usually color-coded red, green, and blue. Component video connections are unusual in consumer-grade video equipment, but they provide superior video quality to coaxial, composite and S-Video connections. *See also* analog, coaxial, composite video, S-Video.

composite video: A connection type for analog video, typically using a single video-connector cable (color-coded yellow). The connector type is also sometimes called an *RCA connector,* usually found paired with audio cables that have red and white connectors. Composite video signals are inferior to S-Video or component video because they tend to allow more signal noise and artifacts in the video signal. *See also* analog, coaxial, component video, S-Video.

DAT (digital audio tape): A digital tape format often used in audio recorders by professional video producers.

data rate: The amount of data that can pass over a connection in a second while contained in a signal. The data rate of DV-format video is 3.6MB (megabytes) per second.

device control: A technology that allows a computer to control the playback functions on a digital camcorder (such as play, stop, and rewind). Clicking Rewind in the program window on the computer causes the camcorder tape to actually rewind.

digital: A method of recording sound and light by converting them into data made up of discrete, binary values (expressed as ones and zeros). *See also* analog.

Digital 8: A digital camcorder format that uses Hi8 tapes. *See also* digital, DV, MicroMV, MiniDV.

DIMM (Dual Inline Memory Module): A memory module for a computer. Most computer RAM today comes on easily replaced DIMM cards. *See also* RAM.

driver: Pre-1980, the person in control of a car or horse-drawn carriage. Post-1980, a piece of software that allows a computer to utilize a piece of hardware, such as a video card or a printer.

drop-frame timecode: A type of timecode specified by the NTSC video standard, usually with a frame rate of 29.97fps. To maintain continuity, two frames are dropped at the beginning of each minute, except for every tenth minute. *See also* timecode.

DV (Digital Video): A standard format and codec for digital video. Digital camcorders that include a FireWire interface usually record DV-format video. *See also* codec, FireWire.

DVCAM: A professional-grade version of the MiniDV digital-tape format developed by Sony. DVCAM camcorders are usually pretty expensive. *See also* digital, DVCPro, MiniDV.

DVCPro: A professional-grade version of the MiniDV digital-tape format developed by Panasonic. Like DVCAM camcorders, DVCPro camcorders are usually very expensive. *See also* digital, DVCAM, MiniDV.

DVD (Digital Versatile Disc): A category of disc formats that allows capacities from 4.7GB up to 17GB. DVDs are quickly becoming the most popular format for distributing movies. Recordable DVDs (DVD-Rs) are becoming a common and affordable recording medium for home users.

EDL (Edit Decision List): A file or list that contains information about all edits performed in a program. This list can then be used to reproduce the same edits on another system, such as at a professional video-editing facility. Most advanced editing programs can generate EDLs automatically.

EIDE (Enhanced Integrated Drive Electronics): Most modern PCs have hard drives that connect to the computer using an EIDE interface. For digital video, you should try to use EIDE disks with a speed of 7200 rpm.

field: One of two separate sets of scan lines in an interlaced video frame. Each field contains every other horizontal resolution line. Immediately after one field is drawn on the screen, the other is drawn in a separate pass while the previous frame is still glowing, resulting in a complete image. *See also* frame.

FireWire: Also known by its official designation IEEE-1394, or by other names such as i.Link, FireWire is a high-speed computer peripheral interface standard developed by Apple Computer. FireWire is often used to connect digital camcorders, external hard drives, and some other devices to a computer. The speed of FireWire has contributed greatly to the affordability of modern video editing.

frame: Still image, one in a sequence of many that make up a moving picture. *See also* frame rate.

frame rate: The speed at which the frames in a moving picture change. Video images usually display 25 to 30 frames per second, providing the illusion of movement to the human eye. Slower frame rates save storage space, but can produce jerky motion; faster frame rates produce smoother motion but have to use more of the recording medium to store and present the images.

gamut: *See* color gamut.

generational loss: A worsening of the signal-to-noise ratio (less signal, more noise) that occurs every time an analog recording is copied; some values are lost in the copying process. Each copy (especially if it's a copy of a copy) represents a later, lower-quality *generation* of the original. *See also* analog.

HDTV (High-Definition Television): A new set of broadcast-video standards that incorporates resolutions and frame rates higher than those used for traditional analog video. *See also* NTSC, PAL, SECAM.

IEEE-1394: *See* FireWire.

i.Link: *See* FireWire.

interlacing: Producing an image by alternating sets of scan lines on-screen. Most video images are actually composed of two separate fields, drawn on consecutive passes of the electron gun in the video tube. Each field contains every other horizontal resolution line of a video image. Each field is drawn so quickly that the human eye perceives a complete image. *See also* progressive scan, field.

jog: *See* scrub.

lavalier: A tiny microphone designed to clip to a subject's clothing. Lavalier mics are often clipped to the lapels of TV newscasters.

lens flare: A light point or artifact that appears in a video image when the sun or other bright light source reflects on the lens.

luminance: A fancy word for brightness in video images. *See also* chrominance.

MicroMV: A small digital-camcorder tape format developed by Sony for ultra-compact camcorders. *See also* digital, Digital 8, DV, MiniDV.

MiniDV: The most common tape format used by digital camcorders. *See also* digital, Digital 8, DV, MicroMV.

moiré pattern: A wavy or shimmering artifact that appears in video images when tight parallel lines appear in the image. This problem often occurs when a subject wears a pinstriped suit or coarse corduroy.

NLE (nonlinear editor): A computer program that can edit video, audio, or other multimedia information without confining the user to an unchangeable sequence of frames from first to last. Using an NLE, you can edit the work in any order you choose. Popular video NLEs include Apple iMovie, Pinnacle Studio, and Windows Movie Maker.

NTSC (National Television Standards Committee): The broadcast-video standard used in North America, Japan, the Philippines, and elsewhere. *See also* PAL, SECAM.

online/offline editing: When you edit using full-quality footage, you are performing *online* editing. If you perform edits using lower-quality captures, and intend to apply those edits to the full-quality footage later, you are performing *offline* editing.

overscan: What happens when a TV cuts off portions of the video image at the edges of the screen. Most standard TVs overscan to some extent.

PAL (Phase Alternating Line): The broadcast-video standard used in Western Europe, Australia, Southeast Asia, South America, and elsewhere. *See also* NTSC, SECAM.

PCI: Peripheral Component Interconnect, a standard type of connection for computer expansion cards (such as FireWire cards). Any new card must be placed in an empty PCI slot on the computer's motherboard.

pixel: The smallest element of a video image, also called a *picture element*. Bitmapped still images are made up of grids containing thousands, even millions, of pixels. A screen or image size that has a resolution of 640 x 480 is 640 pixels wide by 480 pixels high.

Plug and Play: A hardware technology that allows you to easily connect devices such as digital camcorders to your computer. The computer automatically detects the device when it is connected and turned on.

progressive scan: A scan display that draws all the horizontal resolution lines in a single pass. Most computer monitors use progressive scan. *See also* interlacing.

RAM (Random-Access Memory): The electronic working space for your computer's processor and software. To use digital video on your computer, you need lots of RAM.

render: To produce a playable version of an altered video image. If an effect, speed change, or transition is applied to a video image, your video-editing program must figure out how each frame of the image should look after the change. Rendering is the process of applying these changes. Usually, the rendering process generates a preview file that is stored on the hard drive. *See also* transition.

RGB (Red-Green-Blue): The color space (method of creating on-screen colors) used in computer monitors; all the available colors result from combining red, green, and blue pixels. *See also* color space, YUV.

sampling rate: The number of samples obtained per second during a digital audio recording. When audio is recorded digitally, the sound is sampled thousands of times per second. 48-kHz audio has 48,000 samples per second.

scrub: To move back and forth through a video program, one frame at a time. Some video-editing programs have a scrub bar located underneath the video preview window (also called the *jog control*). *See also* shuttle.

SECAM (Sequential Couleur Avec Memoire): Broadcast video standard used in France, Russia, Eastern Europe, Central Asia, and elsewhere. *See also* NTSC, PAL.

shuttle: To roll a video image slowly forward or back, often to check a detail of motion. Professional video decks and cameras often have shuttle controls. Some video-editing programs also have shuttle controls in their capture windows. *See also* scrub.

slate: The black-and-white hinged board that moviemakers snap closed in front of the camera just before action commences. The noise made by the snapping slate is used later to synchronize video with sound recorded by other audio recorders during the shoot.

SMPTE (Society for Motion Picture and Television Engineers): This organization develops standards for professional broadcasting equipment and formats. Among other things, the SMPTE defines standards for bars and tone, counting leaders, and timecode.

S-VHS: A higher-quality version of the VHS videotape format. S-VHS VCRs usually have S-Video connectors. *See also* S-Video.

S-Video: A high-quality connection technology for analog video. S-Video connectors separate the color and brightness signals, resulting in less signal noise and fewer artifacts. Most digital camcorders include S-Video connectors for analog output. Analog capture cards and S-VHS VCRs usually have S-Video connectors as well. *See also* analog, capture, coaxial, composite video, component video, S-VHS.

timecode: The standard system for identifying individual frames in a movie or video program. Timecode is expressed as *hours:minutes:seconds:frames* (as in 01:20:31:02). This format has been standardized by the SMPTE. Non-drop-frame timecode uses colons between the numbers; drop-frame timecode uses semicolons. *See also* drop-frame timecode, SMPTE, timecode break.

timecode break: An inconsistency in the timecode on a camcorder tape. *See also* timecode.

Timeline: The working space in most video editing programs. Clips are arranged along a line, which may include different video tracks, audio tracks, or other features. *See also* clip.

title: Text that appears on-screen to display the name of the movie, or to give credit to the people who made the movie. *Subtitles* are a special type of title, often used during a video program to show translations of dialogue spoken in foreign languages.

transition: The method by which one clip ends and another begins in a video program. A common type of transition is when one clip gradually fades out as the next clip fades in. *See also* clip, render.

USB (Universal Serial Bus): This is a computer-port technology that makes it easy to connect a mouse, printer, or other device to a computer. Although USB usually isn't fast enough for digital-video capture, some digital camcorders have USB ports. Connected to a computer's USB port, these cameras can often be used as Web cams. Most computers built after Spring 2002 use a newer, faster version of USB called USB 2.0.

vectorscope: A tool that monitors the color of a video image. Adobe Premiere Pro has a built-in vectorscope.

video card: This term can refer to either of two different kinds of devices inside a computer: the device that generates a video signal for the computer's monitor, or the card that captures video from VCRs and camcorders onto the computer's hard drive. Some hardware manufacturers refer to their FireWire cards as video cards because FireWire cards are most often used to capture video from digital camcorders. *See also* capture, FireWire.

waveform: A visual representation of an audio signal. Viewing a waveform on a computer screen allows precise synchronization of sound and video.

waveform monitor: A tool that displays brightness information for a video image. Adobe Premiere Pro has a built-in waveform monitor.

YCbCr: An alternative acronym for the YUV color space. *See also* YUV.

YUV: The acronym for the color space used by most TVs and digital camcorders. For some obscure reason, YUV stands for *luminance-chrominance*. *See also* chrominance, color space, luminance, RGB.

zebra pattern: An overexposure-warning feature that some high-end camcorders have. A striped pattern appears in the viewfinder over areas of the image that will be overexposed unless the camcorder is adjusted to compensate.

Index

Notes

Notes

Notes

FOR DUMMIES®

The easy way to get more done and have more fun

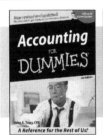

FOR DUMMIES®

A world of resources to help you grow

HOME, GARDEN & HOBBIES

Feng Shui For Dummies
0-7645-5295-3

Gardening For Dummies
0-7645-5130-2

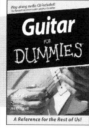
Guitar For Dummies
0-7645-5106-X

Also available:

Auto Repair For Dummies
(0-7645-5089-6)

Chess For Dummies
(0-7645-5003-9)

Home Maintenance For Dummies
(0-7645-5215-5)

Organizing For Dummies
(0-7645-5300-3)

Piano For Dummies
(0-7645-5105-1)

Poker For Dummies
(0-7645-5232-5)

Quilting For Dummies
(0-7645-5118-3)

Rock Guitar For Dummies
(0-7645-5356-9)

Roses For Dummies
(0-7645-5202-3)

Sewing For Dummies
(0-7645-5137-X)

FOOD & WINE

Cooking For Dummies
0-7645-5250-3

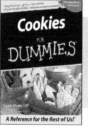
Cookies For Dummies
0-7645-5390-9

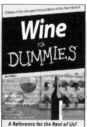
Wine For Dummies
0-7645-5114-0

Also available:

Bartending For Dummies
(0-7645-5051-9)

Chinese Cooking For Dummies
(0-7645-5247-3)

Christmas Cooking For Dummies
(0-7645-5407-7)

Diabetes Cookbook For Dummies
(0-7645-5230-9)

Grilling For Dummies
(0-7645-5076-4)

Low-Fat Cooking For Dummies
(0-7645-5035-7)

Slow Cookers For Dummies
(0-7645-5240-6)

TRAVEL

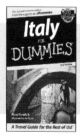
Italy For Dummies
0-7645-5453-0

Hawaii For Dummies
0-7645-5438-7

Las Vegas For Dummies
0-7645-5448-4

Also available:

America's National Parks For Dummies
(0-7645-6204-5)

Caribbean For Dummies
(0-7645-5445-X)

Cruise Vacations For Dummies 2003
(0-7645-5459-X)

Europe For Dummies
(0-7645-5456-5)

Ireland For Dummies
(0-7645-6199-5)

France For Dummies
(0-7645-6292-4)

London For Dummies
(0-7645-5416-6)

Mexico's Beach Resorts For Dummies
(0-7645-6262-2)

Paris For Dummies
(0-7645-5494-8)

RV Vacations For Dummies
(0-7645-5443-3)

Walt Disney World & Orlando For Dummies
(0-7645-5444-1)

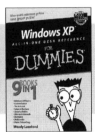
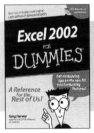
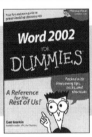

FOR DUMMIES®

Helping you expand your horizons and realize your potential

INTERNET

0-7645-0894-6

0-7645-1659-0

0-7645-1642-6

Also available:

America Online 7.0 For Dummies
(0-7645-1624-8)

Genealogy Online For Dummies
(0-7645-0807-5)

The Internet All-in-One Desk Reference For Dummies
(0-7645-1659-0)

Internet Explorer 6 For Dummies
(0-7645-1344-3)

The Internet For Dummies Quick Reference
(0-7645-1645-0)

Internet Privacy For Dummies
(0-7645-0846-6)

Researching Online For Dummies
(0-7645-0546-7)

Starting an Online Business For Dummies
(0-7645-1655-8)

DIGITAL MEDIA

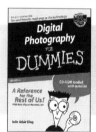

0-7645-1664-7

0-7645-1675-2

0-7645-0806-7

Also available:

CD and DVD Recording For Dummies
(0-7645-1627-2)

Digital Photography All-in-One Desk Reference For Dummies
(0-7645-1800-3)

Digital Photography For Dummies Quick Reference
(0-7645-0750-8)

Home Recording for Musicians For Dummies
(0-7645-1634-5)

MP3 For Dummies
(0-7645-0858-X)

Paint Shop Pro "X" For Dummies
(0-7645-2440-2)

Photo Retouching & Restoration For Dummies
(0-7645-1662-0)

Scanners For Dummies
(0-7645-0783-4)

GRAPHICS

0-7645-0817-2

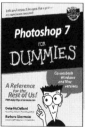

0-7645-1651-5

0-7645-0895-4

Also available:

Adobe Acrobat 5 PDF For Dummies
(0-7645-1652-3)

Fireworks 4 For Dummies
(0-7645-0804-0)

Illustrator 10 For Dummies
(0-7645-3636-2)

QuarkXPress 5 For Dummies
(0-7645-0643-9)

Visio 2000 For Dummies
(0-7645-0635-8)

Available wherever books are sold. Go to www.dummies.com or call 1-877-762-2974 to order direct.

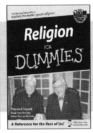
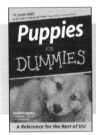

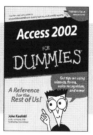

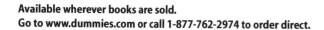

44874909R00216

Made in the USA
Middletown, DE
18 June 2017